FREEING
Shakespeare's
VOICE

FREEING
Shakespeare's
VOICE

The Actor's Guide to
Talking the Text

KRISTIN LINKLATER

Theatre Communications Group
1992

Freeing Shakespeare's Voice is published by Theatre Communications Group, Inc., 355 Lexington Ave., New York, NY 10017.

TCG gratefully acknowledges public funds from the National Endowment for the Arts, the New York State Council on the Arts and the New York City Department of Cultural Affairs in addition to the generous support of the following foundations and corporations: Alcoa Foundation, Ameritech Foundation, ARCO Foundation, AT&T Foundation, Citibank N.A., Consolidated Edison Company of New York, Council of Literary Magazines and Presses, Nathan Cummings Foundation, Dayton Hudson Foundation, Exxon Corporation, Ford Foundation, James Irvine Foundation, Jerome Foundation, Andrew W. Mellon Foundation, Metropolitan Life Foundation, National Broadcasting Company, Pew Charitable Trusts, Philip Morris Companies Inc., Scherman Foundation, Shubert Foundation, L. J. and Mary C. Skaggs Foundation, Lila Wallace-Reader's Digest Fund.

Quotations of Shakespeare throughout the text are based on the Arden edition, published by Methuen & Co. Used by permission. Excerpt from *The Tragedie of King Lear* copyright © 1991 by Folio Scripts, 2515 Caledonia Avenue, Deep Cove, District of North Vancouver, British Columbia, Canada V7G 1T8. Reproduced by the kind permission of Neil Freeman. Quotation from *Writing in Restaurants* by David Mamet copyright © 1986 by David Mamet. Used by permission of Viking Penguin, a division of Penguin Books USA Inc. Quotation from *Et Cetera Et Cetera: Notes of a Word-Watcher* by Lewis Thomas copyright © 1990 by Lewis Thomas. By permission of Little, Brown and Company. The text of Pablo Neruda's "Verbo" reprinted by permission of Agencia Literaria Carmen Balcells, S.A.

Cover photo: Detail of a Vortex by Hans Jenny from *Cymatics: The Structure and Dynamics of Waves and Vibrations*. Used by permission.

Author photo by Marie-Louise Avery

Linklater, Kristin.
    Freeing Shakespeare's voice: the actor's guide to talking the text / Kristin Linklater—1st ed.
ISBN 1-55936-031-3 (paper)
    1. Shakespeare, William, 1564–1616—Dramatic production.
2. Shakespeare, William, 1564–1616—Language. 3. Voice culture. 4. Acting.
I. Title.
PR3091.L56 1991
822.3'3—dc20   91-23801
                                                                             CIP

Design and composition by G&H/SOHO, Ltd.

First Edition, April 1992

Second Printing, July 1993

*I dedicate this book to my son Hamish,
my mother Marjorie,
and to the memory of my father Eric.*

◆▶ Contents ◆▶

FREEING
Shakespeare's
VOICE

◄► Prologue ◄►

This book draws upon my life—in the classroom as teacher and student, on the rehearsal floor as coach and director, on the stage as actor, and in the audience as spectator/listener. The exercises that I have developed for talking Shakespeare's text I owe to my students, to what they could not achieve and to what they could. My attempt as a teacher has been to create exercises that would arouse organically the desire for the necessary result and provide causal stimulus for its realization; for that reason my guide to speaking Shakespeare is experiential rather than prescriptive.

There are books on speaking Shakespeare which every serious actor should read and which are by no means replaced by this one. In this book the actor will find an organic approach to the language which s/he may not find elsewhere, but the information on verse-speaking, rhetoric, Elizabethan language structures and Shakespearean word-use can be found in many other places. The wealth of information is such that no one teacher can encompass the whole field. The serious student will accumulate nuggets of vital knowledge from a variety of sources; the manner in which the information is delivered by different teachers and writers may speak to one student and not to another. *Freeing Shakespeare's Voice* speaks to the polished professional as much as to the absolute beginner. I hope it will also speak to the director, be of interest to the scholar and help the playwright to enter the physicality of language.

The most useful books that I know of for the actor who performs Shakespeare are the following: John Barton's *Playing Shakespeare* (Methuen), Cicely Berry's *The Actor and his Text* (Scribners), Bertram Joseph's *Acting Shakespeare* (Theatre Arts) and Delbert Spain's *Shakespeare Sounded Soundly* (Garland-Clarke Editions/Capra Press). Added to these practical textbooks are invaluable reference books such as Caroline Spurgeon's *Shakespeare's Imagery* (Cambridge), E.M.W. Tillyard's *The Elizabethan World Picture* (Vintage), C.W. Onions's *A Shakespeare Glossary* (Oxford), Eric Partridge's *Shakespeare's Bawdy* (Routledge), and *The Oxford English Dictionary*.

I myself owe a great deal to Walter Ong's *The Presence of the Word* (Yale University Press), Richard Foster Jones's *The Triumph of the English Language* (Stanford University Press), many of Frances A. Yates's books, but in particular *Theatre of the World* (Routledge & K. Paul) and Paul Fussell's inspiring *Poetic Meter and Poetic Form* (Random House). I am most recently grateful to Carol Gilligan and her book *In a Different Voice* (Harvard University Press).

My heartfelt acknowledgments go to those teachers and fellow workers and students and brave actors who have contributed to my Shakespearean journey: to Tina Packer, Artistic Director of Shakespeare & Company; to the actors and teachers of Shakespeare & Company (specifically, I owe thanks to Jonathan Epstein for information on "un" and to John Hadden for inspiration on breath and line-beginnings); to John Barton, Michael Langham, Wallace Chappell, Jill Balcon and Barry Boys; and to those no longer on this earth to accept my loving thanks, Michael MacOwan, Bertram Joseph, Michael Warre, Tyrone Guthrie and Wal Cherry.

It is with pride and affection that I salute those teachers who, over the past twenty years, have trained and traveled with me; they carry on and develop Iris Warren's voice work and the text work that I have done—notably Fran Bennett, Andrea Haring and Cecil Mackinnon. Each "generation" of teachers brings fresh energy and new ideas, and this book is dedicated to their talent and creativity: Normi Noel, Natsuko Ohama, Zoe Alexander, Virginia Ness, Michael Morgan, Christine Adaire, Peter Wittrock, Louis Colaianni, Judith Jablonka, Ariel Bock, Malcolm Ingram, Keely Eastley and Tim Douglas. The teachers of 1991 are worthy of the tradition: Claudia Anderson, Joe Gilday, Brent Blair, Elizabeth Ingram, Trudie Kessler, Paula Langton, James Rice, Patricia Riggin, Judith Shahn, Larissa Solovieva, Eva Wielgat, Walton Wilson and Joanna Weir. I would like also to acknowledge Joseph Jacquinet and Francoise Walot in Belgium and Dianne Eden and Isobel Kirk in Australia.

I am grateful to the Guggenheim Foundation for the fellowship in 1981 which allowed me the breathing-space to explore and test my work without pressure.

Duncan Nelson deserves every ounce of the appreciation I feel for his caring and careful editing. And I am deeply grateful to my beloved brother, Andro Linklater, for last-minute quality control.

Neil Freeman! Thank you!

Always I acknowledge my teacher, Iris Warren, with respect and gratitude.

◀▶ Introduction ◀▶

My intention in this book is to offer a de-mystifying approach to speaking Shakespeare's text. It is often the most sensitive and talented actors who confess to being terrified of playing Shakespeare and this may well be because they have a strong sense of "truth" in their acting which depends on their personal emotional commitment to the characters they play and the words the characters speak. "Personal" truth sometimes seems too small for Shakespeare's poetic grandeur.

It is the actor's own raw material that makes a character believable. Out of the actor/person's own emotions, intellect, memories, imagination, tragedies, loves, hates, family history, dreams, soul, voice and body a "character" is forged who is a believable inhabitant of whatever world occupies the stage.

Most actors, if they are earning a proper living through acting, play twentieth-century characters for most of their careers. Most films, television drama, and stage plays "hold the mirror up to [*contemporary*] Nature," which is exactly what they should be doing. The prime responsibility of the theatre is to show a culture its own face so that it may reflect upon it. But art also has a responsibility to preserve the past, so that a culture may reflect upon itself in the light of its history. Great art lasts, and when the theatre wants to re-produce its past, performers are confronted by artistic demands very different from those posed by contemporary fare. Classical music is played on instruments that bear a distinct resemblance to their ancestors, but classical drama has to be played on a human instrument that experiences and expresses life in a manner radically altered even from a hundred years ago. The Western human behaves, thinks and speaks quite differently now from the days four hundred years ago when Shakespeare's classics were contemporary.

The huge subject matter of Shakespeare's plays is not the problem. Human nature still spawns extreme acts: old men are cast out into the storm to go mad; teenage lovers commit suicide; women scream at men as Margaret does to York, "Why art thou patient, man? Thou

3

shouldst be mad/And I, to make thee mad do mock thee thus," and men reply as does York, "How ill-beseeming is it in thy sex/To triumph like an Amazonian trull . . . 'Tis beauty that doth oft make woman proud/But God he knows thy share thereof is small"; men strangle their wives, falsely suspecting infidelity; political leaders are assassinated; innocent citizens are slaughtered on the streets and on the battlefield—still.

Such extreme events are still the stuff of theatre as they are still the stuff of life, but the big difference between contemporary drama and Shakespeare's drama lies in the language that expresses extremity. Today the unspoken is as dramatic as the spoken on stage because that's how it is in contemporary life. We do not express our passions regularly and the twentieth-century voice goes pretty much unexercised in the language of extreme expression. The general public does not get together and indulge in full-throated singing three or four times a week; families do not regularly sit around and read out loud to each other or discuss matters of substance at length around the dinner table. The industrial revolution, the technological revolution, the rapid growth in literacy and the influence of print have diminished the need for the human voice over the past one hundred fifty years, and we are moving at breakneck speed, in evolutionary terms, further and further away from tens of thousands of years of oral/aural civilization. The oral tradition kept the voice alive in the body but now the *experience* of thought and language has moved from the body into the head. In general, the *experience* of "who I am" now exists in the head, behind the face. The function of the body is merely to transport the "I think, therefore I am" person from one place to another and to organize its fuel intake and output. The body has become a vehicle for a "self" that lives above it.

The basis of all my work is the belief that voice and language belong to the whole body rather than the head alone and that the function of the voice is to reveal the self. This book, in consequence, has a more ambitious aim than that of a verse-speaking manual. It aims to recondition both mind and body so that the voice can express the visceral and spiritual urgency that was its subject matter in Shakespeare's day.

The voice *mechanism* is in the body. The mechanics of voice depend on breath passing through the vocal folds in the throat to create the vibrations which are ultimately recognized as an individual voice. Breath lives in the lungs and the lungs extend down to the middle of the torso. The breathing *musculature* is woven around the rib cage, continues underneath the lungs in the diaphragm, is connected to the spinal column and roots itself deep into the pelvic floor. It is not metaphorical to say "the body breathes."

The muscles that govern the breath are part of a human being's most profound, instinctual life force energies. When a baby is born, breath is its life. The connection of survival impulses with the baby's breath and voice is essential to its life, and a baby's voice communicates essential information long before words are learnt. A baby's voice *is* emotion: happily gurgling and crowing, yelling angrily, crying—a potent wordless message is sent and received. The baby's whole body swells and deflates, ripples and convulses with the forces of breath, emotion and sound that inhabit it. That is the "natural" function of our voices. The "selfhood" of the baby is undivided instinct-impulse-emotion-breath-voice-body.

Today's adult voice is deprived of the nourishment of emotion and free breathing. Society has taught us that it is wrong to express ourselves freely. Conventional child-raising ("poisonous pedagogy" as Alice Miller calls it in *For Your Own Good*), tells children that it is not nice to shout, that it is ugly and dangerous to get angry, that it is upsetting to others to cry in public and that loud hoots of laughter are disturbing. The adult voice is the product of other people's voices—"that's bad," "it's weak to cry," "you'll frighten the men away with that big voice," "never use that tone of voice to me." All too often the breathing musculature has been dislocated from its instinctual connections by physical blows as well as psychological ones.

The adult voice is, in most instances, conditioned to talk *about* feelings rather than to *reveal* them, given that feelings have not been scared away completely as is often the case. The breath that fuels this descriptive mechanism comes from the top portion of the lungs. The throat, tongue and jaw muscles deflect the impulse to communicate from the danger zone of the diaphragm to more manageable areas; just enough breath to interact with the vocal folds is engaged, and the act of speaking is centered in the throat and mouth. Much more is left unspoken than is spoken, and the sensorium of the body stores what it knows, seldom getting the opportunity to discharge its banked-up cargo.

It would not, I think, be going too far to say that the twentieth-century experience of emotion is actually the experience of neurosis: that is, the deflection of emotion from breath and voice to nerve endings and external muscles. The twitching jaw muscle, biting back feelings, is immediately recognizable on the movie screen as a strong man's strong emotion.

The twentieth-century actor, playing twentieth-century characters, experiences "truthful" emotions through these accepted response mechanisms. The voice *must* squeeze out through a narrow throat, clenched jaw and nasal resonance in order to be culturally accurate. The resultant tone is flat and undifferentiated. A richer, more varied range of sounds may be suspect. The reference points of "truth" are made by the culture we live in.

Yet we know more than we say. A crowd of inner voices whispers, "What will they think of you?" "You'll never make it." "Stupid!" "Am I getting it right?" "They're all better (cleverer, prettier, more handsome, more talented, etc.) than me." But, muted through disuse, another voice that is utterly your own can be heard. It is murmuring wilder, more outrageous, more passionate things than all the other voices. It may not speak familiar "truths" but it is truer to our larger, original selves than the limited, correct, proven, out-loud voice that has learnt to conform to the language of a judgmental outside world. Our true voices have been tamed, confined within the bounds of twentieth-century behavior.

Mistrust of the spoken word is understandable, and thus it is that in today's acting classes we hear repeated again and again: "Stop thinking. Get beyond the words. It's not the words that count, it's the behavior. The truth of what you are *doing* is where the truth lies, not what you're *saying*. Play the *subtext* not the *text*. Play the *action*, play the *objective*, play the *intention*. Whatever you do, *don't play the words*!" This is excellent advice for performing an accurate reproduction of contemporary life. Today it is true that "One picture is worth a thousand words" and "Actions speak louder than words."

But it isn't true for Shakespeare. He says to actors: "Suit the action to the word and the word to the action." When a two-year-old jumps up and down, red in the face, throws a plate of food on the floor and shouts "NO, NO, NO," s/he is carrying out Shakespeare's advice for good acting. A baby's emotional/vocal behavior is truer to Shakespearean behavior than the civilized comportment we are led to believe is a sign of intelligent maturity.

Shakespeare's text integrates words, emotions, objectives, intentions and actions, and in so doing it accurately reflects the Elizabethan society to whom it spoke. Elizabethan men and women spoke in a language four hundred years *younger* than ours. It was a language that was still part of the oral culture that had shaped all human interaction for thousands of years. Language lived in the body. Thought was experienced in the body. Emotions inhabited the organs of the body. Filled with thought and feeling, the sound waves of the voice flowed out through the body and were received sensorially by other bodies which directly experienced the thought-feeling content of the sound waves. We can picture the speaker's body as all mouth and the listener's body as all ear.

Shakespeare's "truth," therefore, is different from our daily experience of "truth." The scale is larger than our domestic reality. But he does not express his truth in a different language, he expresses it in a different experience of language. When today's actor starts to *experience* Shakespeare's language as a whole-body process, s/he is led to a larger and deeper experience of thought and emotion, and from there to a more fundamental, more individual and enlarged experience of "truth." Understanding of the text is immediately illuminated. The words become instantly speakable. The speaker's reality expands to fill Shakespeare's reality, and as familiarity with larger, wilder, more outrageous expression grows, so does the confidence that this is "true."

In the course of this book, I will show you how to tap into the enormous range of physical and emotional resources which can feed your voice. Beginning with the fundamental building blocks of language, vowels and consonants, a series of exercises will enable you to feel and to process for yourself the sounds, words, emotions, language forms and verse structure that constitute a Shakespearean text.

I would urge the actor who knows that his or her voice is not yet ready for big demands to find a good teacher and start work on its release and development. Too little emphasis is given in the actor-training field to the importance of the actor's voice, but live theatre is first and foremost a verbal art form. Until actors realize that their voices are integral to the creative process they will never arrive at the core of their art. My book, *Freeing the Natural Voice*—a practical basic textbook—is the best preparation for the work you will find in this book. The natural voice has two to three octaves of speaking notes capable of expressing the full gamut of human emotion and all the subtleties and nuances of thought. To release its potential we must dissolve the limitations imposed by twentieth-century upbringing and awaken the dormant power that brings breath into every cell of the body and rstores largesse of expression and stature to the human-actor-being.

Instinctively, actors know that Shakespeare offers them this greater scope. The steps that can take you from instinct to accomplishment occupy the following pages of *Freeing Shakespeare's Voice.*

THE CONTENT
◆▶
Language

1

◄► Vowels and Consonants ◄►

Within the structure of words is encoded the evolution of language and therefore of thought. Vowels and consonants in one form or another have been around for tens (perhaps hundreds) of thousands of years and, taking that perspective, it is only in the last millisecond of time that they have moved from an oral to a written culture, from the body to the printed page.

Within the last two hundred years the growing influence of print has increasingly cut language off from the sensorium. One might say that language, thus denied emotional and sensual nourishment, has become anemic. The severance creates for the actor a chasm between creativity and verbal communication which poses a major obstacle to playing Shakespeare. When words are mainly experienced in the head and the mouth they convey cerebral meaning. In order to transfer Shakespeare's full emotional, intellectual and philosophical intent from the page to the stage, words must connect with the full human range of intellect and emotion, body and voice. They must be allowed to rediscover old neuro-physiological routes of appetite to bring back taste and texture to speaking, and to spark the animal response mechanisms which fire creative processes long buried under layers of "civilized" and "rational" behavior. Only the fullest access to the humanity of the speaker allows one to speak Shakespeare fully.

Nobody knows how language began. According to my own constantly shifting state of mind and being, I can subscribe one day to the idea that language descended to us from the gods and on another day be convinced that it began as open-throated, appetite-related grunts and groans dealing with life and death issues such as food and the procreation of the species; hunger and sex; pure appetite; hunger and lust experienced in the belly and the groin, expressed with a roar that originated deep in the body, indivisible from the experience. The quantum leap (or crawl) in the evolution of speech, if speech began thus, was articulation, and the agents that articulated, interrupted and shaped the flow of roaring sound were parts of the mouth which had hitherto been used for appetite-related functions: chewing, biting, licking, sucking. Appetite and communication presumably occupied the same brain cells until the tongue, the teeth and the lips were fully adapted to new demands. Taste, smell and texture—pleasure, desire and satisfaction—must have permeated the process of speech for thousands of years. Speaking would have been on a par with sex and eating—an extreme experience.

But I think that Lewis Thomas, in his book *Et Cetera, Et Cetera*, has a more imaginative vision of language origins and therefore probably a truer one. Looking at a two-hundred-year-old horse-chestnut tree in his backyard he says:

> If I were an early, primitive man, instead of the man that I feel these days, and if I had not yet built a language for naming my tree, dumb-struck, I would go looking for a small child. What is it, I would ask. The child would say a word never heard before, pointing up into the tree in eagerness for my attention. The word would have the sound of *ai*, then a gentle breath, *aiw*, and it would sound right for this tree. The word would then enter the language by way of me, I would tell it to my friends, and thousands of generations later, long after my time, it would be used to describe many things, not trees but the *feeling* that was contained in that particular tree. *Aiw* would become EVER, and AYE, and EON and AGE. The Sanskrit language would have built it into the word *ayua*, meaning life. Gothic would have used it for a word, *aiwos*, eternity. Latin would have placed it in *aevem* and *aetas*, for the connected ideas of age and eternity. The Greeks would put it into *aion*, vital force, and we would receive it in our word EON. German would have it as *ewig*, the word sung over and over in a high voice in Mahler's *Das Lied von der Erde*. And some of the languages, in their hopes, would insert a *yeu* sound as a prefix, and the new sound would form words for YOUTH, YOUNG, JUVENILE. By this time all trace of meaning of the chestnut tree would be gone.
>
> In order to get a language really to work from the outset, as a means of human communication by speech, it must have been technically obligatory to make, first off, the words needed to express the feelings aroused by things, particularly living things in the world. Naming as a taxonomic problem could come later and would take care of itself. But for ideas to begin flowing in and out of minds, so that the deepest indispensability of language could take hold, the feelings would have to come first into speech, and that sense of the roots must persist like genes in all the words to follow.

Lewis Thomas, scientist and artist, reminds us that words connect us with the natural world around us as well as with each other, and tales are told of Eskimo tribes that have only recently lost their ability to find their way home after three- or four-month long hunting treks into uncharted wilds by "singing the landscape." Their voices and the shapes of the hills, rivers and valleys, merged to make a journey-song which mapped and navigated their travels. When they were taught to read, this skill was erased. The Australian Aborigines were similarly gifted. These people are of a tribe to which we all once belonged.

Those who dig below the surface of history in a search for traces of lost knowledge, esoteric truths or gnostic religion unearth clear evidence of earlier times when human beings experienced themselves as part of the fabric of nature and the cosmos. As late as Shakespeare's day men and women spoke of the harmony of the spheres and the desire to be in harmony with them. The music within us still sings and so does Nature's music, but we seldom listen to ourselves or Nature with an ear tuned to such subtle vibrations. If we could actually experience that we live in a universe made of sound and light waves, there might be a reunion between the body and the brain and the world around us.

The neuro-physiological pathways connecting words with the sensory apparatus of the body and with nature have not disappeared, but they have been short-circuited as the technology of communication has "progressed." It is not difficult to re-wire the circuitry. Not, of course, with the intention of reviving an old and incomprehensible way of speaking, but to awaken dormant energies of speech and tap into subterranean channels that may reverberate with unsuspected, sub-verbal meaning. By indulging sensory, sensual, emotional and physical responses to vowels and consonants—the component parts of words—we begin to resurrect the life of language.

The vowels and consonants of the English language have been badly treated over the last hundred years. I don't mean that "good speech has deteriorated," I mean that artificial standards of "correct speech" have associated any mention of vowels and consonants with judgments of correct and incorrect, good or bad, upper or lower class, intelligent or stupid, educated or illiterate. Most speech training employs the International Phonetics Alphabet to analyze regionalisms and train the ear to change individual usage. Phonetics is the science of sounds, the orthographic representation of vocal sounds. It was invented some hundred fifty years ago to attempt a more accurate spelling system for the English language. It failed to catch on as spelling but remained to be refined as a system for distinguishing the different sound usage in different languages and dialects. The I.P.A. is a sophisticated scientific language tool which has been overused in speech-training for actors to the detriment of the aesthetics of language.

The beauty of a vowel does not lie in the correctness of its pronunciation according to some arbitrary standard; it lies in its intrinsic musicality, its sensuality, its expressiveness. Vowels are compounded from the vibrations of the human voice molded by subtle changes in the shape of the channels through which those vibrations flow. As the channels narrow or broaden, get larger or smaller, the vibrations change both shape and pitch to create the fundamental elements of the music of speech. When the vowel pitches mix with inflections of thought the result is kaleidoscopic harmony.

Consciously or unconsciously, a great poet uses the sounds within words to communicate mood and accentuate meaning. Shakespeare's use of words can paint scenery, change day into night, provoke attack and evoke emotion, not only through imagery but through the sounds that make the words that hold the imagery. Consonants and vowels are sensory agents of speech communicating information on sound waves which carry subliminal messages from speaker to listener. Twentieth-century listeners are conditioned to translate what they hear more cerebrally than in the age of oral communication, but "whole-body" speaking and listening is still operative even though we may not be consciously tuned in to it.

Actors who want to tune in to Shakespeare's text and communicate it fully to their audiences can/should/must become sensitive to the *feel* of vowels and consonants, to the *anatomy* of words as well as their meaning. They can/should/must re-connect the neuro-physiological circuitry that allows the senses and the emotions to be informed by the taste, touch, color and pitch of words.

WARNING! *All this will sound ABOMINABLE if the voice lacks freedom and truth.*

A recurring instruction given by directors and acting teachers to the actor playing Shakespeare is "Let the *words* play *you*, don't play the words." (An alarming number say that the text is not to be dwelt upon, and encourage the actor to change any word that is hard to understand—these mentors are best ignored.) Of course, if the actor is working on a contemporary text the advice may be, "Don't think about the words, they are unimportant; it's the behavior that counts." And for all kinds of dramatic literature a teacher may counsel, "You're getting in the way of yourself, don't think, let it happen to you." These instructions need translation—they represent the Zen state of the art. But "Don't think" and "Let the words play you" best and most simply mean, "Don't think cerebrally" and "Let the words create an experience in you that you register sensorily, emotionally, imaginatively, and that you respond to impulsively." This is quite different from "not thinking." It is, rather, whole-body thinking, or experiential thinking, or incarnated thinking, or the Word made Flesh dwelling among us.

HOW this apotheosis is to be accomplished is the subject of this book; the goal is to supply the means by which the actor can act as though the brain were in the belly, united with emotion and impulse. This is for acting purposes. In daily life the actor should be able to resort to the accepted social mode in which the emotions are held in rein by a watchful, assessing brain.

To a certain extent, vowels can be seen as the emotional component in word-construction and the consonants as the intellectual component. This is an over-simplification but a useful place from which to start. Vowels require an open passageway from the breath source on out through the mouth. Consonants are formed by a closure or near-closure of some part of the mouth, creating an explosive, reverberative, buzzing or liquid sound with breath or vibration. Because of the direct and uninterrupted connection with the breath source, vowels can be directly connected with emotion, but only if the breath source is as deep as the diaphragm. The solar plexus is knit into the fiber of the diaphragm and is the primary emotional receiving and transmitting nerve center. Many people breathe high up in their chests and in these cases there would be no experience of vowels as emotionally connected. Many actors have been trained to experience vowels only in their mouths and ears—for them also the emotional content will be missing. But anyone who can relax the stomach muscles and allow the breath to drop deep down into the belly, and then drop the thought of a vowel down after the breath, will immediately understand that vowels are the emotional component of words. Emotion and appetite and creative impulse are inextricably connected in the central nervous system.

Consonants provide a sensory experience which can translate into mood and they can curb and channel the vowel in ways that make sense of its emotion. Effective speaking balances emotion and intellect. If the intellect dominates, the speaking is dry and dull; if emotion overcomes the speaker, the audience is embarrassed, suspicious, and usually fails to get the message. An individual habit of speech in which consonants are slurred or swallowed usually reflects a lack of clear thinking; an overly rich vowel-dominated mode may reveal a dedication to emotional expression that is sentimental in effect; and a crisp, staccato style that barely allows the vowels to coexist with the consonants belongs prototypically to the dry academic.

Speaking Shakespeare demands a balance of emotion and intellect to the highest degree. This equipoise is achieved little by little, first by balancing emotion and intellect in the formation of the words, then in combining them to formulate the emotional and intellectual story of the text.

Here is a famous example of Shakespeare's textual scene-painting which illustrates the importance of fulfilling the role played by vowels and consonants in the realization of his artistry. It is the fourth Chorus in *Henry V* at the beginning of Act IV:

> Now entertain conjecture of a time
> When creeping murmur and the pouring dark

> Fills the wide vessel of the universe.
> From camp to camp through the foul womb of night
> The hum of either army stilly sounds,
> That the fix'd sentinels almost receive
> The secret whispers of each others' watch:
> Fire answers fire, and through their palely flames
> Each battle sees the other's umber'd face:
> Steed threatens steed, in high and boastful neighs
> Piercing the night's dull ear; and from the tents
> The armourers, accomplishing the knights,
> With busy hammers closing rivets up,
> Give dreadful note of preparation.

I shall come back to this passage in later chapters, recommending its use as an exercise for the Shakespeare speaker in accomplishing images and onomatopeia. But first of all I would like to highlight the anatomy of onomatopeia as heard here in vowels and consonants.

Say the words *murmur, pouring dark, universe, foul womb, hum*; and now say the words *camp to camp, stilly sounds, fixed sentinels, receive, secret whispers, watch*. The darkness and weight of the first group are in striking contrast to the hissing and cutting sounds of the second. The whispering guards and the dark night acquire a menace through the accumulation of the sounds chosen to represent them. The use of *umber'd* has more dark threat than, for instance, *shadowed* would have had. *Steed threatens steed* creates the sound of *high and boastful neighs* more than *horse threatens horse* would. And so on.

How does this work? The following exercise will allow you to experience the physical, sensory, sensual, emotional content of vowels and consonants, and it could change for ever your relationship with them. The aim of the exercise is to find ways to let the sound affect you, even move you, physically, so prepare yourself for this both in mind and body. You can work lying down, standing or sitting. Lying down may provide the most receptive, relaxed conditions, standing the most productive result in terms of energy, and sitting will be pleasant.

PREPARATION

■ *Feed in a deep sigh of relief that opens you all the way down to your pelvis and then let the feeling of relief **fall out** of you without restraint, on a free breath, without sound. Feed in another deeply felt sigh of relief and this time let it release out through your voice and your body on the vibrations of sound.*

Picture spaces within you that go from the head down through the chest, the belly, the pelvic cradle and the thighs to the toes.

Feel the breath moving into you and out of you in its own rhythm.

Picture the solar plexus as a warm, internal sun whose rays take the energy of your breath and thought down through your legs and feet, out through your arms and hands, up through your head.

Allow the sound to create space in you from head to toe
Allow the sound to move in pitch texture warmth of each "space"

EXERCISE

■ ***Think*** *the sound **OOOOO** (as in **MOO**N) and give it the autonomy to move around through the spaces of your body. See whether it prefers to occupy any particular area of your body more than another.*

*Let the **OOOOO** find the vibrations of your **voice**.*

*Let the **OOOOO** find the emotion that suits it, the mood it wants, the color that matches.*

*Let the **OOOOO** move your body as it pleases.*

*Now expel the thought of **OOOOO** from your body and mind by deliberately blowing it out of you with a strong puff of breath.*

■ *Now **think** the sound **EEEEEE** (as in **SEE**) and let the thought of the sound establish itself where it feels most at home in your body.*

*Let the **EEEEE** find your voice.*

Let the vibrations arouse whatever associations and/or emotions they want.

*Let the **EEEEE** move whatever parts of your body it pleases.*

■ *Follow the same procedure for **AAAAA** (as in **FATHER**).*

Notice that the AAAAA demands a wide open throat and an expansive voice to be fully realized. If your throat doesn't want to open, yawn prodigiously and offer the yawn opening to the AAAAA sound.

■ *Take the **OOOOO** again and this time picture it as a **deep purple** sound, living and moving around in the lower regions of your body. Experience the sound sensually. Imagine it as made of **velvet**. Let it move your body.*

■ *Now let the **EEEEE** inhabit you. Picture it **silver**. Let it glitter and sparkle in you. Allow it to stream up into your head on the highest vibrations of your voice. Let it sound like the **wind**. Imagine yourself ice-skating, calling out on a high, excited **eeeeee**.*

■ *Open up for the **AAAAA**. Let out whatever feeling is going on in you through that wide, uninhibited channel. Open your arms out wide. Feel your chest becoming expansive, generous. Picture the vibrations pouring* *through your heart and out to the horizon. Picture the sound as a warm, rich **red**.*

LET THE BREATH GO INTO YOUR BELLY AND RELEASE OUT FREELY FROM YOUR BELLY WITH EACH NEW EXPLORATION.

THOUGHT/FEELING IMPULSE INSPIRES THE BREATH—BREATH CREATES SOUND—SOUND MOVES THE BODY.

■ *Now let three small sounds play with you: **I** (as in **HIT**), **E** (as in **PET**) and **A** (as in **HAT**). These sounds are intrinsically short. Look for the differences in their nature. Do they express different energies? Find their different colors. If nothing comes to you, try a daffodil **yellow** for **I**, a bright, grass **green** for **E**, a clear **sky-blue** for **A**.*

*Let these sounds fly up into your face and head. Your mouth will be activated, so will your face muscles. **I** will go up above the eyebrows if you let it; **E** likes to ring through your upper cheekbones and **A** snaps out through the roof of your mouth and your cheeks.*

*Notice what subtly different feelings are aroused and expressed with each of these: perhaps **surprise, contempt, aggression, playfulness, delight, silliness**.*

*As these small but energetic sounds activate your body they will probably create **sharp, staccato, angular, quick** movements.*

■ *The next sound to explore is again a long one and belongs in the middle of your body. Think and then sound **O** (as in **HOPE**). Feel it in your belly. Let it express whatever emotion it suggests to you. Does it have a color? If nothing else occurs, give it a dark **blue**.*

■ *And now explore a sound that is somewhere between the **O** and the **AAAAA**. Think and then sound **AW** (as in **WALL**). Imagine it trying to emerge from the solar plexus, right at the bottom of the rib cage. It may have a somewhat anguished content. Lengthen it and feel what it wants to say. See if the color **orange** suits it.*

■ *Above **AW** but lacking the freedom of **AAAAA** is a short, strong sound that has to fight to burst out of the middle of the chest. It is the short **O** sound that occurs in the word **HOT** (the exact pronunciation of this or any of these sounds is not very important—an awareness of their differentiation is the object.) Its color is perhaps a bright **scarlet**.*

■ *For a change of energy explore the sound **EY** (as in **FATE**). It is long and light and arouses interesting responses when allowed to fly out as though through the eyes. Up there it is a very vulnerable sound, even* *naive. It may express **surprise** or **panic** or **wonder**. Perhaps **pink** is its color.*

■ *Now a short, unformed, neutral sound that pops out **HUh** (as in BUT).*

■ *And finally sigh the vibrations of sound out through a relaxed mouth that is not trying to form any particular shape. An unformed, neutral, rather vague stream of sound will easily pour out. It is **grey**, **misty**; perhaps it expresses **relief** or **pleading** or **pleasure**. It moves the body in wavy undulations and flowing soft gestures.*

These are the building-block "simple" vowel sounds and you will have noticed that each one has its own pitch. The mouth and throat are like a wind instrument that changes musical pitch by making the aperture through which the breath escapes larger or smaller. Each vowel has a different set of frequencies and its own intrinsic musical pitch. When the musculature of the mouth and throat is free of habitual tensions that distort organic vowel formation, music is a natural component of speech, with the vowel scale covering at least two octaves. When there is tension in the back of the tongue or throat the music flattens and the range diminishes to a monotonous two or three notes.

IT IS IMPORTANT TO REMEMBER THAT THIS MUSIC <u>HAPPENS</u>. IT MUST NOT BE <u>MADE TO HAPPEN</u> OR THE WORST KIND OF PHONY, AFFECTED SPEAKING WILL RESULT.

The preceding exercise is best used for awareness and for generally connecting the voice with sensory, sensual, emotional and imaginative processes. The resultant psycho-physical conditioning *serves* the refashioning of language use. The enriched enjoyment of vowels should be thought of as consciousness-raising. If pursued for its own sake and used to "beautify" speech the result will be orotund and empty.

CONSONANTS

The same kind of exploration can be undertaken for consonants. The experience will be found to differ considerably, as the sounds communicate more externally through the body, creating moods and effects more than emotions. The vibrations of consonants travel through skin and muscle and bone to the senses, while vowels have direct access to the solar plexus, making them more immediately emotional.

The characters of consonants are multifarious. For the purposes of consciousness-raising and the heightened enjoyment of the language of poetry, I suggest you go through a series of consonant experiences that deliberately connect consonants with your senses and your imagination.

The gymnasium of the mouth offers, for the exercise of twenty distinct consonants, two lips, a versatile tongue, the upper gum ridge, teeth, the dome of the roof of the mouth and the back of the hard palate. The variegated relationships that these few surfaces provide produce an astonishing spectrum of sounds.

The two large categories which define consonants are "plosives" and "continuants"; i.e., short or long. For example, **B** is plosive, it explodes; **M** is continuant, it lasts longer. Subcategories are defined as nasal, labial, fricative, breathed or voiced. The labels, however, are not important. For our purposes we can trust the involuntary processes that know these sounds organically. Somewhere in the old brain these sounds are stored and when we present the possibility of *experiencing* thought and language, consonants and vowels respond as though liberated from prison. We may find them restored in better condition than that in which we acquired them as children.

The exercise that follows is much the same as for the vowels, the goal being to recircuit words from *frontal lobe → mouth* to *brain → solar plexus → body → mouth*. This constitutes a neuro-physiological reconditioning, daunting perhaps, were it not also pleasurable. It is a restoration of natural functions and should be performed in a spirit of play. For the process to bear fruit you must be in agreement with its goal, which is to *experience words in the body*, and you must agree to immerse yourself fully in the exercise with a willingness to be surprised by what happens.

This exercise works best standing, ready to be physically active. Try not to be watchful, critical or result-oriented. Be willing to be physically activated by the sound.

PREPARATION

■ *Shake your body free from tension or lethargy, first generally, then limb by limb.*

■ *Imagine your body is made of the vibrations of sound and shake sound out through each part of your body. Allow a new breath-impulse for each shake-out.*

Each part of your body has its own frequency of vibration and will express itself differently from every other part if you tune in and give it freedom of speech. Try not to invent and impose sounds. Let the sounds galvanize the movement, rather than the body generate the sound.

EXERCISE

■ *Let the **thought** of the **sound** of the consonant **M** enter your mind. Let the thought strengthen and lengthen until you sense it choosing your lips as its means of realization.*

Delay the actualization of the sound until you can't resist it any longer.

*Yield to the long **MMMMMM** and indulge the spreading vibrations as they flow from your lips to other parts of your body.*

■ *Give the sound the power to move your body. Let yourself be activated by the sound. Feel its character. Is it **warm**, **sensuous**, **comforting**, **disturbing**, **irritating**, **nice**, **nasty**?*

■ *Let the sound move you around the room as if it were fuel.*

*Explore the **sound** of the consonants **N** and **NG** (as in SONG) in the same way as **M**, noticing the parts of the mouth these consonants choose—the front of the tongue and the upper gum ridge for **N** and the back of the tongue against the back of the hard palate for **NG**.*

Experience the similarities in mood and character between the three consonants and the **differences**.

Try not to impose ideas on the sounds—let THEM tell YOU who and what they are.

■ *Go through the same procedure with **B**. Let the **thought** of the **sound** of the consonant **B** ("buh"—not "bee") enter your mind's ear. In slow motion allow the thought to become more and more active until you feel an irresistible reaction in your lips to which you yield.*

Try not to **make** the sound, let it **happen** to your lips.
This sound will explode off the lips. It has force.

■ *Let the explosion of energy increase and affect other parts of your body until the **B** sound makes you jump.*

■ *Let the character of this sound affect you. Is it **aggressive**, **funny**, **surprising**, **proud**?*

Your lips may have to acquire extra muscle power to deal with this sound.

■ *Explore the **sound** of the consonants **D** ("duh") and **G** (the hard **G** sound, "guh"—not "gee") in the same way as **B**.*

What are the similarities and **differences** in the character and effect of the sounds?
These exploding sounds need strong muscles in the lips and the

tongue and the ability to respond to them exactly as the mind's ear and the speech cortex request. If you impose your will or invention on them, you will be in danger of pushing and straining in your throat. The formation of each sound is precise, economical and organically understood by your motor cortex. If there is any strain it is contributed by unnecessary effort which could spring from misguided enthusiasm, exaggeration or doing the exercise from outside in rather than from inside out.

The next sounds to play with are those that create friction between the surfaces of the mouth where they are formed—the resulting vibrations easily travel from the mouth through to the body.

■ *Follow the same initial procedure as for the previous sounds with the* **thought** *of the* **sound** *of the consonant* **V**, *letting it lengthen and strengthen until it is irresistibly realized between the bottom lip and the top teeth.*

■ *Let the long, buzzing* **VVVVV** *take and move your body, telling you about its nature. Let it arouse sensations, evoke associations.*

■ *Shake the* **VVVVV** *out of your body and replace it with* **ZZZZZ**. *Let it play on you.*

■ *Shake the* **ZZZZZ** *out of you and replace it with the consonant sound in the middle of the word "PLEASURE" (**ZJ**). This last sound will occupy a place between the middle of your tongue and the roof of your mouth.*

All the above sounds employ vibrations in order to be realized. They are VOICED.

The last two sets of sounds have **unvoiced** (or **breathed**) equivalents, which means that the same surfaces of the mouth as in the voiced version respond to the thought of the sound, but they handle breath rather than vibration.

■ **Think** *the sound of the consonant* **P**. *Eliminate all additional sounds. Let it be realized. You will find that it activates the lips in the same way that* **B** *did but without the vibrations of sound. A small puff of breath will be caught behind the lips and then released, causing a small explosive noise. It is breathed out as a whispered "puh."*

■ *Let its character be made manifest. Let its particular energy move whichever parts of your body seem responsive.*

Be sure not to introduce the vibrations of sound. **P** is unvoiced.

■ *Follow the exploration of* **P**, *with* **T** *(whispered* **tuh**), *and then* **K** *(whispered* **kuh**).

Each has its own precise characteristics and evokes subtly different responses.

B and **P**, **D** and **T**, **G** and **K** are voiced and unvoiced consonant pairs.

The unvoiced equivalents of **V**, **Z** and **ZJ** (as in **pleasure**) are **F**, **S**, and **SH**.

■ *Allow **FFFFFF**, then **SSSSSSS**, then **SHSHSHSH** the same freedom to play on you , moving you physically, sensorily, sensually, associatively, as you allowed the other sounds to do.*

The final pairs of voiced and unvoiced consonant sounds to be explored are **J, CH** and **TH** (as in **this**) and **TH** (as in **with**).

The same process of exploration should be undergone for **L**, **R**, **W** and **Y**.

L and **R** are chameleons, changing their nature according to their surrounding sounds. **W** and **Y** are hybrids, half vowel, half consonant. If you say them very slowly you will hear **OO-UH** making up **W** and **EE-UH** making up **Y**. They are liquid, powerful and suggestive.

If you have fully given yourself to this exploration—the exploration of *you* by the *sounds*, not the other way around—you will have experienced a wide spectrum of emotions, feelings, moods and sensations. You will also have initiated the re-conditioning process by which words are to be re-routed from brain to body and will have discovered the intrinsic energy of these sounds and how easily they stimulate physical response.

If you have been doing these exercises with another person or several others, you will probably have found that the sounds irresistibly cause interactions. Thus it is clear that even before logical meaning fires the engines of communication, communication of a fairly sophisticated nature can occur. The more alive the brain is to the minutest particles of the matter of speech, the richer the exchange of information.

Here now is a quick, energizing warm-up of vowels and consonants in the body. You will be going through the vowel scale with a different consonant attached to the beginning of each vowel, starting with the lowest sound and working up to the highest. Each sound will be aimed at a different part of your body and your interest should be to let each sound arouse whatever energy, mood, feeling or emotion it wants from you, activating the body into movement as it goes through you.

Use your hands to shape, encourage, stroke, pummel the sounds from your body, as though they too were speaking.

■ *Let the sound **ZZOOO** travel down into your pelvis and legs, moving you and them.*

*Now imagine a huge mouth opening from your belly and let the sound **WO-O-O-Oe** (as in **woe**) emerge, moving you and the middle of your body.*

*Picture the solar plexus and the diaphragm attached to the bottom of your rib cage and let out a long-drawn out **SHAW-AW-AW**.*

*Now put one fist on the center of your chest, over the breastbone, and the other directly behind it between your shoulder blades. With the sense that the sound must break through the bones, let a sharp, strong **GOh** (as in **got**) burst out.*

*Put both hands on your upper chest and start a long **MMMM** which opens into a wide, warm **AAAAA** as your arms gradually stretch out to the sides. Your heart releases its vibrations out through a wide, generous throat and through the expansion of your arms and hands.*

*Fingers on your lips and as if blowing a quick kiss: **FUh** (as in **funny**), light and airy.*

*Now your hands and your mouth are going to release a vague, misty, perhaps rather unsure sound, like a long, unformed sigh: **HU-U-U-H**.*

*Next, place your fingers on your cheeks and explode a sharp, strong, extrovert **BA** (as in **bat**) from your lips straight out through the middle of your cheeks. Let it be bright and confident and cheery.*

*From there, move up to your cheekbones. With your fingertips guiding your thought to the hard, resonant bone-ridge on either side of the bridge of your nose, let your tongue-blade flick the syllable **DEh** (as in **den**) forward and up, to spring jauntily, carelessly into the air.*

*The upward flow of your thought has now reached the level of the eyes. Feel, with your fingers, the bone-structure circling the eye-sockets. Picture the portholes of the eyes. Be aware of the fragility of your eyes and the strong protection that surrounds the "windows to the soul." An almost transparent flow of vibration can stream out at this level on **PE-EY-EY** (as in **pay**), expressing an open vulnerability, perhaps surprise, naiveté, even panic.*

*Then a quick hop up to a pinprick of sound, spitting off the middle of the forehead: **KI** (as in **kit**).*

*The final sound at the top of the scale and spiraling out as though through a small hole in the crown of the head is **RRREEE-EE-EE**. This should lift you off the ground with its sheer ebullient energy. It may be silly, ecstatic, trilling or thrilling, but it can hardly be done without a smile on the face and a jump in the air.*

Having gone all the way up, go all the way down. Let each sound arouse its different energy and mood. Make sure you allow each sound its true pitch frequency. Let your breath be free and your spirit willing to be acted upon. The sounds that on the page have been lengthened with one or more dashes are long sounds, the short ones on the page play short and staccato in your voice and body.

Here is the sequence, bottom to top and then top to bottom:

	crown	
	RREE-EE Start again here and go down	
KI	forehead **KI**	
PE-EY	eyes **PE-EY**	
DEh	cheekbones **DEh**	
BA	mid-cheeks **BA**	
HU-UH-UH	mouth **HU-UH-UH**	
FUh	lips	**FUh**
MA-AA	heart	**MA-AA**
GOh	chest center	**GOh**
SHAW-AW	solar plexus	**SHAW-AW**
WO-Oe	belly	**WO-Oe**
ZZOO-OO	legs & pelvis	**ZZOO-OO**

Start here and go up   end here

To begin with you should allow a new breath impulse for each sound. As you become familiar with this sequence you can put together sound groups as though in sentences:

ZZOO WOE SHAW *breath* **GOh MAAA** *breath* **FUh HU-UH BA DEh** *breath* **PE-EY KI RREEE** *breath* **RREEE KI PE-EY** *breath* **DEh BA HU-UH FUh** *breath* **MAAA GOh SHAW WOe ZZOOO**.

Then graduate to:

      ZZOO WOe SHAW GOh MMAAA
        breath
      FUh HU-UH BA DEh PE-EY KI RREEE
        breath
      RREEE KI PE-EY DEh BA HU-UH FUh
        breath
      MMAAA GOh SHAW WOe ZZOO

And:

ZZOO WOe SHAW GOh MMAA FUh HU-UH BA DEh PE-EY KI
        RREEE
        breath
RREEE KI PE-EY DEh BA HU-UH FUh MMAA GOh SHAW WOe
        ZZOO

This scale should warm you up through a wide spectrum of sounds and pitches, but if that is all that happens you have missed the point. The sounds are intrinsically connected to energies and moods as nuanced and diverse as the spectrum of the rainbow and the gamut of human nature. This scale provides an aerobics of the inner self and it is your inner self that desires communication and needs a language sufficient for its most complex expression. If *you* have remained unawakened in the course of the above exploration, you must submit your *desire to communicate* to a ruthless examination.

These simple vowel sounds combine and modify to form a guide to all the vowel sounds in the English and American-English language. You can quickly become alert to the body-pitch places for diphthongs such as "high" or "how" or "hue" when you are attuned to the fundamentals.

If you now return to the Chorus from *Henry V* at the beginning of this chapter, you will almost inevitably overindulge and overdo the vowels and consonants. I recommend this. With a luxurious disregard for good acting or good taste let yourself wallow in the sounds of the following Choruses from the same play. Without *singing*, allow the pitches of the vowels to dictate the sense of the lines, and if they make you move, wriggle, roll or sway yield to their persuasion. It is good to go to extremes in order to establish brain-body connections. The restraining touch of logic can safely be banished for the time being and will easily reestablish itself when the need for "normal" communication returns.

EXAMPLE:

If you take the ZOOWOE SHAW chart as a guide for the first four lines, the experience of the vowels in the words will travel actively through your body energies. The map is roughly as follows:

> *crown of the head*
> *forehead*
> *eyes*
> *cheekbones*
> *mid-cheeks*
> *mouth*
> *lips*
> *heart*
> *chest center*
> *solar plexus*
> *belly*
> *legs and pelvis*

The first four lines of the Prologue are:

> O, for a Muse of fire, that would ascend
> The brightest heaven of invention;
> A kingdom for a stage, princes to act
> And monarchs to behold the swelling scene!

The words travel something like this:

O   *belly*
    for a   *mouth*
        Muse   *forehead to legs/pelvis* (**I** to **OO**)
           of   *chest center*
              fire   *mouth/heart forehead*
                that   *mid-cheeks*
                  would   *legs/pelvis*
                    ascend   *cheekbones*
The   *lips*
    brightest   *mouth forehead*
      heaven   *cheekbones*
        of   *chest*
          invention   *forehead cheekbones mouth*
A kingdom   *mouth forehead chest*
    for a   *mouth*
        stage   *eyes*
          princes   *forehead*
            to   *legs/pelvis*
              act   *mid-cheeks*
And   *mid-cheeks*
    monarchs   *chest heart*
      to   *legs/pelvis*
        behold   *forehead belly*
          the   *mouth*
            swelling   *cheekbones forehead*
              scene   *crown of head*

DO THIS TO STRETCH YOUR VOICE AND FREE YOUR ENERGY

DO NOT GET STUCK IN PLACING THE PITCHES EXACTLY

THINK WHAT YOU ARE SAYING

Painstakingly slow and pedantic when written out like this and in danger of falling into a doctrine of correctness, the ups and downs of the vowel pitches should GO FAST and will only be liberating once you have become alive to them and allow them to move your spirit within your body.

Consonants that carry vowels can be particularly relished in the M and ZZ of "Muse" and the K's, P's, C's, T's and S's in "kingdom," "princes," "act," "swelling scene."

The interesting element that emerges when the vowel pitches are released in these lines is the amount of high energy that seems to focus in the face and head. Starting from a longing "O" in the belly and a long swoop from head to pelvis in "Muse," the thought/feeling flies into the face with "ascend," "heaven" and "invention" suggesting the level of mental effort it is going to take to imagine what comes next. The energy is maintained in the sounds and the images of "a kingdom for a stage, princes to act," and then drops to an appropriate weight for "monarchs to behold." "The swelling scene" suddenly jumps the excitement back up into the head. The next few lines center more in the middle of the body with the strong image of Harry in "the port of Mars." And so on. The one other phrase that I will pull out of this speech is "can this cockpit": when the consonants are spat out and the sharp vowels catapulted from them the scorn for the tiny stage in comparison to the vast battlefield is instantly created.

From this angle you can now play with the two Choruses below.

> O, for a Muse of fire, that would ascend
> The brightest heaven of invention;
> A kingdom for a stage, princes to act
> And monarchs to behold the swelling scene!
> Then should the warlike Harry, like himself,
> Assume the port of Mars; and at his heels,
> Leash'd in like hounds, should famine, sword and fire
> Crouch for employment. But pardon, gentles all,
> The flat unraised spirits that hath dar'd
> On this unworthy scaffold to bring forth
> So great an object: can this cockpit hold
> The vasty fields of France? or may we cram
> Within this wooden O the very casques
> That did affright the air at Agincourt?
> O, pardon! since a crooked figure may
> Attest in little place a million;
> And let us, ciphers to this great accompt,
> On your imaginary forces work.
> —*Henry V, Prologue*

> Thus with imagin'd wing our swift scene flies
> In motion of no less celerity
> Than that of thought. Suppose that you have seen
> The well-appointed king at Hampton pier
> Embark his royalty; and his brave fleet
> With silken streamers the young Phoebus fanning:
> Play with your fancies, and in them behold
> Upon the hempen tackle ship-boys climbing;
> Hear the shrill whistle which doth order give
> To sounds confus'd; behold the threaden sails,
> Borne with th'invisible and creeping wind,
> Draw the huge bottoms through the furrow'd sea,
> Breasting the lofty surge. O, do but think
> You stand upon the rivage and behold
> A city on th'inconstant billows dancing;

For so appears this fleet majestical,
Holding due course to Harfleur.
            —*Henry V, Act III, Chorus*

I close this chapter with a *caveat*: vowel and consonant awareness can become too seductive. They sometimes create such brilliant "readings" of a line that the speaker ceases to think and falls into a patterned inflection that is as boring as a monotone. They can lead to a "singing" of the text. There is an almost equal potential for the worst kind of pretentious reciting as there is for thrillingly alive dramatic speaking. However the dangers are outweighed by the opportunities and the opportunity for richly expanding your range and interpretive possibilities is worth the risk.

2

◆► Words and Images ◄►

Having spent some time resuscitating vowels and consonants and getting a taste of how much non-verbal information they contain, we now move on to what happens when these elements are juxtaposed in such a way as to form words.

Our conditioned, unconscious relationship with words is utilitarian. They get things done for us. "Language is a tool" is a phrase commonly heard in today's trade-minded society. When attached to "doing," words must go somewhere, move along a horizontal road with linear purpose. The language of poetry is different. It is attached to "being." It expresses inner states and emotional responses to outer events. To speak poetry, words must be plugged in to the inner condition, generating energy on a vertical path running between mind and heart. They must then be allowed to flow out, fully charged, to the hearer. The language energies of spoken poetry run simultaneously on vertical and horizontal pathways, or, if you like, on electrical circuits that are at once introverted and extroverted.

A consciousness of *how* words are spoken is necessary in cultivating the ability to speak poetically. For inspired instruction, here is a poem of Pablo Neruda's, *Verbo*, that I like very much. I have made a literal translation from the original Spanish (with help from Gilda Orlandi-Sanchez).

Verbo	*Word*
Voy a arrugar esta palabra	I'm going to crumple this word,
voy a torcerla,	I'm going to twist it,
si,	yes,
es demasiado lisa,	it's too smooth,
es como si un gran perro o	it's as though a big dog or
un gran rio	a big river
le hubiera repasado	had been licking it over and
lengua o agua	over with tongue or water
durante muchos anos.	for many years.

Quiero que en la palabra
se vea la asperaza,
la sal ferruginosa,
la fuerza desdentada
de la tierra,
la sangre
de los que hablaron y de los que
    no hableron.

Quiero ver la sed
adentro de las silabas:
quiero tocar el fuego
en el sonido:
quiero sentir la oscuridad
del grito. Quiero
palabras asperas,
como piedras virgenes.

I want the word
to reveal the roughness,
the ferruginous salt,
the toothless strength
of the earth,
the blood
of those who talked and of those
    who did not talk.

I want to see the thirst
inside the syllables,
I want to touch the fire
in the sound:
I want to feel the darkness
of the scream. I want
rough words,
like virgin rocks.

Neruda refers to sight, touch, taste and feeling but leaves out the most obvious of the senses belonging to words: hearing. It's as though *hearing* is a trap; it's too easy to assume you have heard and therefore understood the word. It's what we do all day long. Words are habits. Thoughts run in patterns. As long as they stay in their grooves they reassure our existence and keep us safe from new experiences which might awaken us to an alarming new look at ourselves and the world around us. If, however, we *want* a deeper experience, a fresh look, we must shut off the sense of hearing and stop taking it for granted that we know what we heard and what we think about it.

When words are *seen, tasted, touched, felt,* they penetrate and break up patterns of thought. They reach into emotions, memories, associations, and they spark the imagination. They bring life. The *way* you speak Shakespeare's words will determine the *depth* at which you plumb his meaning. Neruda's passionate desire for something rough and tactile in words is indivisible from the passion of his creative process. He says that the words must *be* the senses, must *be* the emotions because only then will they plumb the depths of the human condition and tell the truth. The Shakespeare speaker does well to listen to him.

Channeling words off the page and into the sensorium can easily devolve into sentimental wallowing. It must be done with craftsmanlike care. The discrete character and autonomous function of each word must come to life in the imagination and be experienced in the sensory and emotional nerve centers and nerve-endings. The experienced meaning of the word must then be channeled out through the vowel and consonant paths of vibration and appetite articulators. The word on the page ***becomes*** its meaning-in-the-imagination, the meaning ***becomes*** imagination-experienced-in-the-body (sensorily and/or emotionally), and that experienced-meaning ***becomes*** the spoken word.

Imagination, of course, has to do with images. You can have images in your head and you can look at them purely with your mind's eye, or those images can arouse a response in you. Notice the difference between *appreciating* and *experiencing* in these two possibilities. It is, perhaps, the difference between interior decoration and the art of painting. Some people say, "I hate the color green," and are surprised to experience a peaceful, happy feeling when they breathe the image of the color into the solar plexus, or they may say, "I love red," and, breathing the color in, be shocked into murderous rage. There is no value judgment to be placed on these observations. One demonstrates "thinking about" and the other "experiential thinking" or just "thinking."

Unfortunately, "thinking" and "feeling" have become largely separated in our culture. "Cold reason" is generally upheld as being more reliable than "hot passion," the two being considered mutually incompatible, and "judgment" is presented as dependable where "feelings" are not. The approved compromise is tepid tolerance, "seeing both sides of the question," "trying to be reasonable," "respecting the opposition," "taking time out to cool down." While this may be good for a homogenized society, it is clearly death to drama, and those who want to speak the words of a great poetic dramatist may have to confront a social conditioning in themselves that has fragmented their ability to speak with emotion.

Had King Lear been told as a child, "When you've calmed down, we'll talk about why you're angry," his throat would have clamped shut around the storm without and the storm within that meet in these words:

> Blow, winds, and crack your cheeks! rage, blow!
> You cataracts and hurricanoes, spout
> Till you have drench'd our steeples, drown'd the cocks!
> You sulph'rous and thought-executing fires,
> Vaunt-couriers of oak-cleaving thunderbolts,
> Singe my white head! And thou, all shaking thunder,
> Strike flat the thick rotundity o' th' world!
> Crack nature's moulds, all germains spill at once
> That make ungrateful man!

The source of eloquence is emotion, and the vocal musculature is capable of handling any extreme expression, but we are taught early on that suppression is safer than expression and the muscles of diaphragm and throat learn fast how to clamp down on anger and sorrow. "When you stop crying and pull yourself together you can tell me what's wrong"—this seemingly benign admonition in effect informs the child psycho-physically that tears and words cannot co-exist. The child-rearing theories that formed Constance, in *King John*, were clearly of a different school:

> I am not mad, I would to heaven I were!
> For then 'tis like I should forget myself.
> O if I could what grief should I forget!
> Preach some philosophy to make me mad,
> And thou shalt be canoniz'd, Cardinal;
> For, being not mad, but sensible of grief,
> My reasonable part produces reason
> How I may be deliver'd of these woes,
> And teaches me to kill or hang myself.

and later:

> Grief fills the room up of my absent child,
> Lies in his bed, walks up and down with me,
> Puts on his pretty looks, repeats his words,
> Remembers me of all his gracious parts,
> Stuffs out his vacant garments with his form;
> Then have I reason to be fond of grief.
> *King John, Act III, Scene iii*

She is not "talking *about*" her emotional state, she is revealing it, eloquently. Her body can express it and her brain form it into words. Neither instrument inhibits the other.

These passages deal with extremity and it is redundant to offer them as examples of how images create emotion. The effect is so blatant, however, that they may help to demonstrate that the principle holds for all the imagery in Shakespeare's language. Treat the images as metaphors and you will end up spouting poetry; experience them emotionally and they will create an inner drama to be revealed directly and transparently through the medium of the words. Conflicting images creating conflicting emotions will "act" you and, to a large extent, the genius of the originator of the language will make intelligent sense of your emotions if you just keep on speaking.

Becoming aware of images in language is a process of slowing down. If you go into slow motion mentally and say, "I'll go by the supermarket on my way home from work and get something for dinner," you will start seeing in your mind's eye the supermarket, possibly see and discard several alternative stores; you may see yourself leaving your workplace, may get a flash of the hamburger section of the store or the vegetable stand. You can do this with "I think, therefore I am" or "What is the sound of one hand clapping?" Images are intrinsic to words. Concrete images are relatively easy to see internally but it may take more of a questing spirit to catch sight of the abstract imagery in a phrase such as "an abstract idea." As in the art of painting, the art of language is both representational and abstract. Introduce the sense of sight to the meaning of a word and images will emerge and multiply. Images lead more directly, albeit less explicably, to emotion than logical reasoning does, and the speaker of poetry can trust that such a deep, instinctive connection is the wellspring for a true understanding of the text.

As we move into the exercises with which you can practice and experience the word-image-emotion response, bear in mind that in order to build new habits one must be aware of and suspend the old ones. In the case of reading, you almost certainly have a linear habit— you read quickly along the lines of print to find out what information is in them. This is not wrong, but in the search for Shakespeare's meaning it is not enough. Your linear habit must be suspended, your whole reading process must be arrested and rehabilitated. This may sound as though I am accusing you of criminal behavior and in a way I am, but I offer you a swift means of rehabilitation if you will slow down, be patient and swear off all interest in results for the time being.

Most habitual reading out loud follows the following pattern:

printed word → eye → frontal lobe → thinking about → spoken about.

The exercises you are about to embark upon will re-pattern the mechanical habit to:

printed word → eye → image → breath → feeling → experience/memory/emotion → sound → spoken word.

In the second process, the spoken word *reveals* rather than *describes* the inner content. It is *the word made flesh* rather than *the word as symbol*.

The word/image/sound/action exercises that follow may be thought of as the process of painting a picture. Each word is a different brush stroke; several brush strokes create small parts of the whole picture which, as they accumulate on the canvas, reveal more and more of the eventual whole. Along the way, each part is a whole picture: The drop of water, the wave, the many drops, many waves, their color, the clouds, their color, the sky, its color, the ocean, broken masts, torn sails, ship, rocks. The whole picture in the end is shipwreck.

I am going to ask you to go on a journey of words without knowing where they will lead or what they will eventually say. The fact that I can tell you that they *will* say something in the end both gives a reason for going on the journey and sets up the conflict between old and new habits.

The *new* habit will be exercised as you breathe in words of different natures and release them out in no apparent order. They will enter you, explore you, arouse in you whatever they want; they will find cal access into you so that each has its own autonomous existence. They will then escape from you filled with your experience. The *old* habit may be to control the words, work with them to make them make sense. Your exercise is to *do* nothing but allow a great deal to *happen* to you. Your job is to consciously arrest the wish to make linear sense out of the words as they accumulate.

You are at liberty to look ahead to see what the result of the exercise is, but if you do, you will diminish the effect by about 75%. If, after reading these words, you still are compelled to skip ahead to know what it's about, observe your need for the security of being in control. This is not wrong; it reveals your fear of the unknown, and your discovery of a new way of functioning may take a little longer.

The following exercises will take from two to three hours to explore. They work best in one uninterrupted session, but I have marked two places where you can stop and start again, breaking the work into three one-hour sessions.

PREPARATION

■ *Awaken your body and voice with stretches and the vibration-shaking processes described in Chapter One, then spend enough time with the* **ZooWoeShawGohMaa FuhHu-uhBaDePeyKiReee** *sequence to feel an integration and freedom of breath, voice, body, emotions and inner self throughout your range.*

■ *Standing or lying down, turn your attention inward to the solar plexus-diaphragm-breath-emotion-sound-energy center. Picture, perhaps as though it were a child's painting, a round, golden sun whose rays radiate down through your legs, out through your arms, up through your chest, throat and head. Let that picture become vibrations of sound that, as they radiate out through your body, activate your body into movement.*

Spend some time allowing different impulses of breath-sound-sun-energy to flow, or fly out, through specifically visualized parts of the body—your right leg, your left arm, your shoulder, elbow, etc. Each new impulse starts in the central sun picture. Each new impulse is a new ingoing breath impulse which then releases out; the outgoing breath-sound-energy is sometimes long, sometimes short, sometimes sharp, sometimes flowing, sometimes strong, sometimes gentle.

Your body gradually becomes more and more subtly responsive to the thought-breath-sound impulses until the physical and the mental seem to merge and become one. The dense matter of the body has refined to the subtle matter of sound waves and thought waves.

INSTRUCTIONS

In a moment, you are going to see a word on this page and, breathing it into the solar-plexus-diaphragm-breath-emotion-sound energy center, you will then let it play out on the vibrations of sound through your body, activating it into movement along the paths that the sun picture created. Go step by step in this sequence:

1. Look at the word.
2. Close your eyes.
3. Let the word drop into the solar plexus/sound/energy centre.
4. Let the emotion/sound/energy response release out through the vowel and consonant channels that form the word—running through any or all parts of the body, animating into movement as it goes.
5. Open your eyes and look at the question or instruction on the page.
6. Close your eyes and let the word release through you again.

DO NOT <u>ANSWER</u> THE QUESTION

LET THE WORD ENTER AND RELEASE AGAIN

Repeat 5 and 6 to end of questions.

Go through the process quickly so that you are not stopping to "think" or "be sure" about your response. Bypass the head and let the question or instruction act directly on your solar plexus center with an instantaneous reaction out through any or all channels of your voice/body.

EXERCISE

BRASS

Close eyes—"BRASS"

   WHAT COLOR IS IT?

Close eyes—"BRASS"

   WHAT DOES IT FEEL LIKE TO TOUCH?

Close eyes—"BRASS"

   DO YOU OWN ANY OF THIS?

Close eyes—"BRASS"

   FEEL THE VOWELS AND CONSONANTS.

Close eyes—"BRASS"

STONE

Close eyes—"STONE"

   WHAT DOES IT LOOK LIKE?

Close eyes—"STONE"

   WHAT DOES IT FEEL LIKE TO TOUCH?

Close eyes—"STONE"

   HAVE YOU EVER THROWN THIS AT ANYONE?

Close eyes—"STONE"

   WHAT'S IT LIKE TO BE HIT BY ONE?

Close eyes—"STONE"

   FEEL THE VOWELS AND CONSONANTS.

Close eyes—"STONE"

EARTH

Close eyes—"EARTH"

   WHAT DOES IT SMELL LIKE?

Close eyes—"EARTH"

   WHAT'S IT LIKE TO PUT YOUR HANDS IN?

Close eyes—"EARTH"

   WHAT DOES IT LOOK LIKE FROM A SPACESHIP?

Close eyes—"EARTH"

   DO YOU LIKE GARDENING?

Close eyes—"EARTH"

   FEEL THE VOWELS AND CONSONANTS.

Close eyes—"EARTH"

SEA

Close eyes—"SEA"

WHAT COLOR IS IT?

Close eyes—"SEA"

HOW DOES IT FEEL ON A HOT DAY?

Close eyes—"SEA"

IS IT CALM OR STORMY?

Close eyes—"SEA"

WHEN WERE YOU LAST BY THE SEA?

Close eyes—"SEA"

MORTALITY

Close eyes—"MORTALITY"

WHAT DO YOU SEE?

Close eyes—"MORTALITY"

DO YOU THINK ABOUT YOUR OWN MORTALITY?

Close eyes—"MORTALITY"

WOULD YOU LIKE TO LIVE FOR EVER?

Close eyes—"MORTALITY"

FEEL THE CONSONANTS.

Close eyes—"MORTALITY"

POWER

Close eyes—"POWER"

WHERE DO YOU FEEL IT IN YOUR BODY?

Close eyes—"POWER"

WHAT MAKES YOU FEEL POWERFUL?

Close eyes—"POWER"

ARE OTHER PEOPLE MORE POWERFUL THAN YOU?

Close eyes—"POWER"

WHAT COULD YOU ACHIEVE WITH POWER?

Close eyes—"POWER"

AND..........REST..........RELAX..........STRETCH..........SHAKE IT OUT

COMMENTS

At this point it is a good idea to ask yourself how you feel and to assess the process you have been going through. However and whatever you feel is worth observing, noting and, if necessary, analyzing. It cannot be wrong.

A useful rule is always to express *first* (out loud to yourself or to another person or written in a journal) anything that was new, surprising, illuminating or different.

When you have done that, go on to express those experiences, if any, that were difficult, whether because they were painful, or you were resistant, or you thought you were "doing it wrong," etc. Remember that you are conditioning in a new set of habits and the old ones are going to put up a fight to stay in business. If you immediately say (to yourself or someone else), "I felt nauseous the whole time," or "My throat hurts," or "I couldn't see any images," any fleeting new insight or quiver of fresh experience will evaporate. New experiences "happen" and they need to be reinforced in words that describe them or they will dissolve in a flash. In right/left brain hemisphere terminology, a new experience is recorded in the right (imagining) hemisphere and will only survive if supported by verbal record in the left (verbalizing) hemisphere.

After any of these exercises, it is crucial that you record, in some way, any fresh reactions, new emotional connections, insights into your breathing mechanism or creative impulses, things that jolted your memory or gave you unexpected pleasure or pain.

You will notice that the words are like keys that unlock doors inside you. The doors open on different chambers of your inner dwelling. There are doors that open onto landscapes which lead you to memories—perhaps of childhood events—sometimes pleasant, sometimes unpleasant. There are word-keys that turn in the lock and emotions burst the door open. Some keys are like those entrusted by Bluebeard to his wife with the injunction, "You may open every door but THAT ONE!" How many doors are marked "TABOO"? But there is no such thing as a "negative" emotion for the actor. All emotions are essential to creativity and as you go through Shakespeare's words you will find again and again that any feelings that may have seemed too painful, too "negative," or quite simply taboo in your life have already been expressed by Shakespeare.

I suggest that you take a moment here to record, express and assess your state of mind and being, then prepare to continue.

(Or you may break here.)

<<<<<<< >>>>>>>

I would like you now to copy the following words onto a large sheet of paper:

SAD RAGE BEAUTY PLEA ACTION STRONGER FLOWER SUMMER HONEY BREATH WRACKFUL SIEGE BATTERING DAYS ROCKS IMPREGNABLE STOUT GATES STEEL STRONG TIME DECAYS FEARFUL MEDITATION TIME JEWEL CHEST STRONG HAND SWIFT FOOT SPOIL BEAUTY FORBID NONE MIRACLE BLACK INK LOVE SHINE BRIGHT

With a pair of scissors cut the words out so that they are jumbled up. Pick up a word at random and continue the exercise in the manner started above asking yourself at least three questions about each word. The questions can be categorized to cover the following areas of response:

1) The Senses.
2) The Emotions.
3) Memory.
4) Personal Association.
5) Imagination.
6) Vowel/Consonant Dynamics.

Model your questions on the ones asked in the early part of the exercise. Keep them simple. Don't answer the questions—say the word again under the influence of the question. Try working with someone else who can quickly throw in a one-phrase question to awaken more facets of response in you. *The questions should not be psychoanalytical.*
Sample questions of a useful nature:

SAD—   "Where in your body do you feel this?"
            "What made you sad when you were a kid?"
            "Have you ever looked in the mirror when you're crying?"

FLOWER—   "What's your favorite flower?"
            "Who would you like to give flowers to?"
            "If you were a flower, what kind would you be?"

BATTERING—   "Feel the vowels and consonants in your body."
                "Do you ever feel battered by life?"
                "Have you ever banged at a door that's closed?"
                "Can you make pancake batter?"

HONEY—   "Do you have a sweet tooth?"
                "Is it sticky?"
                "Has anyone ever called you this?"
                "Who do you like to call 'honey?'"

Sample questions of a prurient, exploitative, unhelpful, even dangerous nature:

SAD—   "What's the saddest thing in your life right now?"
                "Did anyone you loved die when you were a child?"

FLOWER—   "What flowers would you like at your funeral?"

BATTERING—   "Were you abused as a child?"
                "Do you feel you want to batter someone to death?"

HONEY—   "Imagine honey all over your skin."
                "Picture a swarm of bees all over you."

The deeper the personal material that comes up in reponse to the word, the more deeply rooted the words will be. However, *you* are in charge of the keys, the doors and the journey, and *you* are the person who knows whether your resistance is *preventing you from growth* or *protecting you from an experience you can't take*. Be honest with yourself and others on this issue.

When a strong emotion comes up in response to a word, YOU MUST SPEAK THE WORD. Do not stop to cry, laugh or scream outside the word. You are exercising the ability to feel and speak at the same time, reconnecting thought/feeling/speaking mechanisms which may have been dislocated from each other at some earlier time in your development. If your throat wants to close on the word, notice that and yawn your throat open while you continue feeling what you are feeling and SPEAK THE WORD OUT THROUGH YOUR WHOLE BODY.

KEEP BREATHING—KEEP RELAXING YOUR MUSCLES
BETWEEN WORDS

Remember:
    word → solar plexus → image → breath → experience/
    memory/emotion
    SPOKEN WORD
    activating the body as it releases out
    QUESTION OR INSTRUCTION

breath to solar plexus
SPOKEN WORD
QUESTION OR INSTRUCTION
SPOKEN WORD

etc.

The process, taking in and releasing every word in your jumbled heap of words, should take at least an hour.

<<<<<<< >>>>>>>

Now look at the words you have been absorbing as they appear on the page.

SAD RAGE BEAUTY PLEA ACTION STRONGER FLOWER SUMMER HONEY BREATH WRACKFUL SIEGE BATTERING DAYS ROCKS IMPREGNABLE STOUT GATES STEEL STRONG TIME DECAYS FEARFUL MEDITATION TIME JEWEL CHEST STRONG HAND SWIFT FOOT SPOIL BEAUTY FORBID NONE MIRACLE BLACK INK LOVE SHINE BRIGHT

As if they were a speech or a poem, speak them, slowly at first and then up to the speed of natural speech.

DO NOT LET THE WORDS WASH INTO EACH OTHER. THEY MUST MAINTAIN THEIR AUTONOMY.

At this point you are exercising two abilities, your ability to sustain a precisely alive inner imaging process that is in contact with your feelings, and the ability of your voice to reveal rapidly changing inner content with flexibility, spontaneity and appropriate variety.

Relax, assess, record, prepare to continue, or break here.

<<<<<<< >>>>>>>

In the words you have absorbed thus far, there are:

- image words (brass, sea, flower, gates)
- emotion words (rage, sad, fearful, love)
- state-of-being words (power, strong, impregnable)
- active words (action, battering, decays)
- impressionistic words (bright, time, spoil, days)

Although you might categorize them differently, the purpose of the exercise is not categorization but the experiential discovery that you undoubtedly made which is that all of them have associations and all connect easily with your emotions and/or senses if you let them. They do so in varying degrees of intensity according to their content. They all by nature arouse either states of being, or moods, or feelings, or emotions, or passions. Language is, by its nature, both emotional and reasonable. These words are powerfully suggestive and all are "representational." They re-present the aroused internal human condition. They are easily seen as imagistic.

There are dozens more words that are of a very different character from the ones experienced thus far. I call them the LITTLE-BIG WORDS. In grammar they are called prepositions and conjunctions and pronouns (I will be including a few little-big verbs as well), but they are more interestingly thought of as relationship words. They have the magical property of metamorphosing from very small to very big and changing the meaning of things, hence my label "little-big," with its suggestion of fairy-tale magic, elf and monster. In image terms little-big words belong in the realm of abstract art, and when detached from their obvious jobs as the builders and breakers of relationships they lead quite an active life of their own within the mind. They are little words with big ripples.

You can get to know the autonomous nature of the little-big words in a meditative manner if you wish or continue with the active, physical process. The first step is quiet and non-doing so that you may clear away preconceptive, grammatical imposition.

DESCRIPTION OF THE EXERCISE

Copy onto a large sheet of paper the following words and then cut them out and jumble them up:

SINCE NOR BUT THEIR HOW WITH THIS SHALL A WHOSE IS NO THAN OH OUT AGAINST THE OF WHEN ARE NOT SO WHERE FROM OR WHAT CAN HIS WHO UNLESS HAVE THAT IN MY MAY STILL

In a relaxed state you are going to look at a cut-out little-big word. You will then close your eyes and *silently* repeat the word in your mind/body. Continue to repeat the word internally in the manner of a mantra, ignoring the written image of it and denying it any connection with another word. Notice its behavior, observe any shapes or actions it creates and what state of mind or being it creates in you.

Once it has gone beyond its printed, grammatical persona and has aroused something, however intangible, in you, *let it speak out loud*.

Then open your eyes and get to know another of the little-big words.

PREPARATION

■ *Sitting or standing, be aware of your body and relax each part of it. Then turn your attention inwards and become aware of your relaxed, involuntary breathing.*

PROCEED WITH THE EXERCISE AS DESCRIBED ABOVE.

When all the words have been experienced, relax, stretch, shake and go on to the second part of the exercise.

■ *Choose four of the little-big words. Let them talk to each other through you.*

■ *Let them move you according to their dynamics, one after another, so that the "quadralogue" becomes actively performed.*

■ *Allow a dialogue, trialogue, quadralogue or crowd scene to develop with other people, each person using only his or her own four little-big words as text. Listen and answer.*

■ *Now look at the collection of little-big words as they appear on the page.*

> SINCE NOR BUT THEIR HOW WITH THIS SHALL A
> WHOSE IS NO THAN OH OUT AGAINST THE OF WHEN
> ARE NOT SO WHERE FROM OR WHAT CAN HIS WHO
> UNLESS HAVE THAT IN MY MAY STILL

*Speak them as if they were a whole speech or poem. Let the words **play you** with all their individuality.*

DO NOT MANIPULATE THE WORDS. LET THEM HAVE THEIR AUTONOMY.

What did you find? There will be all sorts of responses to that question but I think you will agree that whatever else goes on with these units of language, they are inherently dramatic. They are constantly stopping, starting, changing, opening up, doubting, suspending action, suggesting another possibility, slamming the door in your face, widening the horizon. They are full of energy. They are looking for relationships.

In the next chapter we will see what happens when these energetic little-big words latch on to the other autonomous characters in the drama of language, and how the representational, image-replete, and emotion-packed words behave when they find themselves in relationship with each other.

3

◆▶ Words Into Phrases ◀▶

As words are juxtaposed, new pictures flash into the mind.

Take the word EARTH with which you worked in the previous session.

Let the word turn into a picture, breathe it in, let it speak.

Now take the word MOTHER.

Let the word turn into a picture, breathe it in, let it speak

Now put MOTHER in front of EARTH—MOTHER EARTH.

Picture; breathe the picture in; release the picture out through the words.

Now take the words EARTH MOTHER.

Picture; breathe the picture in; release the picture out through the words.

Now take EARTH'S CIRCUMFERENCE.

Picture; breathe the picture in; release the picture out through the words.

And now, ROOTED IN EARTH.

Picture; breathe the picture in; release the picture out through the words.

If your breath and voice are sensitive to the changing picture, the word EARTH will sound subtly different each time you say it because the feeling or mood that accompanies each picture is different. If you are working alone, it may be difficult to recognize any change in the sound that results from the changing picture. Often, one will *feel* different, and be imaginatively delighted with different impulses, and yet *sound* exactly the same. But if you start listening to yourself and try to manipulate the sound, you will lose the integrity of your inner work.

Eventually there is a kind of sensory *hearing* that develops which is different from *listening*; you will *feel/hear* what happens and be able to make adjustments causally on an internal basis that will shift the result; but as long as you are *listening* and *making* a resultant sound change with the help of the ear, you are doing two separate things, thus breaking the unity that leads to a truthful performance.

Checking the relationship of cause and result in a process as subjective as acting and/or speaking leads one into a minefield of contradictions. The next few paragraphs indicate some of the confusion, the quagmire of contingent factors to be traversed before arriving at an assessment of performance as *excellent, true, moving* or *bad, false, self-indulgent*. I am fully aware of the dangers of misinterpretation here, and if you prefer to proceed in the subjective, total-immersion mode, you should skip the following section that discusses ways of judging the success of your work.

OTHERWISE:

With some trepidation I suggest the use of a tape recorder to help you in this phase of your work if you are working by yourself. As in the case of peer group work, and in the case of teachers with their students, the first question to be asked is:
"What am I listening for?"
For the purpose of this exercise in judgment you are listening to yourself on the tape to hear a tone of voice that is true to the inner image/feeling.

It may take some time to tune your ear to the subtleties of tone and truth, therefore question #2 is: **"If the inner image/feeling changes, can I hear the tone of voice reflecting the change?"** This question has three possible answers: **(a) "I can't tell what I'm hearing," (b) "The voice stays the same whatever the image/feeling is,"** and **(c) "I hear the change."**

The only remedy for answer (a) is to start listening to people's voices in a different way. Listen not to what they are saying but to how they say it and ask yourself what is conveyed by the different tones of voice you hear. Asking new questions will awaken new perceptions and attune your listening to fresh possibilities.

Answer (b) leads to question #3: **"If the tone of voice remains the same when the inner image/feeling is different, what should I do about it?"**
To this my response is: First, you must realize that your voice is not sensitive to the imprint of the inner impulse. For your voice to become sensitive you may have to address some fundamental tensions in the vocal musculature, or you may have to practice the introductory steps in Sessions One and Two a little longer, or you may just have to relax and breathe more freely, deeper in your body, and the responses will change.

It is answer (c) that leads to the complicated question #4: **"If the tone of voice changes with the changing image/feeling, does it sound phony or true?"** and from there to the murky depths of the question, **"what is TRUE?"** In this instance, the estimate of "truth" may well depend upon whether or not the listener has an aesthetic which tunes out individual "truthfulness" in favor of an external standard. If the listener prefers Richard Burton's voice, or Claire Bloom's voice, to the current speaker's voice, the TRUTH of the current speaker has no hope of being recognized. If the listener is listening with phony ears, the speaker can be reinforced in phony delivery.

By "phony" I mean "pretentious," which has a dictionary definition of "attempting to pass for more than one is worth; pretending to a superiority not real"; but a delivery that sounds pretentious to me may be full of aesthetic pleasure for you and what sounds true to me may seem crude or messy to you. On the printed page, there is very little I can do to shed light on the dark eternal battle of what constitutes good taste in Shakespearean speaking or what makes a performance TRUE. The only element in the whole process that can be assessed without recourse to the wavering arbitration of individual taste is breath. True emotion engages breath deeply in the body and attention paid to the behavior of the speaker's breathing will be the best litmus test for integrity.

The premise of this book is that the truthful expression of twentieth century emotions is experientially different from the truthful expression of Elizabethan emotions and that within us all is the potential for an outgoing, large, uncensored emotional expression that is more deeply true to us, personally, than our daily life allows. Therefore, to achieve a true Elizabethan mode of expression we need to liberate ourselves from the accepted contemporary mode of inhibition and limitation.

Given this premise, we are faced with question #5: **"Do I like what I hear *better* when the voice changes with the changing inner image/feeling or not?"**

When you are working by yourself that implies questions #6 and #7: **"Am I following my own inner voice of truth or some external standard?" "Do I feel freer, more abandoned, re-energized *and* do I like the result?"**

Question #5 is easier with peer group workers because consensus is usually reliable if the ground rules are clear. The feedback should be relatively simple: **"I liked it better"** or **"I liked it less."**

For the teacher with students it seems to me imperative that the teacher opens question #5 out to the rest of the class so that the arbiter of truth and taste is the community and not the authority figure. By and large the community will provide a reliable sounding-board for the TRUTH.

Leaving the assessment intersection now and picking up on the exploration of words becoming phrases, it will be your investment in the connection of your inner image/feelings with your breath/sound/emotion/energy center that counts in any significant success with the exercise.

THE AIM OF THE EXERCISE IS TO BREAK THE LINEAR READING HABIT AND TRUST THAT THE EXPRESSION OF JUXTAPOSED VERTI-CALLY-EXPERIENCED IMAGE/FEELINGS WILL ACCUMULATE INTO MEANING.

As preparation for this next and crucial phase, practice reading the following "script," observing the punctuation as indications of thought patterns. A comma indicates a slight shift in thought, a semi-colon indicates a statement that is not quite finished, and a period must have finality. After a period there is a fresh, new thought. When your brain and body are connected, thought change and breath change are one and the same. At a comma there may be a tiny new breath, at a semi-colon there will be a new breath, and at a period there will be a clear finishing of the previous breath, with a new breath entering, charged with the content of the next thought to start the new sentence.

I am asking you to redefine the words *word thought breath* for this exercise; *word* means *image/feeling*; *thought* means *words/breath*; *breath* means *thought/impulse*. They all live in the middle of the body.

The following are punctuated versions of the "speech/poems" you performed in the last session.

■ *Brass, stone; earth, boundless sea. Sad mortality, power, rage, beauty, plea. Action stronger flower, summer honey breath hold wrackful siege, battering days rocks impregnable, stout gates steel strong time decays. Fearful meditation, time best jewel, chest lie hid. Strong hand swift foot spoil beauty forbid. None. Miracle. Black ink. Love. Shine bright.*

■ *Since nor nor nor but their, how with this, shall a whose is no than. Oh. How shall out against the of, when are not so, nor so but. Oh. Where, alack. Shall from or what. Can his back or who his of can. Oh; none. Unless; this have that, in my may still.*

Rehearse these as you might any speech to performance level and at the pace of natural speaking.

NOW COMES THE BIG MOMENT!

We have labored mightily to reestablish circuits between the speech cortex and the sensorium and have been focusing on the con-

sciousness of vertical thought energy in order to BREAK THE LIN-
EAR HABIT. But we must sooner or later come back to linear communication—your words must come out of you on horizontal
thought/energy lines and go to a listener who is outside you. If you
can be conscious vertically and horizontally at the same time, you will
be speaking at a heightened level of consciousness. The sheer electrical power it takes to do this means that you will be operating at a
higher voltage than usual and your audience will get its money's
worth.

By the end of this chapter you should have "rehabilitated" your
reading and your speaking to the extent that you experience both processes quite differently, and your audience (of one or two to five hundred or more) is hearing you with twice the ease and double the
excitement. You should not sound as if you are speaking in some
peculiar style or that you have learnt how to speak "Shakespearean
verse which is, of course, an elevated, classical way of speaking far
above the heads of most mortals." Given that we are born breathing
and giving voice "naturally," but then learn to suppress and limit communication to fit society's needs, most people speak "unnaturally"
most of the time. When you have "rehabilitated" your speaking for
Shakespeare, you will have rediscovered your "natural" speech. The
state of nature is a very lively state.

However, it may take long reconditioning practice before your
voice naturally responds to the taste, texture and imagery of words.
You may have to go very slowly and repeat the exercises daily for
some time for organic change to take place. The next stage may throw
you right back to your old habits, so be prepared for this and be
patient. Do not worry about results.

You are now going to take the two collections of independent
words you have been exploring and mix them together so that they
make grammatical sense. Your job will be to make sure the independent words do not drown in the grammar.

The "little-big" words take some attention. They are little on the
page but they are essential for the other words to make sense. They
make relationships between words and sometimes they have a tendency to want to dominate the relationship. "So" and "such" and
"my" and "and" can obliterate "strong" and "wealth" and "love." The
twentieth century seems to have allowed the little-big words a great
deal of authority, particularly in officialese. The announcements in
airports are overrun with little-big words sounding important: "**All**
passengers **may** now proceed **to** the west gate. Those **with** small children **will** be boarded first. Please **have** your boarding passes **in** your
hand."

Some of these words are undoubtedly dramatic: *unless—yet—if—
or—but* can make you hold your breath in anticipation of what comes

next and then insist you make a complete mental turnaround, but they must now be made to serve a greater purpose than their own. As you look at a grammatical line your exercise will be to allow the autonomy of each word while it serves the other words; together, they produce rich meaning.

This does __not__ mean that you give __equal emphasis__ to every word. Because each word has its own autonomy it does __not__ follow that they all have the __same importance__. If you pay attention to the autonomy of each word the dynamics of your reading should be more variegated, not more emphatic.

PREPARATION

Without paying too much attention to the sense of it, copy the following sonnet on to a large sheet of paper.

> SINCE BRASS NOR STONE NOR EARTH NOR BOUNDLESS SEA
> BUT SAD MORTALITY O'ERSWAYS THEIR POWER
> HOW WITH THIS RAGE SHALL BEAUTY HOLD A PLEA
> WHOSE ACTION IS NO STRONGER THAN A FLOWER.
> O HOW SHALL SUMMER'S HONEY BREATH HOLD OUT
> AGAINST THE WRACKFUL SIEGE OF BATTERING DAYS
> WHEN ROCKS IMPREGNABLE ARE NOT SO STOUT
> NOR GATES OF STEEL SO STRONG BUT TIME DECAYS.
> O FEARFUL MEDITATION. WHERE, ALACK,
> SHALL TIME'S BEST JEWEL FROM TIME'S CHEST LIE HID
> OR WHAT STRONG HAND CAN HOLD HIS SWIFT FOOT BACK
> OR WHO HIS SPOIL OF BEAUTY CAN FORBID.
>   O NONE, UNLESS THIS MIRACLE HAVE MIGHT
>   THAT IN BLACK INK MY LOVE MAY STILL SHINE BRIGHT.

Now cut each line out and jumble up the resultant fourteen strips of paper.

PREPARE your voice and body for an active response to these collections of words. When you insist that the words and feelings move your body, you are assuring a disturbance of habitual patterns of thought and speech and this is the object of the exercise.

EXERCISE

STEP ONE

■ *pick up one strip of paper and let the sequence of autonomous words activate your voice and body through the channels of vowels, consonants, images, senses and emotions until you have absorbed that line of words.*

■ *repeat the process for each strip of words.*

STEP TWO

■ *standing still, speak out loud the following four lines,* **transferring to your mind and voice the energy that was activating your body.**

> SINCE BRASS, NOR STONE, NOR EARTH, NOR BOUNDLESS SEA,
> BUT SAD MORTALITY O'ERSWAYS THEIR POWER,
> HOW WITH THIS RAGE SHALL BEAUTY HOLD A PLEA
> WHOSE ACTION IS NO STRONGER THAN A FLOWER?

■ *let these four lines go through you two or three times until the meaning emerges clearly.*

■ *go through the same process for the next four lines*

> O HOW SHALL SUMMER'S HONEY BREATH HOLD OUT
> AGAINST THE WRACKFUL SIEGE OF BATTERING DAYS,
> WHEN ROCKS IMPREGNABLE ARE NOT SO STOUT,
> NOR GATES OF STEEL SO STRONG, BUT TIME DECAYS?

■ *paraphrase these eight lines—that is, say out loud what these lines mean, as specifically as possible, in your own words.*

■ *then continue the process with the next four lines*

> O FEARFUL MEDITATION! WHERE, ALACK,
> SHALL TIME'S BEST JEWEL FROM TIME'S CHEST LIE HID?
> OR WHAT STRONG HAND CAN HOLD HIS SWIFT FOOT BACK?
> OR WHO HIS SPOIL OF BEAUTY CAN FORBID?

■ *ask yourself what "time's best jewel" is*

■ *continue with the final two lines*

> O NONE; UNLESS THIS MIRACLE HAVE MIGHT,
> THAT IN BLACK INK MY LOVE MAY STILL SHINE BRIGHT.

■ *as the meaning becomes clearer and the words become more and more your own, personalize the content so that you attach the "story" to your own feelings of love for someone specific in your life.* **"Time's best jewel"** *is the person you love.*

Do not let your personal emotion wash the sonnet in one color!

Practice letting the conflicting images create the emotion within you.

E.G.:   How with this RAGE shall BEAUTY hold a PLEA

If you can let the emotional response change from rage to beauty to plea within one line and without taking a breath, a turmoil of fear and love will naturally occur, conveying through the shifting colors of the voice the inner condition beneath the grammatical question.

CHECK THE FOLLOWING DANGER SPOTS

■ *Are you making a <u>list</u> of "brass, stone, earth and sea," or do they still have their separate images in your mind and voice?*

Is your rage or sorrow obliterating the "flower?"

Is "summer's honey breath" all one word or three?

Are you seeing and saying "battering <u>days</u>" or have they become "battering <u>rams</u>?"

Can you <u>see</u> TIME?

Are the questions taking over from the images, washing the tone-color of a grammatical question all over the emotional images?

Are you running straight through the next to last line? If so, you've killed the drama. <u>Experience</u> "O NONE" taking you down to empty nothing and then let the "MIRACLE" take you up to the ecstasy of "LOVE" and "SHINE BRIGHT."

As you continue to let this sonnet be spoken through you, you will find it falling into its own pace which will be close to the rhythm and pace of your everyday speaking but with an energy that is charged with the packed emotional content of the meaning. In later work sessions you will discover more of the ingredients that lead to the supreme rendition of a sonnet. For now, it is enough to practice your ability to be played upon by the imagery, thereby developing flexibility of mind and voice.

By the time you reach the personalization stage of your speaking, the images are fleeting, not dwelt upon. They, along with the vowels and consonants and all the sensory, sensual, physical and emotional responses to the words, now serve the meaning.

The sonnet you have been working on is Sonnet 65, which I term a Master Sonnet because it is a model of Shakespearean verse which can be used as a continuing exercise in verse-speaking for the rest of your life. You will never completely master a Master Sonnet.

I recommend another "exer-sonnet," the famous number 29, which graphically demonstrates many of the details of word-structure and imagery you have been exploring. I suggest you work through this sonnet with me before going on to some of the dramatic verse examples which appear at the end of this chapter.

The first two lines of Sonnet 29 are:

> When in disgrace with Fortune and men's eyes
> I all alone beweep my outcast state

If only the horizontal (or linear) meaning affects the speaker, there may be a tendency to wash the lines in a generalized tone of self-pitiful misery.

Say the word "disgrace," letting its felt meaning penetrate your consciousness and lodge itself in the place in your body to which it gravitates. (Explore saying "grace" and then "disgrace.") Going on to speak/feel/picture "Fortune" and "men's eyes," notice the difference in the visualized meanings and what they specifically evoke in you. Notice the vulnerability in the sound of the open-mouthed "eyes."

The first word in the second line is "I." It employs exactly the same open-throated channel as "eyes," but now it has a different meaning— even more vulnerable, open-mouthed, open-throated and open-hearted. If you allow this diphthonged vowel sound to find its organic pitch level you will then be struck by the drop from that level that occurs in the next two words—"all alone." The sounds of the vowels, the weight of the "l"'s and the "n," the felt meaning, plummet the words down into the belly. Immediately, however, the next word's vowel pitch and its image of tears jump you back up into the face—"beweep"—and continuing from there into "my outcast state" you will find, if you allow the vowels and consonants to guide you, that your outcast state is by no means a victimized, gloomy one. When you spit out each of the "s"'s and "t"'s that encase the short, sharp vowels in "cast" and "state," you experience your friendless condition with anger, bitterness, defiance or irony, but with hardly a trace of self-pity.

Within two lines you have now communicated at least four different facets of being rejected by life instead of one monotonous "I'm depressed" moan.

The end of line two is a springboard to line three:

> And trouble deaf heaven with my bootless cries,
> And look upon myself and curse my fate.

The make-up of the word "trouble" troubles the psycho-physical condition in its mere utterance, while the image of God with His hands over His ears, and the crying out of "cries," lead up to the possibly ironic self-knowledge of one who watches his/her own behavior as s/he strikes out impotently against the Fates.

Moving on to the next four lines we find the words "wishing" and "desiring." Before looking at the lines, whisper each word. You will almost certainly discover that "wishing" lives in your head and "desiring" in your belly or pelvic region. The sounds within the words together with the felt meaning of the words impel each to a clearly differentiated home within you. Now explore where this leads in your understanding of the following four lines:

> Wishing me like to one more rich in hope,
> Featured like him, like him with friends possessed,

> Desiring this man's art and that man's scope,
> With what I most enjoy contented least.

Here is an escalation of wants: a more optimistic nature, good looks, friends, talent and enlarged opportunity. The climax is created with the felt contrast between "most enjoy" and "contented least." Note that this climax dumps you down at the bottom of the emotional ladder.

This sonnet adheres to classic (Italian) sonnet form, as does Sonnet 65, by building to an emotional point by the end of the first eight lines (the octet) and creating a major emotional shift in the next six lines (the sestet). Observe how the little-big word that comes next acts like an injection of possibility into your apparently hopeless state—

> yet—

and then the sonnet goes on:

> Yet in these thoughts, myself almost despising (do not ignore the
>   "almost")
> Haply (meaning "by chance") I think on thee, and then my state,
> Like to the lark at break of day arising—

Here, let me elaborate on the importance of accuracy in imaging. Very often, when I ask students to show me with their hands the size of the bird they see when they say "lark," we are confronted with something that suggests a pigeon or a turkey, and when they demonstrate the flight of this bird the arms flap up and down. This image does not have an electrifying effect on the emotional state.

When you see with absolute accuracy the image that Shakespeare intended, and let it impinge upon your emotions, you will experience the emotion Shakespeare intended. The English lark is a tiny bird about the size of a wren. The only New World lark is the horned lark which is twice as large, so that even if the speaker knows the American lark s/he will not come close to the image/emotion Shakespeare was conjuring up. He uses the singular flight of the English skylark to express the sudden surge of joy at the chance thought of "thee," the loved one, instantaneously transforming gloom to ecstasy. The dawn take-off of English larks is vertical; they zoom straight up out of the meadow into the sky. Fifty to a hundred tiny dots trill out a symphonic tapestry of sounds high in the heavens. The collective term is rightly "an exaltation of larks." The spark of that image dropped into the solar plexus will fire a spontaneous emotional combustion that makes the next lines soar and scintillate:

> and then my state
> Like to the lark at break of day arising
> From sullen earth sings hymns at heaven's gate.
> For thy sweet love remembered, such wealth brings,
> That then I scorn to change my state with kings.

Speaking sonnets regularly is very good verse-speaking exercise. Exer-sonnets should be part of your daily regime, as emotional, intellectual, vocal and philosophical work-outs.

You have been practicing a process of stringing together images like individual jewels on the necklace of meaning. You can now apply this process to speeches. You have only to open your *Complete Works* at random to find suitable passages for this exercise, because all the imagery in Shakespeare's writing creates the reality of human thought and feeling and all his writing is imagistic to a greater or lesser degree.

I will offer as examples three speeches with particularly heightened imagery and powerful emotional content, but I recommend choosing passages at random and working with them at length and out of context.

Juliet:
> Or if I live, is it not very like
> The horrible conceit of death and night,
> Together with the terror of the place—
> As in a vault, an ancient receptacle,
> Where for these many years the bones
> Of all my buried ancestors are pack'd,
> Where bloody Tybalt, yet but green in earth,
> Lies fest'ring in his shroud, where, as they say,
> At some hours in the night spirits resort—
> Alack, alack, is it not like that I—
> So early waking—what with loathsome smells,
> And shrieks like mandrakes torn out of the earth,
> That living mortals, hearing them, run mad—
> O, if I wake, shall I not be distraught,
> Environed with all these hideous fears,
> And madly play with my forefathers' joints,
> And pluck the mangled Tybalt from his shroud,
> And in this rage, with some great kinsman's bone,
> As with a club, dash out my desp'rate brains?
> O, look! methinks I see my cousin's ghost
> Seeking out Romeo that did spit his body
> Upon a rapier's point. Stay, Tybalt, stay!
> Romeo, I come! This do I drink to thee.
>> *Romeo and Juliet, Act IV, Scene iii*

Cleopatra:
> I dreamt there was an Emperor Antony.
> O such another sleep, that I might see
> But such another man!
>
> His face was as the heavens, and therein stuck
> A sun and moon, which kept their course, and lighted
> The little O, the earth.

His legs bestrid the ocean, his rear'd arm
Crested the world: his voice was propertied
As all the tuned spheres, and that to friends,
But when he meant to quail, and shake the orb,
He was as rattling thunder. For his bounty,
There was no winter in't: an autumn 'twas
That grew the more by reaping: His delights
Were dolphin-like, they showed his back above
The element they liv'd in: In his livery
Walk'd crowns and crownets; realms and islands were
As plates dropp'd from his pocket.

Antony and Cleopatra, Act V, Scene ii

King Lear:
Blow, winds, and crack your cheeks! rage, blow!
You cataracts and hurricanoes, spout
Till you have drench'd our steeples, drown'd the cocks!
You sulph'rous and thought-executing fires,
Vaunt-couriers of oak-cleaving thunderbolts,
Singe my white head! And thou, all-shaking thunder,
Strike flat the thick rotundity o' th' world!
Crack nature's moulds, all germains spill at once
That make ungrateful man!

King Lear, Act III, Scene ii

Here is an appropriate place to state that it is foolish to speak words if you do not know their meaning. Always have a good dictionary at hand and look up any word about which you have any doubts. Even those you think you know may have other meanings which may be more precise for a particular context. Do not rely slavishly on an editor's notes to do your thinking for you.

There are still many elements to be added before you arrive at an intelligent and intelligible rendition of the text, but the foregoing material is fundamental in bringing life to your final understanding. The practice set out in this section is a lifelong discipleship to the essential matter of spoken poetry, of image and emotion revealed through the voice.

4

◆▶ Organically, Cosmically ◆▶ and Etymologically Speaking

▼

Part One:

Organically Speaking

In the previous chapter I asked you to absorb the sound and meaning of the words "wishing" and "desiring" and to observe the natural gravitation of these words, each to a specific area of the body where it seemed to *belong*. While for us the notion of thoughts and words being part of our bodily and organic functioning may be somewhat odd, for the Elizabethans it was implicit. Any common cultural experience of thinking and speaking reflects the overview of that culture and the sixteenth-century sense of humanity as an integral part of the cosmos offers practical information to the twentieth-century actor probing Shakespeare's thoughts and words.

The belief system that supported the Elizabethan view of the world is far too complex to convey in this book, and the outline that I give here is a pale shadow of the rich, mythic vision of the universe inherited by the Elizabethans from the Middle Ages and not yet supplanted experientially by the Age of Science. E.M.W. Tillyard's *Elizabethan World Picture* is an accessible and useful account of the medieval philosophy of microcosm and macrocosm and is essential study for any actor expecting to do justice to Shakespeare. Certainly no explication of Elizabethan language is possible without some reference to the Elizabethan experience of the human being as a microcosmic model of the cosmos, because that experience was indivisible from the Elizabethan process of thinking and speaking.

Simplistically stated, every part of a person's body was believed to correspond to its equivalent in the universe, from the most mundane element to the most divine extension of the soul. For the purposes of this chapter, this means that whereas for us the organs of the body are parts of a physical machine, for the Elizabethans they each contained different "humors." These had a certain correspondence to the elements of fire, air, earth and water, the fundamental elements from which the cosmos was believed to be constructed. The humors were bodily fluids residing in the body and the four chief humors were blood, phlegm, choler (yellow bile) and melancholy (black bile). Blood corresponded with fire and its home was the liver, phlegm corresponded with air and its home was the lungs, choler was earth and its home was the gall, melancholy was water and its home was the bile.

A person's physical and mental qualities were held to be determined by the relative proportions of these humors. There was nothing simple or one-dimensional in the workings of the humors as they intermingled kaleidoscopically according both to physiological and psychological influences, and our contemporary interpretations of the words melancholy and phlegm should not be taken as quite the same as the Elizabethan meaning. The more meta-physical feelings such as love, compassion, pity, joy and ecstasy had their physical dwelling-places too, largely centered in the heart, but we find "bowels of compassion" spoken of in the King James Bible and, less than a century after Shakespeare's death, we find Macheath in John Gay's *Beggar's Opera* saying, "Have you no bowels, no tenderness, my dear Lucy?"

We still use these physical terms today to represent an emotion, but they have become symbols. We say, "I haven't the heart to do it"; "He had the gall to say . . ."; "I can't stomach this nonsense"; "It takes guts to do that"; "I've had a bellyful"; "It sticks in my craw." But these are now merely turns of phrase. Seldom does the word kindle a coincident experience in the appropriate part of the body. For the Elizabethans, the kindling and the speaking were one and the same thing.

There is great significance in this for the actor. All sorts of acting choices open up when a decision not to treat as metaphor any reference to an organ of the body is accompanied by the experience of thought and word in the organ itself.

In Act I, Scene v of *Macbeth*, Lady Macbeth asks for all her organic functioning to be changed from that of a woman in order to have the courage to murder Duncan. Talking *about* this is quite a difficult stretch for an actress, but if she enters into the physical and organ-ic experience of the words she will reveal the struggle as it unfolds:

> Come, you spirits
> That tend on mortal thoughts, unsex me here,
> And fill me, from the crown to the toe, top-full
> Of direst cruelty! make thick my blood,
> Stop up th'access and passage to remorse . . .

Remorse lies in the heart, which is the repository of pure, redemptive love, a love that can transform all baser emotions to forces of the divine soul. She must not listen to her heart.

> That no compunctious visitings of Nature
> Shake my fell purpose, nor keep peace between
> Th' effect and it! Come to my woman's breasts,
> And take my milk for gall . . .

The breast is almost synonomous with the heart and is the vessel not only for mother's milk but for the milk of human kindness; a moment earlier, Lady Macbeth has said of her husband,

> Yet do I fear thy nature:
> It is too full o' th' milk of human kindness,
> To catch the nearest way.

She asks for "gall" to replace her milk. The gall-bladder is "a vesicle attached to the undersurface of the right lobe of the liver, which stores and concentrates the bile." According to C.T. Onions in *A Shakespeare Glossary*, bile is "a bitter, alkaline, yellow or greenish liquid, secreted by the liver." The metaphorical meaning of "gall" is "bitterness of spirit; rancor" or "the spirit to resent injury or insult." "Bile" has come to mean "ill-temper; peevishness."

The liver, on the other hand, is not only one of the most important and active organs of the body—metabolizing and legislating the intake and outflow of nourishment; literally the central organizer of life and etymologically deriving from the same root as "to live"—but was known in Shakespeare's time as "the seat of love and violent passion" (Onions). Put more directly, lust sprang from the liver. So did courage, although we discover this most vividly in the expression of its opposite, cowardice.

> Go, prick thy face, and over-red thy fear,
> Thou lily-liver'd boy . . .
> > *Macbeth, Act V, Scene iii*

> How many cowards . . .
> > have livers white as milk? . . .
> > *Merchant of Venice, Act III, Scene ii*

> Milk-liver'd man!
> That bear'st a cheek for blows, a head for wrongs . . .
> > *King Lear, Act IV, Scene ii*

> Am I a coward?
> > . . . it cannot be
> But I am pigeon-liver'd and lack gall
> To make oppression bitter . . .
> > *Hamlet, Act II, Scene ii*

When playing Lady Macbeth and Hamlet, who are referring to their own conditions, the connection of the organ-word in question with the area of the body where it resides will arouse an immediate visceral response. The actualization of meaning in a felt state of being is the natural outcome and is a consummation devoutly to be wished by any actor. "Becoming" the character, "being" in the situation, is the ultimate aim of any acting method, and with Shakespeare "being" results from the words becoming flesh, senses and emotions; being spoken organ-ically. From this state of being, the actor has the option to choose from a variety of actions that will organically present themselves.

Hamlet's speech after the Players have left offers a perfect exercise in the creation of inner and outer truth directly through organ-ic speaking:

> O what a rogue and peasant slave am I!

The speech starts with the consciousness of his dulled, unfeeling state of being in comparison with the lively, emotional state so easily conjured up by the Players. It is a gross, base state of being *because* it is unfeeling. As he continues, he becomes aware of, and gives an exact account of, the way he feels:

> Yet I,
> A dull and muddy-mettl'd rascal, peak
> Like John-a-dreams, unpregnant of my cause,
> And can say nothing—

"Mettle" is temperament, spirit, courage; "peak" is to look pale, droop in spirit; and "unpregnant" leads him experientially to his belly, where he feels no life. You can speak this metaphorically and you can speak this experientially. Try it both ways.

Continuing with the speech, allow each part of the body Hamlet talks about to be fully incorporated in your inner consciousness and your words. To begin with, be illustrative. Let your hands go to that part of the body in order to awaken as much of a response there as possible. Be faithful to the implications of that body-part. Eventually you will drop the external illustration and retain an internal condition.

> Am I a coward?
> Who calls me villain, breaks my pate across,
> Plucks off my beard and blows it in my face,
> Tweaks me by the nose, gives me the lie i' th' throat
> As deep as to the lungs—who does me this?
> Ha!

Hamlet's consciousness of these contemptuous challenges leads him from his head down through his face and throat to his lungs. Experientially he destroys his mask and comes to the place where he breathes. Inhabiting his deficiencies, they organically begin to change.

> 'Swounds, I should take it: for it cannot be
> But I am pigeon-liver'd and lack gall

> To make oppression bitter, or ere this
> I should ha' fatted all the region kites
> With this slave's offal.

He drops below the experience of the gall to the rottenness of offal and there the turn around begins. In the lowest regions of the body the seeds of vengeance lie and from them life and energy are rekindled:

> . . . Bloody, bawdy villain!
> Remorseless, treacherous, kindless villain!
> O vengeance!

At this point, he is alive again and can even laugh at himself:

> Why, what an ass am I!

for not "suiting the action to the word, the word to the action":

> This is most brave,
> That I, the son of a dear father murder'd,
> Prompted to my revenge by heaven and hell,
> Must like whore unpack my heart with words
> And fall a-cursing like a very drab.

But now that he has "unpack'd his heart with words" he is free to think, feel and plan, and take action.

It would be a mistake to try and make a neat list of corresponding organs and feelings. Love is the tenant of both the liver and the heart, cohabiting with other lodgers. If the heart is savage, love can turn to lust:

> Moreover, urge his hateful luxury
> And bestial appetite in change of lust,
> Which stretch'd unto their servants, daughters, wives,
> Even where his raging eye or savage heart
> Without control lusted to make a prey . . .
> *Richard III, Act III, Scene v*

The spleen contains a wide variety of emotions ranging from laughter to rage:

> If you desire the spleen, and will laugh yourselves into stitches, follow me.
> *Twelfth Night, Act III, Scene ii*

> By the gods,
> You shall digest the venom of your spleen,
> Though it do split you . . .
> *Julius Caesar, Act IV, Scene iii*

> Our ancient word of courage, fair Saint George,
> Inspire us with the spleen of fiery dragons . . .
> *Richard III, Act V, Scene iii*

We are looking for an awareness that deepens and simplifies the speaking of Shakespeare. To try to find the precise location of the liver and the spleen and develop an exquisite distinction between the discrete sensations within each would be folly. I think that it is enough to introduce the sensation/organ/emotion words to the central energy systems that exist between the sexual organs and the throat and respond accordingly.

There are other words that we now use metaphorically which, when restored to their Elizabethan context, discharge immediately exploitable acting energies. These words have lost their original energy because our world view has changed. The Age of Science eventually dulled our cultural consciousness, shifted our thinking and speaking so that words like "hell" and "devil" and "heaven" and "angel" no longer attach themselves to fires burning beneath our feet and a kingdom above the clouds. Political change has taught us that kings can be toppled and that the common man can control his destiny.

In order to speak Shakespeare's words with authority they must be experienced within their philosophical context. When you do this, they are easy to enact. Thereafter, you may be asked to interpret them according to a particular directorial concept that turns Shakespeare's original intention upside down. There is nothing wrong with this. Indeed, it is a sign of Shakespeare's resilience that he can survive conceptual distortions. But whatever the interpretation, the actor's responsibility is to be understood by the audience, and the closer s/he can get to a pure understanding of the original intention, the richer will be the creative twists and turns of interpretive performance.

▼

Part Two:

Cosmically Speaking

Tillyard's *Elizabethan World Picture* gives a description of the medieval philosophy that implicitly governed the way in which the Elizabethans lived in their world. The serious actor will spend time studying the history and cultural influences behind the writing of any play which s/he performs, and the brief account I offer here will, I hope, serve as stimulus for further reading.

Our relationship with the universe today is very different from that of Shakespeare and his contemporaries and we can only bring their language to its fullest life when we re-create their philosophical experience. Elizabethan man knew he was part of Nature, whereas we in the twentieth century have been taught by science and the industrial revolution that Nature can be controlled by man. (It is tempting to speculate on where we will be in this regard a hundred years from now, as Nature, in her vulnerability, commands our attention again and reminds us that our mortality and hers are indeed inseparable.)

The Elizabethan world picture was inherited from the Middle Ages and incorporated the idea of the Great Chain of Being. In order to create the social order in Shakespeare's plays this idea must be understood and embodied. Relationships and conflicts both personal and political lose credibility without the knowledge of hierarchy that the Chain of Being illustrates. In lieu of a summary of this picture of the universe which would only diminish its grandeur, here is Ulysses' famous speech from *Troilus and Cressida*, Act I, Scene iii. It passionately represents the belief that without the maintenance of "degree"— that is, each part of the universe having its allotted rung on the ladder between heaven and hell—chaos will return. Harmony and order are dependent on respect for degree. It is perhaps useful to note that the word "cosmos" has two etymological roots: *cossmos* is Middle English for "world" and *kosmos* is the Greek word for "order, form, the world or universe."

> The heavens themselves, the planets, and this centre
> Observe degree, priority, and place,
> Insisture, course, proportion, season, form,
> Office, and custom, all in line of order.
> And therefore is the glorious planet Sol
> In noble eminence enthron'd and spher'd
> Amidst the other; whose med'cinable eye
> Corrects the influence of evil planets,
> And posts like the commandment of a king,
> Sans check, to good or bad. But when the planets
> In evil mixture to disorder wander,
> What plagues and what portents, what mutiny,
> What raging of the sea, shaking of earth,
> Commotion in the winds, frights, changes, horrors,
> Divert and crack, rend and deracinate
> The unity and married calm of states
> Quite from their fixture! O, when degree is shak'd,
> Which is the ladder of all high designs,
> The enterprise is sick. How could communities,
> Degrees in schools, and brotherhoods in cities,
> Peaceful commerce from dividable shores,
> The primogenity and due of birth,
> Prerogative of age, crowns, sceptres, laurels,
> But by degree stand in authentic place?
> Take but degree away, untune that string,

> And hark what discord follows. Each thing melts
> In mere oppugnancy; the bounded waters
> Should lift their bosoms higher than the shores,
> And make a sop of all this solid globe;
> Strength should be lord of imbecility,
> And the rude son should strike his father dead;
> Force should be right—or rather, right and wrong,
> Between whose endless jars justice resides,
> Should lose their names, and so should justice too.
> Then everything includes itself in power,
> Power into will, will into appetite,
> And appetite, an universal wolf,
> So doubly seconded with will and power,
> Must make perforce an universal prey,
> And last eat up himself. Great Agamemnon,
> This chaos, when degree is suffocate,
> Follows the choking . . .

Postmodernist scholars see this picture through the prisms of Marxism, feminism, colonialism and other -isms, continuing proof of Shakespeare's relevance to any current or future examination of the world. But for the actor to be able to speak this text with authenticity, s/he must embark upon a search for Shakespeare's relationship with the world he lived in. Shakespeare's world was governed by a consciousness of degree which is subtly different from class consciousness.

For actors, some of the most alarming and electrifying improvisational work in the past few years has been centered round "status exercises." These have reached a high level of sophistication in Keith Johnstone's Theater Sports, in which everyone can recognize the humiliations and rewards of status competition. We may no longer ostensibly believe in the class system, but we have internalized the kings and queens and still bow down before some people and psychologically step on others. When we admit this, we can flesh out the worlds that Shakespeare creates in more than outward posture and "style," marrying the age of psychology with the age when Man, Nature and the Cosmos coexisted in immutable degree.

The infinite intricacy of the cosmic game covered every species of living creature, plant life, mineral life, devils in hell, angels in heaven, mankind and man's inner world. The links of the Great Chain of Being began underneath the earth and ended in God, and only man had the potential and free will to change his degree, climbing up the links, moving up the ladder towards the Kingdom of God. With this privilege came the penalty of slipping down towards hell. Inner harmony led one up, internal disorder pulled one down. The lower parts of the body were inhabited by unruly passions, corresponding to the lower degrees of the animal kingdom, which drew one down towards everlasting damnation. In the head dwelt divine reason and the soul, aspiring towards God. Between these extremes lay the unpredictable humors in the organs and the supreme alchemist of Love, infusing the heart with the power to transform the dull, venomous lead of the dark passions to the pure, shining gold of the soul.

What is today's actor to do with this? A combination of imaginative visualization and ancestral sense memory, along with attention to breath and voice, will bring past and present to points of creative collision.

PREPARATION

After having ingested the density of information given in this chapter so far, it is necessary to spend a good half-hour getting out of the head and back into the body before entering the next process.

- *Stretch, shake and undo your body, letting it speak, moan, groan, sigh, squeak and whine as it wishes.*

- *Then take yourself through the **ZOO WOe SHAW GOh MAA FUh HU-U-Uh BAh DEh PE-EY-EY KI RREEE** sequence.*

If you are working on your own, READ THE NEXT SET OF INSTRUCTIONS ONTO A TAPE and then take yourself through the process with your eyes closed. If you are working with another person or in a group, one person should lead the exercise, reading the instructions while the others work with their eyes closed.

Work standing up, not lying down.

Whoever is leading this is hereby advised:

*DO **NOT** enter into a long or deep preparation.*

DO NOT ATTEMPT TO INDUCE ANY KIND OF HYPNOTIC STATE.

DO NOT ADOPT A SPECIAL TONE OF VOICE; SPEAK IN AN ORDINARY CONVERSATIONAL TONE.

MOVE QUITE QUICKLY THROUGH THE PICTURES WITHOUT DWELLING ON ANY OF THEM FOR ANY LENGTH OF TIME.

THIS IS A POWERFUL VISUALIZATION AND CAN RELEASE CONSIDERABLE EMOTIONAL ENERGY.

AT ANY TIME THE PARTICIPANT MAY OPEN HIS OR HER EYES AND TAKE TIME OUT FROM THE EXERCISE.

EXERCISE

Close your eyes.

Relax your stomach muscles and be aware of your natural breathing rhythm. Let your mind be in the solar plexus, breath, sound, energy center, so that you hear these words in the middle of your body.

Be aware of the soles of your feet on the floor.

Let your mind's eye travel from your feet up through your legs, your pelvis, your genitals, your lower belly and intestines, your stomach, diaphragm, solar plexus, rib cage, lungs, heart, throat, mouth, face, and out through the top of your head.

Spread your arms wide and reach them into the air above your head.

Drop your arms.

Sigh.

Be aware of your whole body in space.

Now picture the ground beneath your feet and transform it into a grassy field.

The grassy field is a field in Elizabethan England.

Let your mind's eye travel from your feet down through the earth.

See the bonfires of hell, with Satan sitting on his throne and the Devils attending him.

Bring your mind's eye back up through the earth's crust to the ground you are standing upon and look around at the lowest degrees of animate existence—beetles, worms, snakes, toads, hedgehogs—then expand your vision to catch a quick glimpse of the order of:

> *the plant world—from the weed to the oak*
> *the mineral world—from a grain of sand to gold*
> *the insect world—from the flea to the praying mantis*
> *the reptile world—from the worm to the boa constrictor*
> *the animal world—from the shrew to the lion*
> *the sea world—from the clam to the whale*
> *the bird world—from the wren to the eagle*
> *the human world—from the beggar to the monarch*
> *the elemental world—from the imp to the fairy king*
> *the angelic world—from the cherubim to God*

Bring your mind's eye back down to the ground.

Shake your body out with sound.

Sigh.

If you need a break here, open your eyes and walk around, loosening up and letting sound out. Then close your eyes again and continue:

Be aware of your whole body and let your mind's eye move again down to your pelvic region.

See *the parts of your lower body that house your animal passions:*

lust   rage   hate   revenge   jealousy

Travel your mind's eye through your belly where the fires glow with:

appetite   courage   fear

Then to the airy region of your chest where your heart lives and breathes with:

pure, redemptive love
which transforms all that is below into
divine reason
which lives in the head and, becoming the soul, aspires to heaven.

Bring your mind's eye back down through the head and chest and let it rest in the solar plexus, breathing center.

Shake your body out.

Sigh.

If you need a break here, open your eyes, walk about and loosen up.

Read or listen to these instructions all the way through before you begin:

*Once more you are going to look with your mind's eye down through your body and under the earth. This time let **your voice** travel with your mind's eye so that the **vibrations of sound** move from the image of hell through an upwardly moving picture of the order of the universe merged with your corresponding sensory, organic, emotional, spiritual inner self until you and **your voice** mingle with the angelic choir. Then bring **your voice** and vision back down to the center of your body. Allow as many breaths as are needed.*

CLOSE YOUR EYES AND, STARTING WITH YOUR MIND'S EYE DEEP BELOW EARTH'S SURFACE, **BEGIN** . . .

(At this point the voice should travel from the very bottom of its range to the very top and back down to the middle. This may happen on one breath or several. The object is the actualization of imagination in voice, breath and body.)

Now relax, sigh deeply, shake out, and gradually open your eyes and walk around the room.

Some time should be taken to debrief on this process, either writing in your journal or exchanging experiences. While images of hell may be all too vivid for some, they may be inaccessible to others. To play Shakespeare, hell and heaven have to become "facts of life."

Having reported your experience during this process, you can begin applying it to the text.

The purpose is to fill in the reality of the personal, political and philosophical lives of the characters in Shakespeare's plays, and to make real the words that express this reality.

When, in Act I, Scene ii of *Richard III*, Lady Anne, accompanying the body of her murdered father-in-law to its burial, sees Richard, his killer, she says:

> What black magician conjures up this fiend
> To stop devoted, charitable deeds?

If the actor playing Anne believes that hell is just beneath her feet and that Richard is indeed a fiend from hell, her terror will be rooted in reality. She goes on to say to the coffin-bearers :

> What, do you tremble? are you all afraid?
> Alas, I blame you not, for you are mortal,
> And mortal eyes cannot endure the devil.
> Avaunt, thou dreadful minister of hell!
> Thou hadst but power over his mortal body,
> His soul thou canst not have; therefore begone.

The twentieth-century use of "devil," "minister of hell," and "fiend," is bound to be metaphorical, and the voice, saying the words, will be at a subtle remove from the absolute concrete reality of sixteenth-century demons who *can* appear, *can* be conjured up, as can angels and other spirits of the elemental or celestial worlds. When the voice accepts these images and actualizes them, the actor enters Shakespeare's reality and is able to create a believable life on stage.

Throughout *Richard III* Richard is referred to by epithets linking him to close-to-the-earth creatures whose natural affinity was towards hell. Anne curses him thus:

> More direful hap betide that hated wretch,
> That makes us wretched by the death of him,
> Than I can wish to adders, spiders, toads,
> Or any creeping, venom'd thing that lives.

Later in this scene she calls him "hedgehog" and "toad," Queen Margaret calls him "dog" and "carnal cur." She even describes his mother's womb as a "kennel":

> From forth the kennel of thy womb hath crept
> A hell-hound that will hunt us all to death.

"Bottled spider" and "poisonous, bunch-backed toad": all this name-calling connects Richard with the form of animate life whose relationship is with hell. Without a clear commitment to the forces of Heaven and Hell, Good and Evil, the play will be hard for today's actors to bring to life. Given that commitment, the extremities of outrageous behavior and violent expression become more accessible.

Switching to *Romeo and Juliet*, we find at the opposite end of the pendulum-swing the power of light in Romeo's sudden discovery of true love. Again, the ability to accept the reality of pure love as the transforming agent for Good, and the inevitability of tragic penalty when Romeo kills Tybalt, will direct the enactment of emotions that may otherwise seem beyond credibility.

The meeting of Romeo and Juliet is encapsulated in a sonnet and the words reveal the nature of the love that blooms in an instant:

> Romeo:
>> If I profane with my unworthiest hand
>> This holy shrine, the gentle sin is this:
>> My lips, two blushing pilgrims, ready stand
>> To smooth that rough touch with a tender kiss.
>
> Juliet:
>> Good pilgrim, you do wrong your hand too much,
>> Which mannerly devotion shows in this;
>> For saints have hands which pilgrims' hands do touch,
>> And palm to palm is holy palmers' kiss.
>
> Romeo:
>> Have not saints lips, and holy palmers too?
>
> Juliet:
>> Ay, pilgrim, lips that they must use in prayer.
>
> Romeo:
>> O then, dear saint, let lips do what hands do:
>> They pray: grant thou lest faith turn to despair.
>
> Juliet:
>> Saints do not move, though grant for prayers' sake.
>
> Romeo:
>> Then move not, while my prayer's effect I take.

The religious imagery shows a different quality of love from his previous love for Rosaline; it is the difference between desire and pure love:

> Chorus:
>> Now old desire doth in his deathbed lie
>> And young affection gapes to be his heir . . .

The words with which Romeo addresses Juliet in the Balcony Scene are full of angelic, heavenly and planetary imagery. When these images are clearly seen and attached to heart's love, Romeo's passion is possible. Without this leap of imagination, today's young man may find such adoration beyond his capacity.

The following passage is a perfect exercise for both men and women—an exercise in the expression of excitement and ecstasy. Daily life affords us little opportunity for such exercise and the ecstatic musculature tends to atrophy. When the channels for such feelings are opened and reactivated, the feelings themselves will emerge more readily.

> But soft, what light through yonder window breaks?
> It is the east and Juliet is the sun!
> Arise fair sun and kill the envious moon
> Who is already sick and pale with grief
> That thou her maid art far more fair than she.
> Be not her maid since she is envious,
> Her vestal livery is but sick and green
> And none but fools do wear it. Cast it off.
> It is my lady, O it is my love!
> O that she knew she were!
> She speaks, yet she says nothing. What of that?
> Her eye discourses, I will answer it.
> I am too bold. 'Tis not to me she speaks.
> Two of the fairest stars in all the heaven,
> Having some business, do entreat her eyes
> To twinkle in their spheres till they return.
> What if her eyes were there, they in her head?
> The brightness of her cheek would shame those stars
> As daylight doth a lamp. Her eyes in heaven
> Would through the airy region stream so bright
> That birds would sing and think it were not night.
> See how she leans her cheek upon her hand.
> O that I were a glove upon that hand,
> That I might touch that cheek.
>
> > She speaks.
> O speak again bright angel, for thou art
> As glorious to this night, being o'er my head,
> As is a winged messenger of heaven
> Unto the white-upturned wondering eyes
> Of mortals that fall back to gaze on him
> When he bestrides the lazy-puffing clouds
> And sails upon the bosom of the air.

Juliet's nature is wonderfully down to earth compared with Romeo's; experience the contrast between her images and his:

O Romeo, Romeo, wherefore art thou Romeo?
Deny thy father and refuse thy name.
Or if thou wilt not, be but sworn my love
And I'll no longer be a Capulet.

'Tis but thy name that is my enemy:
Thou art thyself, though not a Montague.
What's Montague? It is nor hand nor foot
Nor arm nor face nor any other part
Belonging to a man.

Here I am running ahead somewhat to the question of character discovery through language, but these issues cannot be completely compartmentalized. The main intention of this chapter is to alert the actor/speaker to the implications of words that may have lost their Elizabethan charge over the centuries.

With this attention to cosmic context we may seem to be teetering on the precipice of interpretation. But I would like to claim that this is not interpretation, it is reading the clues. In coming as close as possible to Shakespeare's mind and voice we can feel our feet on intelligent ground and can use this ground as a jumping-off place for interpretive choice. We are *grounding* and *rooting* language which can then be adapted to all sorts of conceptual use.

A volume of language clues could be put together for each play, but my hope is that the text will naturally be made available to the informed seeker, once s/he is alerted to and exercised in the clues. Here is one more graphic example of the struggle between the pull of heaven and hell, again an exercise in powerful emotional response to powerful images. Macbeth is contemplating the murder of Duncan, his King:

If it were done, when 'tis done, then 'twere well
It were done quickly: if th' assassination
Could trammel up the consequence, and catch
With his surcease success; that but this blow
Might be the be-all and the end-all here,
But here, upon this bank and shoal of time,
We'd jump the life to come. —But in these cases,
We still have judgment here; that we but teach
Bloody instructions, which, being taught, return
To plague th'inventor: this even-handed Justice
Commends th' ingredients of our poison'd chalice
To our own lips. He's here in double trust:
First, as I am his kinsman and his subject,
Strong both against the deed; then, as his host,
Who should against the murderer shut the door,
Not bear the knife myself. Besides, this Duncan
Hath borne his faculties so meek, hath been

> So clear in his great office, that his virtues
> Will plead like angels, trumpet-tongu'd, against
> The deep damnation of his taking-off;
> And Pity, like a naked new-born babe,
> Striding the blast, or heaven's Cherubins, hors'd
> Upon the sightless couriers of the air,
> Shall blow the horrid deed in every eye,
> That tears shall drown the wind—I have no spur
> To prick the sides of my intent, but only
> Vaulting ambition, which o'erleaps itself
> And falls on th' other . . .

I shall come back to this speech later, as it holds so many clues to speaking Shakespeare's verse. For now my context is words in the body, organ-ically sensed, and the extension of these into an Elizabethan world picture.

Looking first at the end of the speech, it is significant that Ambition, for the Elizabethans, belonged in the region of the animal passions, along with revenge, hate, rage and lust, and this was the region of hell. We are given Ambition in the image of a horse to be spurred.

Letting the images work in you and for you, start speaking the words slowly from the beginning. However difficult the murder of a king may be to envisage, this is the imaginative necessity. Now place yourself mentally in the center of the cosmic picture with hell below and heaven above and the world between them, where "success" offers earthly rewards and "judgment" cannot be avoided. Visualize clearly each step of the argument for and against Duncan's murder. Let yourself experience the rise and fall of the dilemma. When you reach the "angels, trumpet-tongu'd," let your spirit, your inner vision and your voice riding on the vowels and consonants go to the heavens, and from there experience the sudden fall to "deep damnation." "Pity" springs you back up again, only more vulnerable this time as the images turn from grown-up angels to a "naked new-born babe" and cherubim riding blind horses. It may even be that as you see the "horrid deed" being blown into the eyes of all the world, these images work upon you to the point that tears come to your eyes and "drown" your "wind." The wind is knocked out of Macbeth and, empty of spirit, he "has no spur to prick the sides" of his intent. His "spur" enters at that moment in the form of his wife, and sexual, sensual, physical imagery dominates the following scene which culminates in his renewed ambition to do the deed.

It is almost impossible to play the "big stuff" in Shakespeare without connecting the language to the Elizabethan philosophical context. It strains our contemporary psycho-physical machinery. Once you have flexed your muscles on this material, the more everyday parts of the text will come very easily.

▼

Part Three:
Etymologically Speaking

"**E**tymology" is "an account of the history of a particular word." Certain word juxtapositions that Shakespeare makes create wonderfully subtle effects; with some intellectual stretch the Shakespeare speaker can develop a sensitivity to the history of words that will enrich the understanding and expression of the text. There is nothing inherently academic about linguistic development, although the academic study of linguistics is about as academic as one can get. Language developed and continues to develop as a result of human intercourse. New influences on language come in the wake of war, religion and trade. The conqueror and the conquered, the missionary and the convert, the merchant and the buyer must communicate, and language is the beneficiary.

By the fourteenth century, English was a mix of Anglo-Saxon, a language with strong Germanic roots, and French, which came in with the Norman Conquest. The language of education and religion was Latin. By the mid-sixteenth century the Bible had been translated from Latin into English. In the ensuing hundred years education yielded to the "vulgar," as English was termed.

Socially, these changes had huge ramifications. Religion no longer belonged to an elite with an exclusive relationship with God, and education became, theoretically if not in fact, accessible to everyone. Everyday English began to absorb and expand with the hitherto elitist Latin. The power of knowledge began to seep down to the general population, and society began the long slow hierarchical change that continues today.

Anglo-Saxon English was the language of the people, Latin the language of the educated. Linguistically, it was as though a strong, down-to-earth woman had married a brilliant, philosophically-inclined intellectual. It was a marriage made in heaven and on earth, and it gave birth to a multitudinous family of new words.

Anglo-Saxon words tend to be the one-syllable or two-syllable words in our language. Most of the polysyllabic words that we take for granted in our everyday speaking and writing were crafted from Latin in Shakespeare's time and many of them by him. Although it is hard to be certain, it appears that about 1700 words were either concocted by Shakespeare or recorded for the first time by him: words such as *hostile, vulnerable, manager, obscene, illumination, traditional, investment, addiction*. They struck the Elizabethan ear with a fresh shock that is almost unimaginable for us. Poets delighted in coining new words to express their inner worlds as they expanded to match the expanding horizons of the real world. The Age of Science was opening up new perceptions of the Old World and explorers were introducing an actual New World. New words were vital to name new experiences.

Latin was a language that could name experiences of the soul and of science which were beyond the ken of Anglo-Saxon English. Latin could argue legal issues. But Anglo-Saxon English could ring into and out of the body with a veracity that shook the brain down into the bowels. So to a certain extent it is true to say that the Latin words express the intellectual and the Anglo-Saxon words express the visceral. But this should not be taken too simplistically.

In the hands of a great poet it is the *juxtapositioning* of Anglo-Saxon words with Latin-based words that is stunning. The Shakespeare speaker who is sensorily aware of these word juxtapositions wields a delicate and delicious power that is something akin to brushstroke and color in the hands of a great painter. One of the most graphic instances of the dramatic linking of monosyllabic, Anglo-Saxon words with Latin-based words is Macbeth's extraordinary vision after he has murdered Duncan:

> this my hand will rather
> The multitudinous seas incarnadine,
> Making the green one red.

In this and other cases it seems as though the coupling of polysyllabic and monosyllabic words reveals a struggle to bring the intelligence to bear on a powerful emotion. When Cleopatra dies, Charmian says:

> So, fare thee well.
> Now boast thee, death, in thy possession lies
> A lass unparallel'd.

The great Empress is called by the simplest female term, "lass," but the adjective that describes what kind of lass she was is made up from a term emerging from the newly popularized sciences of geography and geometry. The word "parallel" is daringly brought into play in a moment of deep emotion, and the emotion is powerfully heightened by the tension between head and heart, by the rhythmic contrast between polysyllables and monosyllables.

A little earlier, Cleopatra puts the asp to her breast and says:

> With thy sharp teeth this knot intrinsicate
> Of life at once untie . . .

Monosyllabic, Anglo-Saxon words express the direct, immediate action Cleopatra seeks, all except "intrinsicate," a marvelous combination of "intrinsic" and "intricate." If I were playing Cleopatra I would feel the asp's bite on that word. She then says,

> Poor venomous fool,

another coupling of Latin-based and Anglo-Saxon words that goes beyond linear meaning to a felt condition. "Venomous" almost leads the poison into the body with its buzzing consonants; "fool" accepts the fact and laughs at it.

> Be angry, and dispatch. O, couldst thou speak,
> That I might hear thee call great Caesar ass
> Unpolicied!

Here again is the juxtaposition of Anglo-Saxon monosyllable with Latin-based polysyllables in a linear meaning that is almost irrelevant except in its emotional context. Seconds later, Charmian echoes "ass unpolicied" with "lass unparallel'd."

Shakespeare's use of the prefix "un" is almost as a separate word. It seems that he added to the then more common usage of "im" as a negative prefix the solidity of "un" and put it in front of words that had never been handled in that way before. "Y' have," says Portia in *Julius Caesar*, "ungently, Brutus,/Stole from my bed"; "You star'd upon me with ungentle looks"; "Is Brutus sick, and is it physical/To walk unbraced . . ." And Beatrice in *Much Ado About Nothing*: "What, bear her in hand until they come to take hands, and then with public accusation, uncovered slander, unmitigated rancor—O God that I were a man!" When we say *un* as we do today, as a throwaway syllable—'n—we miss something in the thought that can add weight or significance. "Un" bore an intention in Shakespeare's mind and made an impact on his audience.

Etymological appreciatian is not the object of the exercise. You must practice allowing these words to play on you, sensorily, sensually, emotionally and physically, so that they create in you their effect.

When you allow these words to travel through the channels that you have been opening up through the exploration of vowels and consonants, images and emotion-words, they will lead you to an exactness of inner condition and outer expression that no refinement of "acting" could do.

Once you have experienced a few examples of the drama created by the juxtapositioning of Anglo-Saxon and Latin-based words you will become sensitive to their presence in a speech and let their electricity inform you. A good dictionary will tell you the etymology of any word if you need to go beyond a "feeling" for the language to a "knowledge" of it.

Here is some acting information drawn from etymological awareness in the speech of Macbeth's we have already looked at:

> If it were done, when 'tis done, then 'twere well
> It were done quickly:

He is talking about murder. He can't even name the deed. The tiny word "it" represents an almost unimaginable act. "It" is murder, "done" first means "finished—over and done with," then it means the actual act of killing, and finally "done" in the sense of "committed." He tries to confront the thought of the act directly in order to get it "done," over with. He uses monosyllabic Anglo-Saxon words to make it a simple matter. But the matter is not simple and he has not galvanized himself into action. So he starts to think about it more:

> If th' assassination

(a polysyllabic, Latin-based word, intellectualizing and distancing the act)

> Could trammel up the consequence . . .

(A "trammel" was a net used to catch birds and the word derives from Old English and Middle French and Latin; "consequence" is Latin-based. His thoughts are becoming more complex on the subject of murder.)

> . . . and catch
> With his surcease success . . .

("Catch" is sharp, direct, Anglo-Saxon; "surcease," deriving from English, French, and Latin, is a major softening of the idea of "death"; "success" is Latin-based and implies, without spelling it out, the crown.)

> . . . that but this blow
> Might be the be-all and the end-all—here,
> But here, upon this bank and shoal of time,
> We'd jump the life to come.

(The hesitation in the thinking is gone. The thoughts spill out in Anglo-Saxon monosyllables saying what he really wants. Then, the opposite argument arrives.)

> But in these cases,
> We still have judgment here; that we but teach
> Bloody instructions, which being taught, return
> To plague th'inventor . . .

("Bloody" is Anglo-Saxon, "instructions" is Latin-based. "Plague" is Anglo-Saxon, "inventor" is Latin-based. "Instructions" and "inventions" come from the head, "blood" and "plague" live in the body. The conflict between the desire and ambition in Macbeth's body and the intellectual argument against murder is experienced in the turmoil created when those words are juxtapositioned.)

> this even-handed Justice
> Commends th' ingredients of our poison'd chalice
> To our own lips.

("Even-handed" is simple, direct Anglo-Saxon; calculating "justice" is Latin-based; "commends" and "ingredients" are Latin-based and full of devious thought; "poison'd chalice" presents the picture of a holy cup filled with a deathly drink in textured English-French-Latin terms, and "to our own lips" brings the speaker to stark realization of cause and effect. From here, Macbeth begins to argue *for* Duncan and his ambition dissolves.)

If the actor is responsive to the clues that lie in the language, he will *feel* the shift that happens at this point in the soliloquy. The struggle to decide is over. Three lines follow with nothing but Anglo-Saxon words and clear thought; the relationship between subject and king, host and guest, the actual words "murderer" and "knife" tumble out:

> He's here in double trust:
> First, as I am his kinsman and his subject,
> Strong both against the deed; then, as his host,
> Who should against the murderer shut the door,
> Not bear the knife myself.

Then images of Duncan flood him, Latin-based and Anglo-Saxon words again tug at each other, revealing the pain of his inner conflict:

> Besides, this Duncan
> Hath borne his **faculties** (L) so **meek** (A-S), hath been
> So clear in his great office, that his **virtues** (L)
> Will **plead** (A-S) like **angels** (L), **trumpet-tongu'd** (A-S),
> Against the **deep** (A-S) **damnation** (L) of his taking-off;

In the final six-and-a-half lines there are only four Latin-based words, as increasingly apocalyptic images reveal his emotional choice; the thinking is over, finally petering out in a dispirited rejection of the whole idea of murdering the king:

> And pity, like a naked new-born babe,
> Striding the blast, or heaven's **Cherubins** (L), hors'd
> Upon the sightless **couriers** (L) of the air,
> Shall blow the horrid deed in every eye,
> That tears shall drown the wind—I have no spur
> To prick the sides of my **intent** (L), but only
> Vaulting **ambition** (L), which o'erleaps itself
> And falls on th'other . . .

It is tempting to go on through the next scene following the etymological signs, but I suggest you look at it yourself and note that when Lady Macbeth first speaks she does so almost entirely in Anglo-Saxon based words which convey strongly and directly her anger and contempt for her husband's feebleness. Her three Latin-based words are to do with thinking and planning: "account," "esteem'st," "enterprise." Once she has convinced Macbeth, her tone changes, and as she lays out her plan of action, helping him think it through, more Latin-based words creep in.

This is an example of word-use in moments of heightened emotion, or rather an example of how the *experience* of those words can create varying shades of emotion from convoluted anguish to something direct and visceral.

I will give one last example of how this awareness contributes to the playing of a scene. It is in Hermione's speech at her trial, Act III,

Scene ii of *The Winter's Tale*. She has just given birth in the prison cell, her baby daughter has been taken from her, she is weak. She is being tried in public on a false accusation of adultery.

Her first line consists of nothing but little words of one syllable which convey the minimal energy she has in her:

> Since what I am to say, must be but that

but by the second line two strong, Latin-based words communicate and create the beginnings of renewed power:

> Which contradicts my accusation, and

That little word at the end of the line says that she can't sustain the effort. The third line manages one more big polysyllabic word—"testimony"—but, as though Hermoine is exhausted by it, the next half-line and following line-and-a-half fall away into little mono- and di-syllables:

> The testimony on my part, no other
> But what comes from myself, it shall scarce boot me
> To say "not guilty" . . .

However, she does not give in to her weakness; a word comes to her that rallies her:

> Mine integrity

and although she falters again for a line-and-a-half, the tide has turned and she can confront her accuser and defend her honor:

> Being counted falsehood, shall, as I express it,
> Be so receiv'd. But thus, if powers divine
> Behold our human actions (as they do),
> I doubt not then but **innocence** (L) shall make
> False **accusation** (L) blush, and **tyranny** (L)
> Tremble at **patience** (L).

Once having invoked the powers divine, her words gain in power and directness without the switching language which discloses inner conflict.

Etymological awareness is a potent ingredient in the search for ways to tap the lifeblood in Shakespeare's language. The large proportion of his words are of Anglo-Saxon and French derivation, designated in the dictionary as Old English, Middle English, Old French and Middle French (O.E., M.E., O.F., M.F.) Very often, but not always, the use of a Latin-based word can be a signal to the actor that something special is occurring in the mind of the character. Words that have become common currency with us were glinting with new-coined significance to the Elizabethans.

5

◄► Figures of Speech ◄►

I have worked with actors who could spot and name figures of speech in Shakespeare's text that I have never heard of, and yet be incapable of applying their knowledge to their craft. By that I mean that the erudition shed no light on the rendition. Shakespeare makes constant and conscious use of figures of speech because Rhetoric was a natural instrument of communication at that time. Every educated person had practiced the art, and the practice of Rhetoric was very close to an actor's training. For today's actor, it is the *practice* of rhetorical forms that will clarify his or her performance, not the mere study of them.

The Elizabethan schoolboy learnt his lessons by reciting them out loud according to the rules of Rhetoric. These rules demanded gestures appropriate to the content of the speech, an emotionally truthful expression whose goal was to excite the *passions* of the hearers, and a mastery of the devices of logical argument that would persuade the *reason* of the hearers. In a nutshell, the rules of Rhetoric demand good acting. For the actor it is useful to remember that the Art of Rhetoric developed from the analysis of successful persuasion, and successful persuasion was originally the result of inspiration, not study.

Figures of speech are the foot soldiers of rhetorical expertise, and although the term "figures of speech" sounds dry and academic, we are perfectly familiar with them and use them automatically in our everyday speaking. Becoming aware of figures of speech allows us to notice the moments when Shakespeare uses them for a particular effect, whether consciously or with the unconscious brilliance of natural genius. If you let them affect you sensorily, they perform one or all of the following services:

1) lead you to discoveries about the character you are playing;
2) create the emotional tone of a scene;
3) do half your acting for you.

The figures of speech which Shakespeare uses most often for dramatic effect are: *alliteration, assonance, onomatopoeia, antithesis, double and triple antithesis, puns,* and *the ladder*.

ALLITERATION, ASSONANCE, ONOMATOPOEIA

Alliteration is the repetition of a vowel or a consonant at the beginning of two or more words in a phrase.

In Act I, Scene ii of *Henry V*, the Ambassador of France presents the young King Henry with a "tun of treasure" which turns out to be tennis balls. The insult well-taken provokes Henry to a response peppered with alliterations. These actually create in the actor the sarcasm, the reined-in anger of the moment:

> We are glad the Dauphin is so **p**leasant with us;
> His **p**resent and your **p**ains we thank you for:
> When we have match'd our rackets to these balls,
> **W**e **w**ill in France, by **G**od's **g**race, play a set
> Shall strike his father's crown into the hazard.

and later in the same speech:

> And tell the **p**leasant **P**rince this mock of his
> Hath turn'd his balls to gunstones; and his **s**oul
> Shall **s**tand **s**ore-charged for the wasteful vengeance
> That shall fly with them: for many a thousand widows
> Shall this his **m**ock **m**ock out their dear husbands;
> **M**ock **m**others from their sons, mock castles down;
> And some are yet ungotten and unborn
> That shall have **cause** to **curse** the Dauphin's scorn.

This speech offers examples not only of alliteration but of *assonance* (the resemblance of sounds) and an interesting instance of *onomatopoeia* (words with sounds imitative of their meaning). In the last line, the assonant "cause to curse" has the same consonants with different vowel sounds between them which, when savored, give the phrase weight, deliberation, menace. The onomatopoeic device of the word "mock" refers to the tennis balls Henry has just received. When the lips strongly explode the "m" and the "o" sounds, the word makes the sound of ball on racquet.

If the actor is capable of putting together the exploding sound on lips and tongue, the image of a hard-hitting tennis game with husbands and sons and mothers and castles as the balls, anger at the Dauphin's insult and grief at the "wasteful vengeance" of war, he will discover the character of this young man. Not just angry, not cocksure, but dangerous and witty at the height of passion.

In Chapter One we looked at the fourth Chorus from *Henry V* for the way in which the sounds of vowels and consonants helped to create the environment. A mixture of *alliteration* (broadening from its pure definition of "repetition of vowels or consonants at *the beginning* of words" to "repetition of vowels and consonants *in* words," sometimes also called consonance) and *onomatopoeia* makes us hear the sentinels as they whisper to each other, standing on guard the night before the battle:

> The hum of either army stilly sounds,
> That the fix'd sentinels almost receive
> The secret whispers of each other's watch:

A little later in the speech, alliteration again helps the sense become almost onomatopoeic:

> The country cocks do crow, the clocks do toll,
> And the third hour of drowsy morning name.

The sharp, hard "c" sounds juxtaposed with the long, heavy vowel sounds in the next line create the effect of sleep broken into by outside noises.

In Act I, Scene ii of *A Midsummer Night's Dream*, Helena bemoans her lovelorn state, spurned by Demetrius who has rejected her for her friend Hermia. The repeated, alliterative "h's," if they come right from her suffering heart, will actualize her hapless, perhaps almost sobbing, perhaps scornful condition:

> For, ere Demetrius look'd on Hermia's eyne,
> He hail'd down oaths that he was only mine;
> But when this hail some heat from Hermia felt,
> So he dissolv'd and show'rs of oaths did melt.

The repetition of "h's" and "f's" indicates excitement of the breath from some vulnerable emotion. In *Twelfth Night*, Act I, Scene v, Olivia falls in love with the disguised Viola/Cesario, and after she/he has left, Olivia says:

> I do I know not what, and fear to find
> Mine eye too great a flatterer for my mind.
> Fate, show thy force; ourselves we do not owe.
> What is decreed, must be: and be this so.

In Sonnet 116, the weight of repeated "m's" gives a profundity to the first statement:

> Let me not to the marriage of true minds
> Admit impediments.

Most often the repetition reveals and re-engenders some form of anger, contempt, sarcasm or mockery:

> Beatrice: But manhood is melted into curtsies, valour into compliment,
> and men are only turned into tongue, and trim ones too . . .
> *Much Ado About Nothing, Act IV, Scene i*

Queen Margaret:
> For **Q**ueen, a very **c**aitiff, **c**rown'd with **c**are . . .
>> *Richard III, Act IV, Scene iv*

Hotspur:
> To be so **p**ester'd with a **pop**injay . . .
>> *Henry IV, Part I, Act I, Scene iii*

Iago:
> Didst thou not see her **p**addle with the **p**alm of his hand?
> . . . When these **m**utualities so **m**arshal the way, **h**ard at **h**and, comes
> the **m**aster and **m**ain exercise, th'in**c**orporate **c**onclusion.
>> *Othello, Act II, Scene i*

Iago, in those lines, using Latin-based euphemisms for the sexual act, leans on the sensual "m's," the heavy-breathing "h's" and the exclamatory "c's" to thrust home his meaning for the incredulous Roderigo.

And for comic effect:

Bottom:
> The **r**aging **r**ocks,
> And **sh**ivering **sh**ocks,
> Shall break the locks
> Of prison gates;
> And Phibbus' car
> **Sh**all **sh**ine from **f**ar
> And **m**ake and **m**ar
> The **f**oolish **f**ates.
>> *A Midsummer Night's Dream, Act I, Scene ii*

> Whereat with **b**lade, with **b**loody **b**lameful **b**lade,
> He **b**ravely **b**roach'd his **b**oiling **b**loody **b**reast . . .
>> *A Midsummer Night's Dream, Act V, Scene i*

The actor who can absorb and play these sounds so that they inform performance will be in an excellent working partnership with the text. The actor who can take advantage of Romeo's self-conscious use of assonance in the midst of his agonised questions to the Nurse about his love will add artistry to emotional expression:

> Where is she? and how doth she?
> And what says my **conceal'd** lady to our **cancell'd** love?

Not only does the assonance provide a poignancy to his feeling, but the fact that the sounds are part of a *double antithesis* gives an even weightier finality to his speech.

ANTITHESIS

Antithesis, as John Barton says in his *Playing Shakespeare*, is far too dry a word for a way of thinking and speaking that is inherently dramatic. "Setting the word against the word" is Shakespeare's description of antithesis. Sometimes antithesis is more like a balancing act, as in "suit the action to the word and the word to the action," which has a swinging rhythm to it, but at its most dramatic it lobs opposites to and fro between the protagonists or juxtaposes contrasting words in such a way as to create and reveal inner turmoil in the speaker. The latter case is graphically demonstrated in Romeo's reaction to the evidence he sees of the fight between the Capulets and the Montagues in Act I, Scene i of *Romeo and Juliet*. He appears to be ridiculing his own agony and ecstasy:

> O me! What fray was here?
> Yet tell me not, for I have heard it all.
> Here's much to do with hate, but more with love.
> Why then, O brawling love, O loving hate,
> O anything of nothing first create!
> O heavy lightness, serious vanity,
> Misshapen chaos of well-seeming forms!
> Feather of lead, bright smoke, cold fire, sick health,
> Still-waking sleep, that is not what it is!
> This love feel I that feel no love in this.
> Dost thou not laugh?

This speech, which could be perhaps a conscious exercise on Shakespeare's part, becomes for the actor an entré into Romeo's possible behavior through the assumption that it is *Romeo* who is consciously using antithesis to make fun of his lovelorn condition. Another way of seeing the speech is that Romeo is in such a state of frustrated love that the fight in the street sparks off a wild alternation of rage and longing which spouts forth in pendulum-swing imagery. One way or another, if he really experiences the roller-coaster extremes of these closely juxtaposed images and emotions he will be thrown into such exaggeration that he makes melodrama both from the drama of his inner condition and the drama that has just happened in the street.

One cannot begin to give examples of *antithesis* without producing examples of *double* and *triple antithesis*. In this speech, textbook instances of antithesis are seen in "bright↔smoke, cold↔fire, sick↔health" and in "heavy↔lightness, serious↔vanity." When the antitheses of "brawling love" and "loving hate" are set against each other they form a textbook instance of *double antithesis*. "Brawling" sets against "loving" and "love" against "hate." A good example of *triple antithesis* lies in "Mis-shapen chaos of well-seeming forms": mis↔well; shapen↔seeming; chaos↔forms.

How is the actor helped by this awareness? First of all, by exercising her/his ability to think/feel/speak antitheses accurately. They are the barbells of eloquence. Practice first with the simple weights of simple antithesis. Romeo's speech and Sonnet 65 provide excellent material. Then advance to the heavier matter of double antithesis and triple antithesis. If you use a tape recorder for this, listen for the equality of attention given each side of the contest. None of the weights can be dropped.

> E.G.:   "**heavy** lightness! serious **vanity**!" is unbalanced;
> "heavy **lightness**! serious **vanity**!" is unbalanced;
> "**heavy** *lightness*! **serious** *vanity*!" balances.
> "**Mis**-shapen *chaos* of well-***seeming* forms**" is unbalanced;
> "**Mis**-*shapen* *chaos* of **well**-*seeming* *forms*" is balanced

because the mind has taken the three elements of the antithesis and pitted each of them individually against its counterpart in order to come up with the whole intellectual-emotional burden. It takes a great deal of brain muscle to accomplish this—really to think each bit of it—without which one has missed the intensity of the moment that is occurring mentally and emotionally for the character.

The words and ideas that make up antitheses are not always extreme opposites and do not always create emotional extremity; quite often they sharpen an argument or make a witticism through more shaded counterpoint.

> Iago:
> In Venice they do *let* **God** *see* the pranks
> They *dare not show* their **husbands**: their best conscience
> Is not to **leave't undone**, but **keep't unknown**.
> *Othello, Act III, Scene iii*

There is a clever double or, arguably, triple antithesis, well worth playing, in "let God see" and "dare not show their husbands." "Let see" suggests a subtle opposition to "dare not show," and "God" is set clearly against "husband." This is made even more telling in performance as "God" comes on a weak stress of the iambic beat which now strengthens because of the demand of the antithesis. These three strong stresses in the middle of the line allow a heavy innuendo to build into the next line. The diabolical insinuation is neatly capped by the double antithesis "leave't undone" against "keep't unknown." These words do not have opposite meanings but offer shaded contrast with devastating effect.

Do not make the mistake of oversimplifying the idea of antithesis, and thereby bludgeoning the performance of it. I employed a double antithesis in that sentence to show that this is not an outdated procedure ("oversimplifying ↔ bludgeoning" and "idea ↔ performance"). It is part of our everyday language use, for example:

> "Shall I tell you the **good** news or the **bad** news first?"

> "**Loved** the ***book*, hated** the *movie*."

> "The man's a **liar**, and he *stole* **money** that *belonged* to the **STATE**"
> "No, he's a **politician**, and he *re-allocated* **resources** *sequestered within his jurisdiction* on behalf of his **CONSTITUENTS**."

One can go on, doubling, tripling, quintupling; indeed, Shakespeare uses the device as naturally as he speaks and in all sorts of variations. The term "antithesis" is not his; it belongs to those of us who dissect and anatomize the forms of genius in order to probe into its content.

The conflict and drama in two of the most powerful scenes in *Richard III* depend almost entirely on the use of antithesis and its variables. In acting terms this means that the most important element in the playing of the scene is LISTENING. The characters do not know that they are speaking in a series of brilliant antitheses. They HEAR/FEEL what is said, and the words that they hear/feel stimulate a related and oppositional word/feeling response. The actor's process must be to *absorb* the experiential meaning of the words into the body, *absorb* the form and logic of the antithesis and then LISTEN for the trigger words in what the other person is saying. The trigger words spark the apparently unpremeditated response.

This may seem a simplistic description of the natural outcome of good acting. Unfortunately, a combination of spontaneity and comprehension of the text is very rare on the Shakespearean stage at present; those actors who are able to create spontaneous, moment-to-moment life on the stage tend to sacrifice the text to their creativity, while those "who know how to speak Shakespeare" tend to be dead from the neck down.

This book is an attempt to bring creativity and intelligibility together, to marry form and content. As we wade through the minutiae of rhetorical forms and figures of speech, there is grave danger of losing sight of the fact that such forms and figures are the natural components of eloquence which is itself a natural attribute. Eloquence is released when a flood of emotion swirls into the brain, sweeping all the right words into the most satisfying constructions and pouring them forth to carry the listener to new understanding. This natural force can be cultivated and raised to an art by noting the most effective forms arrived at by passion and conviction and consciously exploiting them. The danger is that the *form* will be so seductive, because it demands less emotional energy to reproduce than *content*, that the speaker will resort to empty "rhetoric," forgetting that it is the commitment of his/her own true feelings that makes the difference between lying and telling the truth.

Ralph Waldo Emerson on the subject of eloquence may provide a *caveat* for the whole study of form.

> Eloquence . . . shows the power and possibility of man . . . The orator is the physician . . . There is no true orator who is not a hero . . . No act indicates more universal health than eloquence. The special

ingredients of this force are clear perceptions, memory, power of statement, logic, imagination or the skill to clothe your thought in natural images, passion which is the heat, and then a grand will . . . But this power which so fascinates and astonishes and commands, is only the exaggeration of a talent which is universal. All men are competitors in this art. Eloquence is as natural as swimming,—an art which all men might learn, though so few do. The orator must command the whole scale of the language, from the most elegant to the most low and vile. Everyone has felt how superior in force is the language of the street to that of the academy. The street must be one of his schools. Ought not the scholar to be able to convey his meaning in terms as short and strong as the porter or truckman uses to convey his? The speech of the man on the street is invariably strong, nor can you mend it by making it what you call parliamentary. The power of his speech is, that it is understood by all . . . but we must come to the main matter, of power of statement,—know your fact; hug your fact. For the essential thing is heat, and heat comes of sincerity. Speak what you know and believe. Eloquence is the power to translate a truth into language perfectly intelligible to the person to whom you speak.

Coming back to the barbells of eloquent brain-muscle—figures of speech—I emphasize once more that you can only exercise usefully when you involve your creative, thinking, feeling apparatus in the activity.

Antithesis is so much a part of Shakespeare's lexicon that the antithesis gymnasium offered here will be substantial. Antithesis springs into play very often at peak moments of conflict; it must never be divorced from feeling. A classic case is Hamlet's confrontation with his mother:

Gertrude:
Hamlet, thou hast thy father much offended.

Hamlet:
Mother, you have my father much offended.

Gertrude:
Come, come, you answer with an idle tongue.

Hamlet:
Go, go, you question with a wicked tongue.

An analysis of these exchanges presents all sorts of detailed indications of relationship, story and character for the actors to *play* not just *say*.

1. "Hamlet," says Gertrude. "Mother," says Hamlet.
2. "Thou," says Gertrude, using the familiar address, suggesting a relatively gentle opening approach. "You," says Hamlet, rejecting the intimacy.
3. "Thy father," says Gertrude, meaning Claudius. "My father," says

Hamlet, meaning his dead father, King Hamlet . The actor playing Hamlet must be very clear in his imaging and intention in
these two words. The antithesis is not "**thy** father ↔ **my** father,"
it is "**thy father** ↔ **my father**," so that Gertrude very clearly
gets it that Hamlet does not accept his uncle as his father and is
bringing the memory of her former husband into the argument.

4. Feeling his intent, her next line is addressed in the formal "you"
as she scolds him with maternal authority: "Come, come," she
says. "Go, go," he mocks her.

5. "You **answer**" ↔ "You **question**."

6. "An **idle** tongue," the mother reprimands, and the avenging
moralist lashes back with, "A **wicked** tongue."

Here is a three-act play packed into four lines. If realized in all its
detail and played at speed, it will kick the scene off on an emotional
energy which can support the killing of Polonius and the ensuing
escalation of the mother/son confrontation.

Let us return now to *Richard III*. Lady Anne, as she accompanies
the coffin containing the body of her father-in-law, is confronted by
the man who murdered both him and her husband. The passion that
surely mounts within her is terror ("clever" interpretations of character could arrive at a different conclusion, but here we start from what
is most apparent from the given circumstance and the text). Richard's
passions are more hidden, but ambition is the driving one, and in this
scene he must convince Anne that he passionately loves her. As in the
famous question, "Does Lady Macbeth *really* faint or only pretend to?"
the question here may be, "Does Richard *really* fall in love with Anne
or only pretend to?" In either case, the other characters on stage must
be convinced—the faint, the falling in love, must seem real. It can only
seem real if it is experienced as real by the protagonist; therefore,
Richard must tell the truth when he says that his love for Anne drove
him to murder:

> Your beauty was the cause of that effect:
> Your beauty, that did haunt me in my sleep
> To undertake the death of all the world,
> So I might live one hour in thy sweet bosom.

When the heat of passion ignites the play of minds there is the
chance that a spontaneous combustion will bring real life to the stage.

His approach to her begins with flattery:

Sweet *saint*

She responds:

Foul *devil*

The double antithesis is framed in the antithesis of heaven and hell.

Anne must *hear* "sweet" to send back "foul" and *hear* "saint" to send back "devil." In her ensuing tirade against the murderer, fueled by the sight of the dead man's congealed wounds suddenly spouting new blood, her appeals to heaven and then to earth for help create natural antitheses:

> O *God!* which this blood **mad'st**, revenge his death;
> O *earth!* which this blood **drink'st**, revenge his death;
> Either **heav'n** with *lightning strike the murderer* **DEAD**,
> Or *earth gape open wide and eat him* **QUICK** . . .
> ("Quick" here with its old meaning of "living"—the opposite of "dead.")

From this point the heat of the passions sparks a pyrotechnical display of antithesis and we can observe and absorb the antitheses so that they in turn help spark the passions.

For the sake of clarity in the next section of the scene, I'd like you to look at the way the antitheses work in terms of a tennis game. Richard serves: Anne returns the ball. Anne serves: Richard returns. Occasionally they rally, or volley at the net. In a rally the shots are exchanged with equal strength for some time—in a volley the ferocity and velocity increase. The actors involved may have some leeway in deciding who wins and who loses the points, but this is primarily an exercise in listening for who originates the thought and who reacts to it. The device of SERVES and RETURNS may help sharpen the hearing.

Richard:	*(Serves)*	**Lady**, **you** know no ***rules*** of *charity*, Which renders good for bad, blessings for curses.
Anne:	*(Returns)* *(Serves)*	**Villain**, **thou** know'st no ***laws*** of *God nor man*. No **beast so fierce** but knows some *touch of pity*.
Richard:	*(Returns)*	But **I** know *none*, and therefore am no **beast**.
Anne:	*(Serves)*	**O** wonderful, when ***devils*** *tell the truth*!
Richard:	*(Returns)* *(Serves)*	**More** wonderful, when ***angels*** *are so angry*. Vouchsafe, **divine *per***fection of a *woman*, Of these **supposed *crimes***, to give me leave, By circumstance, but to **ACQUIT** myself.
Anne:	*(Returns)*	Vouchsafe, **diffus'd *in***fection of a *man*, For these **known *evils***, but to give me leave, By circumstance, to **CURSE** thy cursed self.
Richard:	*(Serves)*	**Fairer** than *tongue* can *name* thee, let me have Some patient leisure to **EXCUSE** myself.
Anne:	*(Returns)*	**Fouler** than *heart* can *think* thee, thou canst make No excuse current but to **HANG** thyself.
Richard:	*(Serves)*	By such despair I should **ac**cuse myself.
Anne:	*(Returns)* *(Serves)*	And by despairing shalt thou stand **EX**cus'd For doing **worthy vengeance** on *thyself* That didst **unworthy slaughter** upon *others*.

Anne wins this set and pursues her advantage with righteous accusations, occasionally provoking further rallies of antithesis:

Richard:	*(Serves)*	I was provoked by **her *sland'rous*** tongue,
		That laid their guilt upon **my *guiltless*** shoulders.
Anne:	*(Returns)*	Thou wast provoked by **thy *bloody*** mind,
		Which never dream'st on ought but butcheries.

But she weakens and the next set goes to Richard as he shatters her defenses with his bald announcement that he is going to sleep with her. He blames her beauty for his murderous acts:

> Your beauty that did haunt me in my sleep
> To undertake the death of all the world,
> So I might live one hour in thy sweet bosom.

Shocked back into energy, Anne delivers a serve from which Richard wins a point and goes on to serve again:

Anne:	*(Serves)*	If I thought that, I tell thee homicide.
		These nails should rent that beauty from my cheeks.
Richard:	*(Returns)*	These eyes could not endure that beauty's wrack;
		You should not blemish it if I stood by.
	(Serves)	As all the **world** is cheered by the ***sun***,
		So **I** by ***that***; it is my day, my life.

The game is alight again and the antitheses fly:

Anne:	*(Returns)*	Black **night** o'ershade thy ***day***, and *death* thy *life*.
Richard:	*(Rally)*	Curse not thyself, fair creature; thou art both.
Anne:	*(Rally)*	I would I were, to be reveng'd on thee.
Richard:	*(Serves)*	It is a quarrel most **unnatural**,
		To be reveng'd on him that ***loveth*** thee.
Anne:	*(Returns)*	It is a quarrel **just and reasonable**,
		To be reveng'd on him that ***kill'd*** my *husband*.
Rich ard:	R	He that bereft thee, lady, of thy husband,
	A	Did it to help thee to a better husband.
Anne:	L	His better doth not breathe upon the earth.
Richard:	L	He lives that loves thee better than he could.
Anne:	Y	Name him.
Richard:	V	Plantagenet.
Anne:	O	Why, that was he.
Richard:	L	The **self-same** *name*, but one of **better** *nature*.
Anne:	L	Where is he?
Richard:	E	Here. *(She spits at him)* Why dost thou spit at me?
Anne:	Y	Would it were mortal poison, for thy sake!
Richard:	*(Serves)*	Never **came** poison *from* so *sweet* a **PLACE**.
Anne:	*(Returns)*	Never **hung** poison *on* a *fouler* **TOAD**.

Although poor Anne wins a few of the rallies and an occasional set, Richard wins the game:

> Richard: Look how **my *ring*** encompasseth **thy *finger*:**
>   Even so **thy *breast*** encloseth **my *poor heart*;**

Once she has left, a final leap over the net and back again celebrates his victory:

> Was ever woman in this humour **woo'd**?
> Was ever woman in this humour **won**?

In his euphoric post-victory re-run of the game, he sets up the image of the odds he had to play against—a huge antithesis—"all the world to nothing." He follows it with the image of Lady Anne's dead husband in antithesis to his deformity:

> A sweeter and a lovelier gentleman, ↔ [On me,] whose all not equals
>   Edward's moi'ty?
> Fram'd in the prodigality of nature, ↔ [On me,] that halts and am
>   misshapen thus?

The antithesis does a flip-flop as he recognizes his power, perhaps for the first time:

> My dukedom to a beggarly denier,
> I do mistake my person all this while!
> Upon my life, she finds—although I cannot—
> Myself to be a marv'llous proper man.

He has found his confidence through Lady Anne, young and vulnerable; at the end of the play he tangles with the former Queen, Elizabeth, a woman of the world, a politician, unafraid for herself, emotionally mature. He attempts the same tactics that worked with Anne, and although there is room for interpretation at the end of the scene, it is clear to me that he, hollow and desperate, misreads Elizabeth totally while she runs rings around him, confronts him, undermines him, and calling down God's judgment destroys him. Her final words are ambiguous, leaving him to draw a false conclusion. He has lost his touch. But the battle between them is a right royal battle of antithesis.

This scene is unbeatable as an exercise in listening and answering with detailed accuracy, and the variety of its emotional topography depends on handling both imagery and antithesis with depth and precision.

There is a short passage near the beginning of this conversation which builds emotional intensity by means of an elaborate antithetical device. The scene starts with some classic single, double and triple antitheses (not to mention assonance and internal rhyme) setting the emotional tone:

Queen Elizabeth:
> Though **far** *more cause*, yet **much** *less* spirit to curse
> Abides in me, I say Amen to her.

King Richard:
> Stay, madam: I must talk a word with you.

Queen Elizabeth:
> I have no more **sons** of the royal blood
> For thee to slaughter. For my **daughters**, Richard,
> They shall be **praying** *nuns*, not **weeping** *queens*;
> And therefore level not to hit their lives.

King Richard:
> You have a daughter call'd Elizabeth,
> **Virtuous** and *fair*, *royal* and *gracious*.

Here, the die is thrown, and each of the attributes Richard assigns the young Elizabeth is rebutted desperately as her mother fights for her daughter's life. Elizabeth must *hear* each word in that last line of Richard's and find an answer for each, which she does, with a half-line to each of the first two words and a whole line to the last two:

Queen Elizabeth:
> And must she die for this? O, let her live,
> **And I'll corrupt her manners**, *stain her beauty*,
> *Slander myself as false to Edward's bed,*
> **Throw over her the veil of infamy;**
> So she may live unscarr'd of bleeding slaughter,
> I will confess she was not Edward's daughter.

King Richard:
> **Wrong** not her *birth*; she is a royal Princess.

Queen Elizabeth:
> To **save** her *life*, I'll say she is not so.

King Richard:
> Her life is safest only in her birth.

Queen Elizabeth:
> And only in that safety died her brothers.

After this mortal play on words comes the *coup de grâce*: six antitheses, if we can count "Lo" and "No":

King Richard:
> **Lo**, *at* their *birth* **good STARS** were *OPPOSITE*.

Queen Elizabeth:
> **No**, *to* their *lives* **ill FRIENDS** were *CONTRARY*.

The scene is a long one, usually cut to a shadow of its full brilliance because it comes late in a long play, and Shakespeare uses antithesis relentlessly to pile up arguments, to score points of life and death, to juggle politics, family, love, hate and destiny until Richard is driven to make a bargain with heaven that cannot but destroy him:

> Myself, myself confound!
> God and fortune, bar me happy hours!
> Day, yield me not thy light, nor night, thy rest!
> Be opposite, all planets of good luck,
> To my proceeding if with dear heart's love,
> Immaculate devotion, holy thoughts,
> I tender not thy beauteous princely daughter.

The enormity of the lie, this extreme antithesis between the words and the truth spells his doom.

Antithesis unlocks doors that open onto rooms full of brilliant argument, chambers crammed with innuendo, great caverns of ideas. The device appears throughout Shakespeare and it should be one of the actor's best friends.

PUNS

A *pun* plays with a word that has two or more meanings in order to twist the sense. *Puns* are not always funny, or rather they are not found only in comedy. When Mercutio is stabbed he says:

> Ask for me tomorrow, and you shall find me a **grave** man.

There is the opportunity for Lady Macbeth to hit a bizarre and chilling note when she says:

> If he do bleed,
> I'll **gild** the faces of the grooms withal,
> For it must seem their **guilt**.

It is quite possible that the adrenalin makes her slightly hysterical and she can't help making the joke.

The person making a pun does so very consciously and for effect. A pun asks to be noticed, if not always laughed at, and the punster must set the pun up, put it in quotes, underline it, push it under people's noses. There is not much virtue in being shy about a pun. The actor's relish is the key to making puns work.

Most punning is for comic effect and is accompanied often with a rude elbow digging the listener's ribs:

> Antipholus of Ephesus: Go fetch me something, I'll break ope the gate.
> Dromio of Syracuse *(Within)*: Break any breaking here, and I'll break your knave's pate.
> Dromio of Ephesus: A man may break a word with you, sir, and words are but wind; Ay, and break it in your face, so he break it not behind.

Dromio of Syracuse *(Within)*: It seem'st thou want'st breaking; out upon thee, hind!

For this to work, the actors must know the different meanings intended each time the word is spoken and relish the building insults through the repetition of the word, and the sound *in* the word, "break." Anything more subtle will not work. *The Comedy of Errors* is stuffed with punnage, and I recommend it as a pun gymnasium.

In *The Taming of the Shrew* comes a classic case of punnage, again dealing with a master, his man, and a door. The comic construction is so perfect it is worth quoting in full:

Petruchio: Here, sirrah Grumio, knock, I say.
Grumio: Knock, sir? Whom should I knock? Is there any man has rebused your worship?
Petruchio: Villain, I say, knock me here soundly.
Grumio: Knock you here, sir? Why, sir, what am I, sir, that I should knock you here, sir?

Petruchio:
Villain, I say, knock me at this gate,
And rap me well, or I'll knock your knave's pate.

Grumio:
My master is grown quarrelsome. I should knock you first,
And then I know after who comes by the worst.

Petruchio:
Faith, sirrah, an you'll not knock, I'll ring it.
I'll try how you can solfa, and sing it. *(He wrings him by the ears)*

Grumio: Help, masters, help! My master is mad.
Petruchio: Now knock when I bid you, sirrah villain.
(Enter Hortensio.)

Hortensio: How now, what's the matter?

. . .

Grumio: Nay, 'tis no matter . . . look you, sir. He bid me knock him and rap him soundly, sir. Well, was it fit for a servant to use his master so, being, perhaps, for aught I see, two and thirty, a pip out?

Whom would to God I had well knock'd at first,
Then had not Grumio come by the worst.

Petruchio:
A senseless villain. Good Hortensio,
I bade the rascal knock upon your gate,
And could not get him for my heart to do it.

Grumio:
Knock at the gate? O heavens!

Spake you not these words plain, "Sirrah knock me here, rap me here, knock me well, and knock me soundly?" And come you not now with "knocking at the gate?"

Some of Shakespeare's punning is used to show the stupidity of the speaker, but in this case the actor has the option of playing Grumio extra dumb or extra wily.

The Fool in *King Lear* uses his gift for punning to soften the blunt blow of the truth:

> Fool: Nuncle, give me an egg, and I'll give thee two crowns.
> Lear: What two crowns shall they be?
> Fool: Why, after I have cut the egg i'th' middle and eat up the meat, the two crowns of the egg. When thou clovest thy crown i'th' middle, and gav'st away both parts, thou bor'st thine ass on thy back o'er the dirt: thou hadst little wit in thy bald crown when thou gav'st thy golden one away.

The actor must develop an ability to "point" certain words in order to arrive at the full effect, and should err on the side of boldness to begin with. It pays off to embody, physicalize, illustrate the joke being made with the word. This imprints the intent of the wordplay in the brain; later one may modify the delivery.

Punning is wordplay, but wordplay is not always punning, as can be found in the following passage from *Richard II*:

> Bolingbroke:
> My gracious uncle—
>
> York:
> Tut, tut! grace me no grace, nor uncle me no uncle,
> I am no traitor's uncle, and that word 'grace'
> In an ungracious mouth is but profane.

The thrill of wordplay is endemic to Elizabethan writing and it is to be played with and played upon to the hilt. So much of Shakespeare's writing is wordplay that producing examples is rather embarrassing. For practice in shading and bending and pointing thoughts so that the voice and the mind learn subtlety and revel in their artfulness, Sonnet 135 is a prototype—wordplay, punnage and bawdy double meanings:

> Whoever hath her wish, thou hast thy Will,
> And Will to boot, and Will in overplus;
> More than enough am I that vex thee still,
> To thy sweet will making addition thus.
> Wilt thou, whose will is large and spacious,
> Not once vouchsafe to hide my will in thine?
> Shall will in others seem right gracious,
> And in my will no fair acceptance shine?
> The sea, all water, yet receives rain still,
> And in abundance addeth to his store,

So thou being rich in Will, add to thy will
One will of mine to make thy large Will more.
  Let no unkind, no fair beseechers kill;
  Think all but one, and me in that one Will.

There are here four meanings for the word "will":

1. Will = William
2. Will = purpose or determination
3. Will = carnal appetite
4. Will = sexual organ, male or female

Your exercise is to accept the four possible meanings of "will" and to image exactly which meaning you are intending as you say each. Know also that your voice is alive to each image. Make sure that your choices add up to a logical overall meaning for the sonnet as spoken by you, and that you are neither coy nor coarse.

THE LADDER

The final figure of rhetorical speech that the actor must be aware of and respond to is the "ladder." This is a device for building the intensity of a feeling. The ladder starts with a statement or an image or a feeling which is capped by one that outdoes the first, and then another and another rising to the top climactic rung of the ladder. Very often a final statement jumps back down to the ground again. The performer of the ladder must find a way to convey the mounting intensity through the use of the voice. According to the law of dynamics, this will either be through growing volume, rising pitch and/or increasing pace, the choice between them being determined by the way in which the imagery, the circumstances, the objective, act on the inner energies of the speaker.

The model ladder is used by Rosalind, the mistress of rhetoric, and used with such a flourish that she lets us know that she knows she is using the ladder. She is describing to Orlando how his brother Oliver and her sister (actually her cousin) Celia fell in love at first sight:

There was never anything so sudden, but the fight of two rams, and Caesar's thrasonical brag of I came, saw, and overcame. For your brother and my sister no sooner met, but they looked; no sooner looked but they loved; no sooner loved, but they sighed; no sooner sighed, but they asked one another the reason; no sooner knew the reason, but they sought the remedy. And in these degrees have they made a pair of stairs to marriage, which they will climb incontinent, or else be incontinent before marriage. They are in the very wrath of love, and they will together. Clubs cannot part them.

Rosalind announces the ladder with a three-rung signal: "I came, saw, and overcame." She then performs the ladder. Then she tells us what she has done: "and in these degrees have they made a pair of stairs to marriage." She then makes a slightly naughty joke, "or else be incontinent before marriage." She wraps up the description with a hyperbolic image for the violence of their love, "Clubs cannot part them."

Here is a pictorial representation of the ladder device:

10	***TO MARRIAGE***
9	***A PAIR OF STAIRS***
8	**AND IN THESE DEGREES HAVE THEY MADE**
7	***BUT THEY SOUGHT THE REMEDY***
6	**NO SOONER KNEW THE REASON**
5	***BUT THEY ASKED ONE ANOTHER THE REASON,***
4	*but they sighed; no sooner sighed*
3	**but they loved; no sooner loved**
2	*but they looked; no sooner looked*
1	for your brother and my sister no sooner met

Rosalind is one of several of Shakespeare's characters who are actors within their stories. She seems to enjoy performing more than, for instance, Viola or Hamlet. She could well play this speech like a stand-up comedian. She has come almost to the end of Orlando's tolerance; he probably knows by now she is not really a man: "Did your brother tell you how I counterfeited to swoon when he show'd your handkerchief?" (She had genuinely fainted when Oliver produced Orlando's kerchief stained with blood.) Orlando replies, "Ay, and greater wonders than that." She must put on a major act to keep the game going a little longer.

There are other ways of interpreting this point in the play, but all is lost if Rosalind merely *reports* in a conversational tone that Oliver and Celia have fallen in love. It is late in the play, the audience needs fireworks to keep taking an interest, and Shakespeare has provided a great display to keep the entertainment and excitement building. And, like any good showman, seeing how well that ladder worked, he gives us another one:

Phebe:
Good shepherd, tell this youth what 'tis to love.

Silvius:
It is to be all made of sighs and tears,
And so am I for Phebe.

Phebe: And I for Ganymede.
Orlando: And I for Rosalind.
Rosalind: And I for no woman.

Silvius:
> It is to be all made of faith and service,
> And so am I for Phebe.

Phebe: And I for Ganymede.
Orlando: And I for Rosalind.
Rosalind: And I for no woman.

Silvius:
> It is to be all made of fantasy,
> All made of passion and all made of wishes;
> All adoration, duty and observance,
> All humbleness, all patience and impatience,
> All purity, all trial all obedience;
> And so am I for Phebe.

Phebe: And so am I for Ganymede.
Orlando: And so am I for Rosalind.
Rosalind: And so am I for no woman.
Phebe: If this be so, why blame you me to love you?
Silvius: If this be so, why blame you me to love you?
Orlando: If this be so, why blame you me to love you?
Rosalind: Why do you speak too, 'Why blame you me to love you?'
Orlando: To her that is not here, nor doth not hear.
Rosalind: Pray you no more of this,'tis like the howling of Irish wolves
> against the moon.

There is one huge ladder and within it three stepladders with four "and I for" rungs, plus one internal ladder of Silvius's extended paean of adoration. The first trickle of love expressed as "sighs and tears" quickly turns to a river and then a flood of passion which results in a vocal outpouring worthy of Rosalind's description, "the howling of Irish wolves against the moon."

Another ladder that exhibits love is mounted by Lorenzo and Jessica in *The Merchant of Venice*. Each of the classical references conjures up a more powerful emotion relating to the trials of love:

Lorenzo:
> The moon shines bright. In such a night as this,
> When the sweet wind did gently kiss the trees,
> And they did make no noise, in such a night
> Troilus methinks mounted the Troyan walls,
> And sigh'd his soul toward the Grecian tents
> Where Cressid lay that night.

Jessica:
> In such a night
> Did Thisby fearfully o'ertrip the dew,
> And saw the lion's shadow ere himself,
> And ran dismayed away.

Lorenzo:
>   In such a night
> Stood Dido with a willow in her hand
> Upon the wild sea-banks, and waft her love
> To come again to Carthage.

Jessica:
>   In such a night
> Medea gathered the enchanted herbs
> That did renew old Aeson.

Lorenzo:
>   In such a night
> Did Jessica steal from the wealthy Jew,
> And with an unthrift love did run from Venice,
> As far as Belmont.

Jessica:
>   In such a night
> Did young Lorenzo swear he lov'd her well,
> Stealing her soul with many vows of faith,
> And ne'er a true one.

Lorenzo:
>   In such a night
> Did pretty Jessica (like a little shrew)
> Slander her love, and he forgave it her.

Jessica:
> I would out-night you, did nobody come . . .

If this scene is played as a generalized love scene, it will have one wash of color. If the details of the stories are taken as clues to the game Lorenzo and Jessica are playing with each other, and the form of the ladder is fulfilled, a wonderfully human, teasing, loving, provocative relationship is revealed.

These devices are theatrical, dramatic, performance devices. Their observance gives the actor a set of acting tools that do half the acting for him/her. Mastering the execution of rhetorical forms is something like mastering *grand jetés* and *pirouettes*. They are the means by which the excitement of performance is raised to dazzling heights but they are also the means by which the audience really understands what is being said, what is being felt, and what the story is. They are the linchpins of intelligibility.

INTERLUDE

◀▶

Chapters One through Five have taken you on an organic journey through the anatomy of language. You experienced the elementary particles of vowels and consonants and how their energy combines into word-cells which in turn form relationships to make a phrase; and the phrases connected to make waves of intelligent matter which stimulated the intellect to orchestrate all the components into an overall meaning. This first section has dealt with those elements of language which, when allowed to penetrate the flesh, blood and spirit of the speaker, to be *incarnated*, create an overflowing abundance of thought-feeling-action **content**.

Abundant **content** *needs* **form; content** is so emotionally, sensorily, imagistically and intellectually energetic that it requires the management of **structure**. Content needs to be channelled in such a way that the energy—through conservation and discipline—is rendered communicable. But if we had started with the discipline of form, we would have found it hard to persuade the energy of the content to emerge at all. Although "form" may sound cold and intellectual, and "structure" hard and ungiving, when we start to work with them we will find that form and structure are also energy fields, offering clues to performance as potent as those discovered in language.

Before moving on, however, there are a few categories of language clues which lie outside my own structure, and I shall present them in this Interlude. They are lively and entertaining and will, perhaps, provide the kind of light relief suitable to an Interlude.

STAGE DIRECTIONS—DOUBLE MEANINGS—BAWDRY— THEE'S, THOU'S, AND YOU'S

Sometimes Shakespeare gives clear **stage directions**. Sometimes there are **double meanings** in the words, sometimes the meaning of a word has changed from what it was in Elizabethan times. Sometimes there are **bawdy double meanings,** or outright **bawdry,** which the ears of prudery might prefer to ignore—character and action will be fundamentally affected by their observance. Our task is to unearth performance possibilities with the help of these clues.

STAGE DIRECTIONS

In a modern playscript stage directions are often set in parenthesis just before a character's lines. When they also indicate the emotional reactions of the characters they are an actor's nightmare.

> John (*Moodily running his hand through his hair*): I hate the way you eat.
> Mary (*Sobbing as she throws her plate at him*): You sound just like my father.
>
> (*The telephone rings. They both start nervously*)

As we have discovered, Shakespeare indicates *how* his text should be spoken—if we know how to listen to him; he does it organically within the words. Outside the text he does not tell his actors how to play the scene, but a stage direction combining inner and outer action often emerges from inside the text when the actor fully embodies and respects the face-value meaning of what is said. For instance:

> I weep for joy
> To stand upon my kingdom once again.
> Dear earth, I do salute thee with my hand,
> Though rebels wound thee with their horses' hoofs.
> As a long-parted mother with her child
> Plays fondly with her tears and smiles in meeting,
> So weeping, smiling, greet I thee, my earth,
> And do thee favors with my royal hands . . .
> *Richard II*

One would have to fabricate a very convoluted character *not* to play that speech with tears and laughter, kneeling, sitting or falling on the ground and touching the earth. "Suit the action to the word, the word to the action." Indeed the stage directions in Richard's text are also clear character indications.

> —of comfort no man speak.
> Let's talk of graves, of worms, and epitaphs,
> Make dust our paper, and with rainy eyes
> Write sorrow on the bosom of the earth.
>
> . . .
>
> For God's sake let us sit upon the ground
> And tell sad stories of the death of Kings.

A little later the Bishop of Carlisle says:

> My lord, wise men ne'er sit and wail their woes . . .
> *Richard II, Act III, Scene ii*

Creating a different mood, there are stage directions within the text throughout the wooing scene between Petruchio and Katherine (*The Taming of the Shrew*, Act II, Scene i). If the actors "suit the action to the word, the word to the action," they will quickly get to what is going on in the scene. They may thereafter want to make some other choices, but the words clearly point the way to physical actions.

Petruchio:
    Myself am mov'd to woo thee for my wife.

Katherine:
    Mov'd, in good time! Let him that mov'd you hither
    Remove you hence. I knew you at the first
    You were a movable.

Petruchio:
                                    Why, what's a moveable?

Katherine:
    A joint-stool.

Petruchio:
    Thou hast hit it. Come, sit on me.

Katherine:
    Asses are made to bear, and so are you.

Petruchio:
    Women are made to bear, and so are you.

Katherine:
    No such jade as you, if me you mean.

Petruchio:
    Alas, good Kate, I will not burden thee!

If he suits the action to the word, Petruchio will pull Katherine onto his lap on "come, sit on me." Following the stage directions literally, in the ensuing struggle she ends up on the floor with him on top of her—"Women are made to bear." From this position she insults his manhood—"No such jade as you"—and he physically disengages on "I will not burden thee." The next few lines are full of movement:

Katherine:
    Too light for such a swain as thee to catch,
    And yet as heavy as my weight should be.

Petruchio:
    Should be? should—buzz!

(This makes sense when played for the onomatopoeia or, as Partridge suggests, delivered as a rude noise, rather than as "sense.")

Katherine:
>   Well ta'en, and like a buzzard.

Petruchio:
>   O slow-wing'd turtle, shall a buzzard take thee?

These lines ask to be spoken with Petruchio in pursuit of Katherine (a "turtle" is a "turtle-dove"). Danger couples with jesting and becomes overtly sexual:

Katherine:
>   Ay, for a turtle, as he takes a buzzard.

Petruchio:
>   Come, come, you wasp; i' faith, you are too angry.

Katherine:
>   If I be waspish, best beware my sting.

Petruchio:
>   My remedy is then to pluck it out.

Katherine:
>   Ay, if the fool could find it where it lies.

Petruchio:
>   Who knows not where a wasp does wear his sting?
>   In his tail.

Katherine:
>   In his tongue.

Petruchio:
>   Whose tongue?

Katherine:
>   Yours, if you talk of tales, and so farewell.

Petruchio:
>   What, with my tongue in your tail? Nay, come again,
>   Good Kate. I am a gentleman—

Katherine:
>   That I'll try.

Petruchio:
>   I swear I'll cuff you, if you strike again.

The bawdy play on "tale" and "tail" and "tongue" needs no explication. Even if your edition does not have written stage directions for Kate to hit Petruchio on "That I'll try," it is stated that she does so in Petruchio's next line. She also does her best to leave the room on "and so farewell," and has no alternative but to be angry at the "buzzard, turtle" exchange because Petruchio tells her she is.

A little later, the lines indicate that she is again trying to get out of the room:

> Petruchio:
> Nay, hear you, Kate—in sooth, you scape not so.
>
> Katherine:
> I chafe you, if I tarry. Let me go.

Somehow he is physically preventing her from leaving—these are physical stage directions. In the next long speech, Petruchio mocks Kate's behavior and by the end of it shows that something physically violent has happened; enough to hurt her foot:

> Why does the world report that Kate doth limp?
> O slanderous world! . . .
> O, let me see thee walk. Thou dost not halt.

"How to play the scene" can start from these active sets of energies. One might think that this is all too obvious to point out, and I would not do so had I not seen so many actors struggle with this scene, trying everything but the obvious physical choices, making no sense of it and having no fun.

A different kind of stage direction is found in Lady Macbeth's comment upon the messenger who brings her the news of Duncan's arrival at her castle:

> The raven himself is hoarse,
> That croaks the fatal entrance of Duncan
> Under my battlements.

It seems obvious that the messenger has been running or riding in haste and is exhausted when he arrives, barely able to croak out his message. He has been given a "stage direction" by Shakespeare and he becomes the symbol of death, the raven.

When Viola says of Olivia:

> She made good view of me, indeed so much,
> That methought her eyes had lost her tongue,
> For she did speak in starts distractedly.
> *Twelfth Night, Act II, Scene ii*

she gives the actor playing Olivia stage directions for Olivia's behavior in Act I, Scene v.

A classic example of "stage directions" within the text is found in the sonnet in the course of whose fourteen lines Romeo and Juliet meet and fall in love. Romeo has been watching Juliet dancing at the Capulets's ball to which he has come uninvited and masked. He approaches her:

Romeo:

    If I profane with my unworthiest hand
    This holy shrine, the gentle fine is this,
    My lips, two blushing pilgrims, ready stand
    To smooth that rough touch with a tender kiss.

Juliet:

    Good pilgrim, you do wrong your hand too much,
    Which mannerly devotion shows in this;
    For saints have hands that pilgrims' hands do touch,
    And palm to palm is holy palmers' kiss.

Romeo:

    Have not saints lips, and holy palmers too?

Juliet:

    Ay, pilgrim, lips that they must use in prayer.

Romeo:

    O then, dear saint, let lips do what hands do:
    They pray: grant thou, lest faith turn to despair.

Juliet:

    Saints do not move, though grant for prayers' sake.

Romeo:

    Then move not, while my prayer's effect I take.

If the actor playing Romeo embodies the words he will, as he says "If I profane with my unworthiest hand/This holy shrine," carefully touch Juliet's hand which is the "holy shrine"; the delicacy of the encounter, softened with little jokes, comes through as he offers to pay for his wrongdoing by kissing the hand he holds, "the gentle fine is this/My lips, two blushing pilgrims, ready stand/To smooth that rough touch with a tender kiss." (Many editions give "sin" instead of "fine." Wrestle with it as I may, I cannot make better sense of the action with "sin" as the choice, so I will proceed with "fine.")

Juliet picks up the play on words—"Good pilgrim, you do wrong your hand too much"—and neatly avoiding the subject of the lips, she moves her hand in relation to his hand so that the two hands are in a praying position between them, thus also keeping him at bay, "Which mannerly devotion shows in this/For saints have hands that pilgrims' hands do touch/And palm to palm is holy palmers' kiss." She has cleverly twisted his words to show that there is no need for him to kiss her hand if she is a saint, because pilgrims kiss saints by touching their hands.

The form of a sonnet requires fourteen lines divided into three quatrains (four lines of verse) each with its own alternating rhyme scheme, and a rhyming couplet. Two quatrains make an octet (eight lines) and the third quatrain plus the couplet add up to a sestet (six lines). You will find more about this form in Chapter Seven. Romeo and Juliet's first two quatrains have, in classic style, presented the theme, the story; the sonnet is now poised between the octet and the sestet, the point in classical sonnet form where a major emotional shift occurs. Romeo intensifies his plea, his emotion compressed into one line, which Juliet quickly answers with gentle encouragement, "lips that they must use in prayer." Romeo begs that their lips may touch in the same manner that their hands are touching, "let lips do what hands do:/They pray:" and, at the end of the third quatrain he discovers how deeply he loves, "grant thou, lest faith turn to despair." In the couplet that ends the sonnet they pledge their troth. The sonnet encapsulates within its fourteen lines the process of Romeo and Juliet falling irrevocably in love.

A more complex example of "stage directions" is found in the parting of Queen Margaret and Suffolk in *Henry VI, Part II*, Act III, Scene ii. This scene is hard because the passions are so huge. It becomes intelligible when the actors suit action to word, and word to action. In this case, the result is almost unbearably sensual and sexual. On the page I will try to show how the words can become actions by writing in the "stage directions" contained in the words. Occasionally a question will be put to you rather than an instruction given. Both the questions and the instructions are designed to make you find in the words the impulses that compel full physical actions. The actions, as you will see, are perhaps too illustrative for actual performance but are spelled out to encourage the actors to go to an extreme; they may then decide on the modifications of artistic and playable choice. Remember that "action" can transfer from outside to inside as much as from inside to outside.

King Henry, urged on by the common people, has banished the Earl of Suffolk from England. Henry's wife, Margaret, and Suffolk have been lovers for many years. Margaret curses Henry and his counsellors. Suffolk begs her to stop:

> Suffolk:
> Cease, gentle Queen, these execrations,
> And let thy Suffolk take his heavy leave.
> *(defeated, ready to go)*

> Queen Margaret:
> Fie, coward woman and soft-hearted wretch!
> Hast thou not spirit to curse thine enemies?
> *(turn your anger on him)*

> Suffolk:
> A plague upon them! Wherefore should I curse them?
> *(not yet angry)*
> Would curses kill as doth the mandrake's groan,
> I would invent as bitter searching terms,
> *(begin to do what you say and "invent")*
> As curst, as harsh, and horrible to hear,

Deliver'd strongly through my fixed teeth,
(teeth clench)
With full as many signs of deadly hate,
As lean-fac'd Envy in her loathsome cave.
My tongue should stumble in mine earnest words;
(tongue stumbles)
Mine eyes should sparkle like the beaten flint;
(eyes open wide)
Mine hair be fix'd on end, as one distract;
(feeling crazy)
Ay, every joint should seem to curse and ban:
(body jerks and tenses)
And even now my burden'd heart would break
Should I not curse them. Poison be their drink!
(the first real curse)
Gall, worse than gall, the daintiest that they taste!
(mouth contorts)
Their sweetest shade a grove of cypress trees!
(start to hallucinate)
Their chiefest prospect murd'ring basilisks!
(see the basilisks' eyes that paralyze)
Their softest touch as smart as lizard's stings!
(feel the stinging)
Their music frightful as the serpent's hiss
And boding screech-owls make the consort full!
(hear the sounds)
All the foul terrors in dark-seated hell—
(fall to the ground)

Queen Margaret:
Enough, sweet Suffolk; thou torments thyself;
And these dread curses, like the sun 'gainst glass,
Or like an overcharged gun, recoil
And turn the force of them upon thyself.
(this is a description of his condition—knocked out by the force of his own cursing)

Suffolk:
You bade me ban, and will you bid me leave?
Now, by the ground that I am banish'd from,
(still on the ground)
Well could I curse away a winter's night,
Though standing naked on a mountain top,
Where biting cold would never let grass grow,
And think it but a minute spent in sport.
(does the body start to shiver in circulatory reaction to the adrenalin flow of the cursing? is there semi-hysterical laughter?)

Queen Margaret (weeping):
O! let me entreat thee cease. Give me thy hand.
That I may dew it with my mournful tears;

(take his hand to your face)
Nor let the rain of heaven wet this place,
To wash away my woeful monuments.
O! could this kiss *(kiss his hand)* be printed in thy hand,
That thou might'st think upon these *(lips)* by this seal *(the kiss)*,
Through whom a thousand sighs are breath'd for thee.
So, get thee gone, that I may know my grief;
(push him away)
'Tis but surmis'd while thou art standing by, *(when did he get up?)*
As one that surfeits thinking on a want.
(hold on to yourself physically as if you might vomit)
I will repeal thee, or, be well assur'd,
Adventure to be banished myself;
And banished I am, if but from thee.
(what happens? do you break down again? does he come to you? he tries to say something)
Go; speak not to me; even now be gone.
(he starts to go)
O! go not yet!
(hold each other)
Even thus two friends condemn'd
Embrace, and kiss and take ten thousand leaves,
(suit the actions to the words)
Loather a hundred times to part than die.
Yet now farewell; and farewell life with thee.
(try to make him go)

Suffolk:
Thus is poor Suffolk ten times banished,
Once by the King and three times thrice by thee.
(do you go? apparently not)
'Tis not the land I care for, wert thou thence;
A wilderness is populous enough,
So Suffolk had thy heavenly company:
For where thou art, there is the world itself,
With every several pleasure in the world,
And where thou art not, desolation.
I can no more: Live thou to joy thy life;
Myself no joy in nought but that thou liv'st.

At this point they are interrupted by someone bringing news to the King; he leaves and they continue:

Queen Margaret:
Now get thee hence: the King, thou know'st, is coming;
If thou be found by me thou art but dead.

Suffolk:
If I depart from thee I cannot live;
(give up: refuse to go)
And in thy sight to die, what were it else

But like a pleasant slumber in thy lap?
(you are either kneeling with your arms around her waist or she is on
her knees and you are lying with your head in her lap)
Here could I breathe my soul into the air,
As mild and gentle as the cradle-babe
Dying with mother's dug between his lips;
Where, from thy sight, I should be raging mad,
And cry out for thee to close up mine eyes,
To have thee with thy lips to stop my mouth:
(kissing)
So should'st thou either turn my flying soul,
Or I should breathe it so *(suit the action to the word)* into thy body,
And then it liv'd in sweet Elysium.
To die by thee were but to die in jest;
From thee to die were torture more than death.
O! let me stay, befall what may befall.

Queen Margaret:
Though parting be a fretful corrosive,
It is applied to a deathful wound.
(make him go)
To France, sweet Suffolk. Let me hear from thee;
For whereso'er thou art in this world's globe,
I'll have an Iris that shall find thee out.
Away!

Suffolk:
I go.
(start to go)

Queen Margaret:
And take my heart with thee
(go to him)

Suffol k:
A jewel, lock'd into the woefull'st cask
That ever did contain a thing of worth.
Even as a splitted bark, so sunder we:
(break away from each other)
This way fall I to death.

Queen Margaret:
This way for me.

My italicized "stage directions" are merely verbalizing what the words will organically make happen when they are actively embodied. Again, I emphasize that this example is intended as a graphic exercise in the physicalization of the text, not as a performance prescription. It is interesting to speculate on how this kind of extremely sensual scene was played by a man and a boy in Elizabethan times.

DOUBLE MEANINGS—BAWDRY

Within the context of the sensual language leading up to the lines "To die by thee were but to die in jest/From thee to die were torture more than death," the words "death" and "die" are redolent of their Elizabethan **double meaning** of orgasm. Even today, modern French retains the connection of the experience of orgasm to a deathlike moment in "la petite mort"—"the little death." Double meanings play a delicate part in performance and are different in effect from puns. Many double meanings are sexual and many innocent-looking words carry sexual innuendo.

The graph of society's tolerance for sexual frankness goes up and down over the centuries, sometimes with rapid fluctuations within decades. The three decades from 1960 to 1990 went from the crest of a tolerance-measuring graph wave to the trough, and it is likely that as sudden a shift occurred with the ascendance of the Puritans, when Oliver Cromwell became Lord Protector of England and her morals in 1653. The Puritan morality was applied with arms and law and only such force, perhaps, could have quelled the ebullience of sensuality that had been rampant in country and city for at least a hundred years.

"Ebullience of sensuality" does not mean to imply an idyllic "Merrie England" replete with amorous shepherds in pursuit of willing milk-maids. The socio-political scene was, from our twentieth-century angle of vision, a grim struggle for existence within a ruthless hierarchical system. But to deny the evidence in the writing of the time, which vividly depicts an energetic society, buzzing with physical interaction, is an equal error. To work on Shakespeare without the spirit of play is to miss his spirit totally. Sex is knit into the fiber of his plays and through the language of the text. When one allows the possibility of a sexual double meaning in the following words, all sorts of extra nuances of performance present themselves:

> death, die: *orgasm*; spirit: *sperm*; merry: *sexy*; will: *penis or sexual desire*; wit: *penis or sexual desire*; reason: (occasionally) *penis or erection*; to stand: *to have an erection*; prick: *penis*; pricking: *sexual desire*; to stir: *to feel sexual desire*; horn: *penis*; tool: *penis*; most weapons—sword, arrow, gun, knife—are used on occasion with a phallic double meaning; hour: *whore*; lap: *vagina*; circle: *vagina*; O, or nothing: *vagina*; burden: *a man's body on top of a woman's*; to bear: *to feel that burden*; medlar: *meddler, a fruit resembling a woman's genitalia*; hell: *venereal disease*; fire, burning: *the symptoms of venereal disease*; conceive: *to think or to become pregnant*; country matters: *a pun on the first syllable of "country."*

This is a small sampling of the words which Shakespeare used to ribald effect. Eric Partridge's book, *Shakespeare's Bawdy*, has two hundred pages or more devoted to a huge range of sexual and scatological double meanings in Shakespeare's text, double meanings which open up rich acting choices.

The fact that there are double meanings in words does not mean that they should always be <u>used</u> with double meaning!

Here are some illustrative passages from *Romeo and Juliet*, *Hamlet*, *As You Like It*, *Cymbeline*, and *Henry IV, Part II*, Act II, Scene iv:

Nurse:
>   I must another way
> To fetch a ladder by the which your love
> Must climb a bird's nest soon when it is dark.
> I am the drudge, and toil in your delight,
> But you shall bear the burden soon at night.

. . .

Nurse: O, there is a nobleman in town, one Paris, that would fain lay knife aboard . . .

. . .

Mercutio:
> This cannot anger him. 'Twould anger him
> To raise a spirit in his mistress' circle
> Of some strange nature, letting it there stand
> Till she had laid it and conjur'd it down . . .

. . .

Mercutio:
> Now will he sit under a medlar tree
> And wish his mistress were that kind of fruit
> As maids call medlars when they laugh alone.

. . .

Celia: Come, lame me with reasons.

Rosalind: Then were there two cousins laid up, when the one should be lamed with reasons and the other mad without any.

Celia: But is all this for your father?

Rosalind: No, some of it is for my child's father.

. . .

Posthumus:
>   Some coiner with his tools
> Made me a counterfeit.

. . .

Hamlet: Lady, shall I lie in your lap?

Ophelia: No, my lord.

Hamlet: I mean, my head upon your lap.

Ophelia: Ay, my lord.

Hamlet: Do you think I meant country matters?

Ophelia: I think nothing, my lord.

Hamlet: That's a fair thought to lie between maids' legs.

Ophelia: What is, my lord?

Hamlet: Nothing.

Ophelia: You are merry, my lord.

. . .

Gregory: To move is to stir, and to be valiant is to stand: therefore if thou art moved thou runn'st away.

Samson: A dog of that house shall move me to stand. I will take the wall of any man or maid of Montague's.

Gregory: That shows thee a weak slave for the weakest goes to the wall.

Samson: 'Tis true, and therefore women, being the weaker vessels, are ever thrust to the wall; therefore I will push Montague's men from the wall, and thrust his maids to the wall.

Gregory: The quarrel is between our masters and us their men.

Samson: 'Tis all one. I will show myself a tyrant: when I have fought with the men I will be civil with the maids, I will cut off their heads.

Gregory: The heads of the maids?

Samson: Ay, the heads of the maids, or their maidenheads; take it in what sense thou wilt.

Gregory: They must take it in sense that feel it.

Samson: Me they shall feel while I am able to stand, and 'tis known I am a pretty piece of flesh.

Gregory: 'Tis well thou art not fish; if thou hadst, thou hadst been Poor John. Draw thy tool—here comes two of the house of Montague.

Samson: My naked weapon is out.

. . .

Falstaff: The fiend hath prick'd down Bardolph irrecoverable; and his face is Lucifer's privy-kitchen, where he doth nothing but roast malt-worms. For the boy—there is a good angel about him; but the devil outbids him too.

Prince: For the women?

Falstaff: For one of them—she's in hell already, and burns poor souls.

And finally, *Sonnet 129*:

Th'expense of spirit in a waste of shame
Is lust in action; and till action, lust
Is perjur'd, murd'rous, bloody, full of blame,
Savage, extreme, rude, cruel, not to trust;
Enjoy'd no sooner but despised straight;
Past reason hunted, and no sooner had,
Past reason hated, as a swallowed bait,

> On purpose laid to make the taker mad—
> Mad in pursuit, and in possession so;
> Had, having, and in quest to have, extreme;
> A bliss in proof, and prov'd, a very woe;
> Before, a joy propos'd; behind, a dream.
>   All this, the world well knows; yet none knows well
>   To shun the heaven that leads men to this hell.

To arrive at the deepest meaning of this sonnet, one must take in the sexual imagery projected by the double meanings of "spirit," "reason" and "hell"; the panting sexuality of the repeated "h's" in "hunted," "had," "hated," "had, having and in quest to have," "heaven" and "hell"; the emphasis of "mad" repeated at the end of one line and the beginning of the next.

There are, in this sonnet, three words that have meanings current in Elizabethan times but not in ours: **rude**, **extreme** and **straight.** "Rude" nearly always means "rough" in Shakespeare; "extreme" is a dangerous state according to Elizabethan philosophy because it goes over the edge of order and harmony, courting disorder and madness; "straight" often means "immediately." There are other words in this category (such as "presently" which also means "immediately," and "nice" which means "neat," and "neat" which can mean "ox") and you should be alert to many possible changes. Footnotes will usually tell you about them and Onions's *Glossary* always will.

THEE'S AND THOU'S AND YOU'S

Finally, in this Interlude, I must touch upon a language issue that often causes confusion when one is first introduced to Shakespeare: the use of **thee**, and **thou**, and **you**. The first and simplest fact about these forms of address is that "thee" and "thou" are always singular, "you" is both singular and plural. Many European languages still retain this double usage of the second personal pronoun, and with much the same subtle mix of rules and social interplay as we find preserved in Elizabethan writing but no longer evident in our everyday speech. The accidental misuse of "tu" and "vous" in French has landed me in situations where the atmosphere has noticeably cooled, or where intimacy was established where none was intended. Thus, with Shakespeare, it is important to pay attention to indications as to status, relationship, degrees of intimacy and shifting internal attitudes, according to whether the character employs "thou" or "you."

These "rules" of language are, as always, observations of actual practice rather than preordained decrees, and they are full of exceptions and open to individual interpretation. I offer a few guidelines against which you may test your perceptions of what is going on within the culture of a particular character or dialogue or scene.

Thou/thee/thy is intimate: you is formal.

Thou/thee conveys contempt: you conveys respect.

God is addressed as Thou/Thee when the speaker feels on good terms with Him, and is often addressed as You when the speaker feels humbled in His presence. Kings and Queens and those in authority are "you": the lower classes are "thee/thou."

Fathers and mothers are "you": children are "thee/thou." On the other hand if the parents are angry with their children they may address them formally as "you." Equally, those in inferior positions may occasionally have the gall to address their superiors as "thee/thou," bringing them down to size. Sometimes the choice of which version of the second personal pronoun is used seems quite arbitrary, but the actor who relishes subtlety will enjoy the niceties of address and the status games offered by this aspect of Elizabethan language usage. One general theory has it that in any status relationship "you" suggests everything is going smoothly while "thou" implies some kind of upset.

I will again use the exchange between Hamlet and his mother to show one or two of the above variations:

Hamlet:
Now, mother, what's the matter?

Queen:
Hamlet, thou hast thy father much offended. *(mother to son, familiar)*

Hamlet:
Mother, you have my father much offended. *(son to mother, formal)*

Queen:
Come, come, you answer with an idle tongue. *(mother—formally reprimanding)*

Hamlet:
Go, go, you question with a wicked tongue.

Queen:
Why, how now, Hamlet?

Hamlet:
What's the matter now?

Queen:
Have you forgot me? *(still in command, reprimanding)*

Hamlet:
No, by the rood, not so.
You are the Queen, your husband's brother's wife,
And, would it were not so, you are my mother.

Queen:
Nay, then I'll set those to you that can speak. *(still in parental superiority)*

Hamlet:
Come, come and sit down, you shall not budge.
You go not till I have set you up a glass
Where you may see the inmost part of you.

Queen:
What wilt thou do? Thou wilt not murder me? *(her status has dropped to that of suppliant)*
Help, ho!

Polonius answers from behind the arras and is stabbed by Hamlet who addresses him as "thou/thee/thy" with mixed contempt and affection and little apparent remorse. He turns from Polonius's dead body to his mother with these words:

(to Polonius) Take thy fortune:
Thou find'st to be too busy is some danger.
(to his mother) Leave wringing of your hands. Peace, sit you down,
And let me wring your heart; for so it shall
If it be made of penetrable stuff,
If damned custom have not braz'd it so,
That it be proof and bulwark against sense.

Queen:
What have I done, that thou dar'st wag thy tongue
In noise so rude against me?

Hamlet proceeds to tell her everything that she has done and more than she wants to hear. His accusations are intimately brutal and crude but always delivered in the form appropriate to his filial relationship. Notice that a shift from "you" to "thou/thy" comes when the object of his harangue shifts from Gertrude herself to Shame personified within her:

What devil was't
That thus hath cozen'd you at hoodman-blind?
Eyes without feeling, feeling without sight,
Ears without hands or eyes, smelling sans all,
Or but a sickly part of one true sense
Could not so mope. O shame, where is thy blush?
Rebellious hell,
If thou canst mutine in a matron's bones,
To flaming youth let virtue be as wax
And melt in her own fire . . .

Gertrude, her guilty conscience undermining her maternal status, continues to address Hamlet in the familiar form "thou/thee" until the Ghost of Hamlet's father appears to Hamlet. Hamlet says "you" to his father's ghost, the ghost calls Hamlet "thou," and Gertrude, fearful of her son's apparent madness, says:

> Alas, how is't with you,
> That you do bend your eye on vacancy,
> And with th'incorporal air do hold discourse?

This change from the familar to the formal suggests perhaps an almost breath-holding inner state, frozen with fear or horror, perhaps the careful respect we owe to madmen; one way or another the shift here creates a momentary distance, and from this perspective she explains away Hamlet's vision as part of his madness:

> This is the very coinage of your brain.
> This bodiless creation ecstasy
> Is very cunning in.

But later, when he has again penetrated her conscience, she reverts to the intimate form:

> O Hamlet, thou hast cleft my heart in twain.

And:

> Be thou assur'd, if words be made of breath,
> And breath of life, I have no life to breathe
> What thou hast said to me.

Emotional status-play can very often be mapped in the shifts from formal to familiar second personal pronouns, and in portraying the turmoil of love and jealousy the sensitive actor can discover exquisite shadings of rage, hate and grief in assessing the distancing effect of a "you," and the intimate effect of a "thou/thee/thy." Othello's accusation of Desdemona in Act IV, Scene ii of *Othello* is worth studying from this point of view. At the beginning of the scene, Othello uses the formal address:

> Let me see your eyes . . .

As he starts to accuse her, his emotion building, he switches to the intimate:

> Why, what art thou?
>
> · · ·
>
> Come, swear it, damn thyself . . .
>
> · · ·
>
> Heaven truly knows, that thou art false as hell.

He reaches the extremity of his passion:

> Heaven stops the nose at it, and the moon winks,
> The bawdy wind, that kisses all it meets,
> Is hush'd within the hollow mine of earth,
> And will not hear't. What committed!
> Impudent strumpet!

Desdemona stops him:

> By heaven, you do me wrong.

And Othello shifts to the formal address:

> Are not you a strumpet?
>
>   . . .
>
>   I cry you mercy,
> I took you for that cunning whore of Venice,
> That married with Othello . . .

Emilia, Desdemona's attendant and Iago's wife, who as an inferior addresses everyone as "you" throughout the play, suddenly finds herself, in Act V, Scene ii, Othello's emotional equal when he confesses that he has murdered Desdemona and slanders her virtue. It is in defense of Desdemona's honor that Emilia finds the strength to meet Othello on his level:

> Othello:
> 'Twas I that kill'd her.

> Emilia:
>   O, the more angel she,
> And you the blacker devil!

> Othello:
> She turn'd to folly, and she was a whore.

> Emilia:
> Thou dost belie her, and thou art a devil.
>
>   . . .
>
> Thou hast not half the power to do me harm
> As I have to be hurt. O gull, O dolt . . .

When Iago enters, Emilia for the first time in the play addresses him in the familiar form; his equal; no longer the subservient wife but the intimate one, even the maternal one. But only for three lines:

> Emilia:
> Disprove this villain, if thou be'st a man;
> He says thou told'st him that his wife was false,
> I know thou didst not, thou art not such a villain:
> Speak, for my heart is full.

> Iago:
> I told him what I thought, and told no more
> Than what he found himself was apt and true.

> Emilia:
> But did you ever tell him she was false?

> Iago:
> I did.

Emilia:
  You told a lie, an odious, damned lie . . .

Emilia dies by her mistress' side, her peer in love and betrayal:

  What did thy song bode, lady?
  Hark, canst thou hear me? I will play the swan,
  And die in music: Willow, willow, willow . . .

These clues provide invaluable detail in the accurate navigation of a character's inner and outer emotional and social state, and the actor who, in learning her/his lines, substitutes "thou's" and "thee's" for "you's" and vice versa, employing the variations on the second personal pronoun with a careless disregard of their significance, will miss a great deal of interesting topography.

The Interlude could well expand to include many more details of grammar and construction and Elizabethan language usage, but these elements can be found elsewhere by the concerned student, and having covered these particular clues in this particular way I am now prepared to consider the role of form in Shakespeare.

THE FORM

◆▶

Verse and Prose

6

◆▶ The Iambic Pentameter ◆▶

"To young people studying for the stage I say, with all solemnity, leave blank verse alone until you have experienced emotion deep enough to crave for poetic expression, at which point verse will seem an absolutely natural and real form of speech to you. Meanwhile if any pedant with an uncultivated heart and a theoretic ear proposes to teach you to recite, send instantly for the police."
George Bernard Shaw

"In any poet's poem, the shape is half the meaning."
Louis MacNeice

One dictionary definition of poetry is that it is "lofty thought or impassioned feeling expressed in imaginative words." The *form* within which that lofty thought or impassioned feeling is contained is part and parcel of the art of poetry. The "form" of verse is the external representation of the internal pulsation of its content. As many clues to Shakespeare's meaning can be found in his verse form as in the language itself. Nearly three-quarters of Shakespeare's text is in verse, therefore "speaking the verse well" becomes synonymous with "speaking Shakespeare well."

I hope that no one reading this chapter has picked the book up and flipped through to this page because s/he just wants to know something about the iambic pentameter. We have arrived at the consideration of form after having opened up content as much as possible. To isolate the rules of poetic form from poetry's source and content would be like separating a skeleton from the flesh, blood and breath that animate it. Form alone has no life. I would go further and say that an appreciation of form without deep experience of content will render an actor stone dead on stage. The practice of form must be plugged into the electrical outlet of thought/feeling impulses or it will leave a mechanical imprint on the brain, and the actor will end up "speaking the verse" but not "acting Shakespeare."

The actor who would play Shakespeare well has to unify form and content, discovering that the skeleton of form is the life support for poetic content and *vice versa*. I hope that the actor who has followed

121

the organic progression of language experiences thus far outlined in this book is proof against the trauma of verse-speaking, primed and ready for the adventure of rhythm. Rhythm takes language and adds an inner drive that moves it, shakes it and channels it. A poet uses rhythm to shape language into dramatic peaks and valleys, and major clues to the topography of any given scene in a Shakespeare play are to be found in its rhythmic dynamics. The verse rhythm that reigns supreme in Shakespeare is the iambic pentameter.

My first great Shakespeare teacher, Michael MacOwan, who was the principal of the London Academy of Music and Dramatic Art when I was a student there, used to hop up and down with excitement, rattling the loose change in his pocket, as he launched us on to the jubilant waves of the iambic pentameter. What I remember him saying was, "It's like riding a racehorse. Sit relaxed in the saddle, grip with your knees, feel the energy under your seat and hold the reins firmly or the horse will run away with you." He would shake his head in wonder at "Old Bill's" cleverness in harnessing the essential rhythms of the English language to his genius. He chortled with glee as we ferreted out the niceties of the sense, carefully nursing the strong beats in the line and bending our brains to accept the changing nuance of meaning when we let "Old Bill" tell us what he wanted. Michael Mac was having too much fun for his students to be intimidated by the iambic pentameter. Exhilaration comes when sense and rhythm merge and one rides the rhythm, sitting firm as on a galloping horse, the bridle of comprehension keeping a rein on the rippling energy.

I am sadly conscious that on the page I am unable to convey the essential information on the iambic pentameter with the high energy sustained by Michael Mac in the classroom. I see no alternative to laying out first some basic working facts in a relatively low-key manner, then reigniting the fire of performance later.

Let me begin by posing and answering some of the questions commonly asked by beginners about the iambic pentameter:

Why did Shakespeare write his verse in the form of the iambic pentameter?

Because the basic rhythm of the English language is iambic and because, by the end of the sixteenth century, the development of prosody ("the art or science of versification") had determined five to be the most satisfying number of iambic feet per line for English dramatic, or heroic, verse.

What does "iambic" mean?

The term "iamb" probably derives from a Greek word meaning *to drive forth, to assail, to shoot*. It comes from the metrical terminology of Greek and Latin classical poetry representing *push, persistency, determination, aspiration*. Its steady thrust forward is ideal for the drive of an ongoing narrative. Its rhythm is a weak beat followed by a strong beat (or stress), represented in this chapter thus:

$$\overset{-}{}\quad\overset{/}{}$$

(weak strong).

This is one "foot" of verse; one iamb.

Why is it called a foot?
Because such measures of rhythm were originated in the march melodies and dance melodies of Ancient Greece, and the foot comes down on the stressed beat. (Poetry, dance and music have been interrelated throughout the ages and the influences they have had upon each other are manifold.)

What is a pentameter?
A line of verse made up of five feet. The "pent" prefix means 5 (from Greek) and "meter" means "measure." The Renaissance brought in a deep admiration for Greek and Latin classical literature, hence the adoption of the metrical terminology of those times. Monometer, Dimeter, Trimeter, Tetrameter, Pentameter, Hexameter mean 1, 2, 3, 4, 5 or 6 measures or feet in the line respectively.

Why is the iambic rhythm the rhythm of the English language?
I have no idea *why* it is, but I can help you observe *that* it is. This is not to say that we speak in steady iambic rhythm all the time but that the prevailing rhythm goes from an unaccented to an accented syllable. Within that prevailing rhythm all sorts of counterstresses elaborate the procedure.

$$-\;/\;\;-\;\;/\;-\;/\;-\;/$$
"I wish you'd take the garbage out"

is strictly iambic.

$$-\;\;/\;-\;-\;/\;-\;/\;-\;/$$
"It's your turn to take the garbage out"

has a little extra weak beat in the second foot but the rhythm remains essentially iambic.

$$-\,/\,-\;/\,-\;/\;-\,/\,-\,/\,-\;/\;-\,-\;/\;\,-\,/$$
"a little extra weak beat in the second foot but the rhythm remains

$$-\;/\,-\,/\,-\,/\;-$$
essentially iambic"

How can I develop a feeling of this rhythm?
Listen to your heartbeat when you have been exerting yourself, or listen to a baby's heartbeat — it goes "de-dum, de-dum, de-dum"; weak strong, weak strong, weak strong; - / - / - /.

How can I remember it?
A well-known mnemonic for the iambic pentameter is

```
  - /    - /    - /    - /    - /
```
" I am(b), I am(b), I am(b), I am(b), I am(bic)"
  1   2   3   4   5

Do I have to be able to count the five feet in an iambic pentameter?

I would love to be able to say "No" but in all honesty I can't. It takes time for some people to develop a feeling for the iambic pentameter but without it we have no check on whether we are using Shakespeare's emphasis or our own. To know where the last strong stress comes in a given line is to know where the thought is driving. Thus it is important to find a way to count five iambic feet. I do it on the five fingers of one hand.

I have worked with a great many actors who have extreme difficulty getting a feel of the five iambic feet, who say, despairingly, "I just have no sense of rhythm." If this is your difficulty also, do not panic—panic destroys all rhythm. Patiently, slowly and calmly, practice this five-finger exercise:

Put your thumb firmly down on the flat surface of a table, then your second finger, then your third, your fourth and your little finger.

Repeat several times, making a strong impact with each finger.

Now say out loud, as you do the five-finger exercise:

"First **one**, then **two**, then **three**, then **four**, then **five**,"

making sure that you say *the number* at exactly the moment your finger hits the table. Repeat this until it comes easily.

Now try it with:

"de-**dum**, de-**dum**, de-**dum**, de-**dum**, de-**dum**"

And now with:

"The **sun** is **ver**y **hot**, so **wear** a **hat**"

"I **wish** you'd **take** me **with** you **to** the **beach** ."

"Since **brass** nor **stone** nor **earth** nor **bound**less **sea**

But **sad** mor**tal**ity o'er**sways** their **power** (or, arguably, **pow**er)."

Keep practicing and observing. Notice that when you say, "I wish you'd take me with you to the beach," you don't *hit* the "to" although it falls on a strong beat, and that "mortality" must be spoken as a recognizable word, not as an example of two iambs. There are many different degrees of emphasis that can modify the regularity of the rhythm. Poetry, in this respect, has more freedom than music or dance. Rhythm does not imply a monotonous regularity in the speaking. The strength of each strong stress is determined by the individual meaning of the word that falls on that stress, together with the overall sense of the line.

Are all Shakespeare's iambic pentameter lines always "de-dum, de-dum, de-dum, de-dum, de-dum?"

Alas (for those who are looking for a simple rule to hang onto), no. The variations on the iambic rhythm are described by different experts differently and I have sat in on classes where the analysis of rhythm in the terminology of classical Greek prosody became a formidable science. I find this approach not readily translatable to performance and I belong to another school which uses English terminology for practical application.

I was, however, taught the classical terms when I was a student, and although I now consider them to be red herrings for the actor, their origins are of interest. Four dominant classical verse rhythms that vary the iamb can be spotted in Shakespeare: the "trochee," the "anapaest," the "dactyl" and the "spondee." Each of these performed a particular function in Greek verse. "Trochee" is taken from the Greek word for "running" and is related to the word for "wheel": its rhythm is / -. The "anapaest" goes - - / and means "struck back," being the reverse of the "dactyl" which goes / - -. The "spondee" was used mainly for hymns and religious expression and has two equal strong beats / /. In the approach to verse-speaking which I favor, all these rhythmic variations can and will be described in terms which, in my experience as an actor and as a teacher of actors, are more accessible and useful because they are not distanced by specialist language and because they directly describe their function.

The basic "rules" of verse rhythm were taught me by Michael MacOwan; my other great initiator into speaking Shakespeare was Bertram Joseph who taught at the London Academy of Dramatic Art when I was a beginning teacher there. He was more of an academic than MacOwan, but he was equally impassioned. He showed me how imagery imprints the voice, and he dealt with the irregularities of the iambic pentameter with pragmatism and artistry. In the course of thirty years' use, I have almost certainly subjected Joseph's teaching to a sea-change, but my debt to him is clear.

The verse-speaker's main task is to be alert to moments when **the stress of the verse** is challenged by **the emphasis of sense**. When this happens, a "sprung rhythm" is the result. A sprung rhythm can be synonymous with a spondee or a dactyl, but the term "sprung rhythm" has more immediate physicality to it for anyone other than an expert prosodist than "spondee" or "dactyl." A sprung rhythm means that a weak stress springs up to meet the strong stress on its own level or even to subdue it. A simple example is found in the third line of Sonnet 65:

> Since brass, nor stone, nor earth, nor boundless sea
> But sad mortality o'ersways their power,
> How with this rage shall beauty hold a plea . . .

The first foot of line 3 could be a regular iamb:

How **with** this **rage**

But it is more likely that the question posed in the first two lines generates enough energy to intensify the force of the "How" to the point where it must be emphasized and thus the rhythm shifts to:

How with this **rage**

The emphasis laid on the first syllable of the third line, making it the first strong stress, gives extra power to the "how" that falls on the *actual* first strong stress in the fourth line, and at the end of that line we find another natural sprung rhythm where the **emphasis of sense** in "hold" almost inevitably matches the **stress of the verse** in "out":

Oh **how** shall **summ**er's **hon**ey **breath hold out** . . .

The next few lines follow the regular iambic rhythm. In the tenth line, however, the **emphasis of sense** again springs up to match the strong **stress of the verse**, not once, but twice:

Shall **Time's best jew**el **from Time's chest** lie **hid** . . .

The accumulating intensity of the questions about the inexorable power of Time, coupled with the graphic imagery within a double antithesis, makes the eleventh line gallop with equal stresses and short, strong monosyllables:

Or **what strong hand** can **hold** his **swift foot back**?

The twelfth line slows down to a regular iambic rhythm again with words that cannot be rushed:

Or **who** his **spoil** of **beau**ty **can** for**bid**?

The final couplet has one almost regular line followed by one with two sprung rhythms:

Oh **none,** un**less** this **mir**acle have **might,**

That **in black ink** my **love** may **still shine bright**.

Traditionally the iambic rhythm would be deemed more influential in this instance (and probably elsewhere) than I have shown. I am suggesting that when the speaker is in touch with the strong emotional content of love and mortality and Time, the emphasis of passionate sense will sometimes spring internal rhymes and antitheses up to match the iambic stress. A more contained interpretation will follow the regularity of five strong beats to a line, but I am asking for something more emotionally risky.

Here now is Sonnet 65, our Master Sonnet, marked out in iambic

pentameter with its sprung rhythms identified with an asterisk (*).
You are familiar with this sonnet from Chapters Two and Three. You
absorbed the individual images through the sensory, sensual, emotional, physical channels of the vowels and consonants into your
body. The images aroused emotional responses which, when strung
together, gradually engaged the intellect so that the meaning of the
sonnet emerged. You then deliberately found a personal connection
for the "story." *You* asked how your love could possibly challenge
Time's destructive force, and you concluded, with William
Shakespeare, that the written word would give her/him immortality.

The work you did, digging and delving, rooting and planting, tapping into your own feelings and life story to bring present truth to the
words you speak, comes under the heading of **content**.

That content must now be molded by **form**. Without form, the content will spread and meander, never rising to the heightened intensity
of expression appropriate to the intensity of the original flash of emotional insight that was the sonnet's conception.

A deliberate choice of rhythmic expression is the element of form
you are exploring. Notice and adopt the subtle shifts in emphasis that
occur when you let the stress of the iambic rhythm influence your
thought. Find out what they offer you as alternatives in your interpretation. The sonnet is marked out in the accents we have already
defined and each foot is given a divider line.

```
    -    /    -   /    -   /    -    /    -   /
Since brass, | nor stone, | nor earth, | nor bound|less sea |

   -   /    - / - -   -      /       -   /
But sad | mortal|ity | o'ersways | their power, |

   *   /    -   /    -    /    -  /    -  /
How with | this rage | shall beau | ty hold | a plea, |

    -   / - /    -    /    - /    -  /
Whose ac|tion is | no strong|er than | a flower? |

  - /    -    /    -   /    - /    *    /
O how | shall summ | er's hon | ey breath | hold out |

  - /    -    /    -   /    - /    -   /
Against | the wrack | ful siege | of batt | 'ring days, |

    -    /    -   /    - -   -   /    -  /
When rocks | impreg | nable | are not | so stout, |

   -   /    -   /    -   /    -  /    -  /
Nor gates | of steel | so strong | but Time | decays? |

  -   /    -  /   - /   -      /    - /
O fear | ful med | ita | tion! Where, | alack, |
```

```
-       /       *    /   -    /      *      /    -   /
```
Shall Time's | best jew | el from | Time's chest | lie hid? |

```
-       /       *       /     -     /     -     /      *     /
```
Or what | strong hand | can hold | his swift | foot back? |

```
-    /    -     /    -     /     -     /     -    /
```
Or who | his spoil | of beau | ty can | forbid? |

```
-     /      -    /    -     /    - -     -       /
```
O none, | unless | this mir | acle | have might, |

```
-     /     *     /    -    /     -    /      *     /
```
That in | black ink | my love | may still | shine bright. |

The sonnet uses the iambic pentameter in a very regular manner most of the time and you should practice molding your thought to the suggestion of the strong stresses. You may well find that you have an unconscious pattern of speech that delivers your thoughts in rhythmic phrasing subtly different from the iambic phrasing. **Do not confuse your *pattern* with your *truth*!**

Patterns of speech are acquired through imitation. The small child picks up the patterns, rhythms and emphases in which the surrounding family speaks. Later, particularly around the early teens, patterns shift to adopt the "in" mode of communication among friends at school or in the street; and again, at nineteeen or twenty, as one enters a still wider outside world. Adopting patterns which the ear picks up from outside the body is an acculturating device that the human speech mechanism naturally possesses.

The only problem is that these patterns can feel like "me"; they can define who I am, and yet they are only a tiny proportion of "me." The actor must shake loose the acquired, unconscious patterns in order to allow the imprint of a completely different pattern of speech belonging, for instance, to a character in a play quite unlike himself or herself. We have a myriad of possible rhythms in our brains, and exercising them releases varying shades of communication and varying shades of who we are. Anyone who says, "This is who I am and how I speak" has locked the door on, "I wonder who I really am and what I might become, and what my real voice is, and what I might say if I spoke my thoughts out freely through my real voice." Shakespeare has the magic key that unlocks the doors to chambers in the brain that we might never have guessed existed. As he flexes our brain-cells we start to think thoughts in ways that are new and old at the same time. Paradoxically, the discipline of obedience to the rhythms of another's genius releases the potential for increased individuality.

The first discipline, therefore, is to practice thinking the sense that emerges when the iambic rhythm determines the shape of the thought. The flexibility of your rhythms of speech exercises the flexibility of your thinking mechanisms and the flexibility of yourSELF.

As you absorb the *regular* rhythm of the lines of Sonnet 65, you will discover that there are obvious exceptions to marking every strong stress, such as the last syllables of "mortality" and "impregnable," which fall on a strong beat; it would be the worst sort of plodding to say, "$_{mor}$**tal**$_i$**tee**" and "$_{im}$**preg**$_{na}$**ble**" in blind obedience to the iambic rule. There are *irregularities*, and the judicious handling of the *ir*regularities of the verse elevates the *re*gularity. To put it more powerfully, the regularity of the iambic pentameter creates the order and harmony to which human nature aspires, and the irregularities which erupt are symptomatic of the disorder and discord of the human condition as it is. Lest "disorder and discord" sound ugly or negative, listen to how Robert Herrick's poem, *Delight in Disorder*, celebrates the artful beauty that lies in the counterpoint between order and disorder:

> A sweet disorder in the dresse
> Kindles in cloathes a wantonnesse:
> A Lawne about the shoulders thrown
> Into a fine distraction:
> An erring Lace, which here and there
> Enthralls the Crimson Stomacher:
> A Cuffe neglectful, and thereby
> Ribbands to flow confusedly:
> A winning wave (deserving Note)
> In the tempestuous petticote:
> A careless shooe-string, in whose tye
> I see a wilde civility:
> Doe more bewitch me, than when Art
> Is too precise in every part.

As you begin to develop a "feel" for the iambic regularity, you will also beget a taste for the irregularities that make verse-speaking the art of heightened speaking rather than recitation. This art does not create distance; it involves the innermost depths of both speaker and listener, using the intelligibility of everyday speaking and the punch of high holiday.

Distinguishing Shakespeare's artful irregularities from your own incompatible patterns and the inadvertent arrogance of personal preference is a challenge. It takes hawk-like vigilance to monitor the tyranny of personality and habitual behavior. The awarenesses cultivated in the preceding chapters and the constant search for language clues must be your allies as you exercise the discipline of form. The reward is sheer delight, for it is an exercise of the soul.

Sonnet 65 honors the iambic pentameter except when certain figures of speech offer an **emphasis of sense** which balances out the

stress of the verse. For instance, "Time's best jewel" is in *antithesis* to "Time's chest" with an *internal rhyme* in "best " and "chest"; "best" and "Time's" are thus sprung from a weak stress to the level of the strong stress. Equally the *antithesis* between "strong hand" and "swift foot" springs "strong" up to meet "swift" and "foot" up to balance "hand." The choice to spring "black" and "shine" up from weak stresses is more a matter of the enjoyment of juxtaposing the two incongruities—and one needs "shine" as the final comeuppance for Time.

Several artistic refinements are yet to come before you are fully equipped to speak this sonnet. For the time being, practice the delicate play upon your thought processes of the iambic demand and the mental precision and poise required by the sprung rhythms.

WARNING! WARNING! WARNING!

Three language viruses have emerged during the twentieth century that can infect Shakespeare's meaning if not treated firmly with the antidote of consciousness.

1) Look out for the language disease called the "twentieth-century dumdee's." The English language is departing rapidly from its heartbeat-based rhythm and a virus carried by the little-big words can throw communication into acute arhythmic spasm.

Take the example given in Chapter Three:

Scene: an airport.
The public address system speaks:

All passengers **now** awaiting the arrival **of** flight 443 **may** proceed directly **to** Gate 14· Passengers **with** small children **will** be given priority boarding·

In Sonnet 65 it is tempting to say:

"Whose action is **no** stronger than a flower"

and

"When rocks impregnable are not **so** stout'

Nor gates of steel **so** strong but Time decays..."

but if you think and listen carefully you will find that the stresses on "stronger," "stout" and "strong" communicate the argument much more cogently than does an emphasis on the small preceding word.

2) A rather more psycho-physical condition that infects English language rhythms is "me-ism." "You-ism" and other personal pronoun superiority complexes also cause complications.

In this sonnet the only vulnerability to the latter contagion is in the last line, "That in black ink **my** love may still shine bright." A far greater emotional punch is packed when the stress stays on "love." Later in this chapter I will point out vital danger spots where this disease can destroy the power of a performance.

3) The symptoms of the third virus are that of a wasting disease: weakness, falling. It tends to strike at the end of an iambic pentameter line, causing a repetitive downward inflection of the voice. I refer to the sickness of "falling inflections."

Superficial treatment for this symptom prescribes upward inflections to replace the downward ones. But this only imposes a dead inflection on a dead inflection. The cause of the downward inflection of the voice is dying thought, and the cure must lie in treating the thinking, not just the vocal tune.

The cause of this problem may be that the velocity of communication has accelerated in the course of the twentieth century and has conditioned our thinking processes to the point where the listener guesses what the speaker intends to say four or five words before the sentence is completed. We have been conditioned by film and television to pick up visual messages from the screen carried in facial expressions and body language; words, in this medium, are very often spoken as an accompaniment to the information carried in the image. We have learnt to understand unconsciously what someone means to say almost as soon as s/he speaks because our whole receiving apparatus is attuned more visually than aurally. The speaker's brain, trained by this culture, is thus conditioned to the experience that the second half of her/his spoken thought is redundant. Thought energy is injected into the first part of a sentence and trails off by the end of it, leaving the vibrations of the voice at the mercy of the pull of gravity.

An irritating corrective to this downward inflection is the implied or verbalized question set at the end of each thought. A plaintive upturn in the inflection asks, "Are you listening?" "Do you agree?" Or tagging along at the end comes, "Y' know?" "D'you get me?" "Understand what I mean?" "Right?"

The cure for falling inflections and the irritating question is to think through to the end of a sentence and to develop the confidence to make statements and stand by them. This is hard to do if there is deep contrary conditioning, but without an energetic drive through to the end of a thought/sentence, Shakespeare's text will be utterly betrayed. Each iambic pentameter moves toward the final word in the line which is, in turn, the springboard on to the first word in the next line. Once the thought energy drive is established and the speaker is naturally thinking through to the end of each line, vocal inflections will go up or down or remain level but will always be full of variety because Shakespeare's thought is full of variety and the ends of his iambic pentameter lines are particularly packed with interest.

Bearing these warnings in mind, we now return to the iambic pentameter. I have outlined the rules that govern the regular iambic pentameter and two of the ways in which that regularity is interfered with: 1) by figures of speech whose demands cause sprung rhythms, and 2) by an emphasis of sense that supersedes the stress of the verse.

The most important fact to grasp about the *ir*regularities in the iambic pentameter scheme is that they indicate something irregular in the thought or feeling of the character. The emotional condition will be reflected in extra syllables in the line, weak stresses becoming strong or a weak extra syllable at the end of the pentameter line. This last condition is traditionally called a "feminine ending."

In Shakespeare's earlier plays, he adhered to the rules of poetic form almost rigidly. Indeed, he seems to have reveled in his ability to make form perform brilliantly in the accomplishment of his creative ends. *Love's Labor's Lost, Richard II, Richard III, A Midsummer Night's Dream* all have a consciousness in their poetic art that adds delight. The later plays—*The Winter's Tale, Macbeth, Hamlet, King Lear, Antony and Cleopatra, The Tempest*—are full of "irregularities" in the verse forms; their author seems here committed to reproducing as accurately as possible the stormy and unpredictable rhythms of emotional expression.

The actor is served by a knowledge of verse form when it highlights the contrast between order and disorder, revealing details of internal emotional states. But s/he must apply this knowledge within the context of Shakespeare's development as a playwright. *The Winter's Tale* and *Lear* often spill over into eleven, twelve or thirteen syllables to a line and emotion rocks the iambic beat out of recognition, but *Romeo and Juliet*, written some ten years earlier, and also full of passionate expression, is still quite faithful to the regular iambic pentameter form. Here is Romeo, mad with grief and rage, hearing of his banishment from Friar Lawrence:

> Hadst thou no poison mix'd, no sharp-ground knife,
> No sudden mean of death, though ne'er so mean,
> But "banished" to kill me? "Banished"?
> O Friar, the damned use that word in hell.
> Howling attends it. How hast thou the heart,
> Being a divine, a ghostly confessor,
> A sin-absolver, and my friend profess'd,
> To mangle me with that word "banished"?

And lest there be any question as to the extremity of the emotional outpouring, he ends thus:

> Thou canst not speak of that thou dost not feel.
> Wert thou as young as I, Juliet thy love,
> An hour but married, Tybalt murdered,
> Doting like me, and like me banished,
> Then mightst thou speak, then mightst thou tear thy hair
> And fall upon the ground as I do now,
> Taking the measure of an unmade grave.

Although there are a few lines that begin with a strong stress—

/ -   -   /

Doting like | me . . .

/ -   -   /

Taking the | measure of an unmade grave—

every line has ten syllables (five feet) despite the searing passion.

In *The Winter's Tale*, Leontes falls inexplicably into a mad jealousy and his passion immediately capsizes the verse-line with an overload of arhythmic syllables. The juxtaposition of Camillo's stoutly regular defense of Hermione's reputation with Leontes's jagged response exemplifies well the acting clues to be found within the verse form:

Camillo:
> I would not be a stander-by, to hear
> My sovereign mistress clouded so, without
> My present vengeance taken: 'shrew my heart,
> You never spoke what did become you less
> Than this; which to reiterate were sin
> As deep as that, though true.

Leontes:
>   Is whispering nothing?
> Is leaning cheek to cheek? Is meeting noses?
> Kissing with inside lip? stopping the career
> Of laughter with a sigh? (a note infallible
> Of breaking honesty)? Horsing foot on foot?
> Skulking in corners? wishing clocks more swift?
> Hours, minutes? noon, midnight? And all eyes
> Blind with the pin and web, but theirs; theirs only.
> That would unseen be wicked? is this nothing?
> Why then the world, and all that's in't, is nothing,
> The covering sky is nothing, Bohemia nothing,
> My wife is nothing, nor nothing have these nothings,
> If this be nothing.

Romeo's wild words reveal his emotional state; Leontes uses simpler, more direct words, but his rhythms are storm-tossed.

Here are the iambic pentameters and the sprung rhythms within them indicated for these passages in the same way as earlier for the Master Sonnet.

Romeo:

    -   / - / - /   -   /   -   /
Hadst thou | no pois | on mix'd, | no sharp-|ground knife,

   -   / -   / -   /   -   / - /
No sudd | en mean | of death, | though ne'er | so mean,

    -    / - / - / -   / - /
But "ban | ished" | to kill | me—"ban | ished"?

  -   /   -   / - / -   / -   /
O Friar, | the dam | ned use | that word | in hell.

    * - - / -   / -   / -   /
Howling | attends | it. How | hast thou | the heart,

  * - - - / - / - / - /
Being a | divine, | a ghost | ly con | fessor,

 - / - / - / - /   - /
A sin- | absolv | er, and | my friend | profess'd,

   -   / - / -   / -   / - /
To mang | le me | with that | word "ban | ished"?

        . . .

   - /   -   / - / - / -   /
Thou canst | not speak | of that | thou dost | not feel.

   -   / -   / -/ - / - /
Wert thou | as young | as I, | Juliet | thy love,

  -   / -   / -   / -   / -/
An hour | but marr | ied, Tyb | alt murd | ered,

  * - -   / - / - / - /
Doting | like me, | and like | me ban | ished,

    -   /   -   / -   / -   / - /
Then mightst | thou speak, | then mightst | thou tear | thy hair

 - / - / -   / -/ - /
And fall | upon | the ground, | as I | do now,

  * - - / -/ - / * /
Taking | the meas | ure of | an un | made grave.

Camillo:

```
 -   /    -  /  -  /   -  /   -  /
I would | not be | a stand | er-by, | to hear

  -   /    -   /    -   /    -  /    -   /
My sov' | reign mis | tress cloud | ed so, | without

  -   /  -   /    -   /   -   /    -   /
My pres | ent veng | eance tak | en: shrew | my heart,

  -   /  -   /    -   /   -  -    -   /
You nev | er spoke | what did | become | you less

  -   /    -    /    -/  - /    -    /
Than this; | which to | reit | erate | were sin

  -   /   -  /    -    /
As deep | as that, | though true.
```

Leontes:

```
                 -   /    -   /   -
              Is whisp | 'ring nothing?

 -   /   -   /    -   /    -   /   -  /  -
Is lean | ing cheek | to cheek? | Is meet | ing noses?      [11 syllables]

 *   -   -   /  *  /    *   -   -   -  /
Kissing | with in | side lip? | stopping | the career      [11 syllables]

 -   /   -   /   -  /    -  /    -  / - -
Of laugh | ter with | a sigh? | (a note | infallible       [12 syllables]

 -   /   -   /   - -    /    -   /   -   /
Of break | ing hon | esty)? Hors | ing foot | on foot?      [11 syllables]

 *   -   -   /   -    /    -   /    -    /
Skulking | in corn | ers? wish | ing clocks | more swift? [10 syllables]

 *   /   -   /   *  /    -   /   *
Hours, min | utes? noon, | midnight? | And all | eyes       [9 syllables]

 *   -   -  /   -   /    -  /   *   /  -
Blind with | the pin | and web, | but theirs; | theirs only. [11 syllables]

 -   /    -  /    -  /    -   -  /   *   -
That would | unseen | be wicked? | is this nothing?      [11 syllables]

 *   /   -   /   -   /   -   /   -  /   -
Why then | the world, | and all | that's in't, | is nothing, [11 syllables]
```

```
   -   /   -  /   -  /   -   -  /   -  /   -
The cove | ring sky | is nothing, | Bohem | ia nothing,    [12 syllables]

   -   /   - /   -   -  /   -  /    -    /    -
My wife | is nothing, | nor noth | ing have | these nothings,
                                                  [12 syllables]
   -  /   -  /   -
If this | be nothing.
```

Romeo's lines have ten syllables apiece, despite his emotional torture which is revealed in the words—"poison," "damned," "hell," "howling," "mangle"—and in the actions demanded by the lines, "Then mightst thou speak, then mightst thou tear thy hair/And fall upon the ground as I do now,/Taking the measure of an unmade grave." By the time *The Winter's Tale* was written, Shakespeare was as likely to communicate emotional content in erratic rhythms of verse as in imagery and passionate language. Camillo's lines have a solid iambic beat and ten ordered syllables to a line as he attempts to calm Leontes down; Leontes spills his passion into disorder, breaking the rule of the verse structure as he breaks the rule of love, trust and harmony that maintains the order and structure of the cosmos.

In the stress and emphasis markings for Leontes's lines you will see how the extra syllables spatter the rhythms into anarchy with, for instance, the strong beat shaking the foundations of the iambic pentameter in "stopping," "kissing" and "skulking." There are variables possible in some of the emphases I have marked with an asterisk, such as "inside lip," "theirs; theirs only" and "Why then," but it is likely that these syllables will rise up to meet the stress of the verse as the emotions release. Every line but one has eleven or twelve syllables, and nine of the thirteen lines end on a weak beat. There is nothing solid or reasonable going on.

The one line with *fewer* than ten syllables ends with the word "eyes" which is nearly always a loaded word in Shakespeare, connoting both "I" and the light of seeing that illuminates truth, leads to love and guides the Self to its divine source. This monosyllable fills out a whole beat with its special meaning. Leontes leans on it, plays with it, intends more than just seeing.

Later on in *The Winter's Tale*, when Leontes has put his wife Hermione on trial for the adultery he imagines, she defends herself in the following words:

> Since what I am to say, must be but that
> Which contradicts my accusation, and
> The testimony on my part, no other
> But what comes from myself, it shall scarce boot me
> To say "not guilty": Mine integrity,
> Being counted falsehood, shall, as I express it,
> Be so receiv'd.

Here is a passage in which the twentieth-century virus of "me-ism" would ravage the character and meaning of Hermione. Each of the first six lines contain either "I" and "me" or "myself" and "mine," yet only the "mine" and the final "I" fall on a strong beat. If the actor fails to observe the stress of the verse in these lines, dwelling instead on Hermione's personal battle, she will make the queen self-pityingly speak in prose:

> Since what **I** am to say, must be but that which contradicts **my** accusation, and the testimony on **my** part, no other but what comes from **myself**, it shall scarce boot **me** to say "Not guilty": **Mine** integrity, being counted falsehood, shall, as **I** express it, be so receiv'd.

When the iambic stresses are the guide to what Hermione is saying, her emphasis is clearly rooted in WHAT she has to say, which is that her INTEGRITY has been impugned. In Chapter Nine we will look again at this exquisitely crafted speech, but for now notice how, when you let the verse shape your thought, you reach an understanding of Hermione's character from her determined focus on her subject matter rather than on her personal condition:

```
 -     /  - / - /   -   /  -    /
Since what I am to say, must be but that
```

```
 -      /  - /  - / - / -     /
Which contradicts my accusation, and
```

```
 -  /- / - / -  /   - / -
The testimony on my part, no other
```

```
 -    /   -     / - / - /   -   /  -
But what comes from myself, it shall scarce boot me
```

```
 -  /  /  / -   /   - / - -
To say "not guilty": mine integrity,
```

```
 -    /  - /   -    /  - / - /  -
Being counted falsehood, shall, as I express it,
```

```
 - / -   /
Be so receiv'd.
```

I shall repeat that the balance between obeying the rules of the verse and finding one's own truthful speaking of the text is always a very delicate one. Bear in mind that Shakespeare, as he wrote (and probably spoke aloud as he wrote) his plays, heard the words in a certain way that dictated their order within the verse line; there was a good reason for a word landing on a strong beat in the line. However brilliant our interpretations may be, we must remind ourselves that we are dealing with genius when we deal with Shakespeare. It behooves us to test the shades of meaning in the text which the iambic rhythm opens up to us before we become wedded to what *we* think it means and how *we* think the emphasis should lie. For instance, Romeo says to the Friar, "Thou canst not speak of that thou dost not feel," and then, after listing the agonies of feeling that would validate the Friar's speech, he says: "Then mightst thou speak." Grammatically, one could easily land on "then" with a strong beat: "**Then** mightst thou **speak**," and continue, "**Then** mightst thou **tear thy hair**." However, the nicety of Romeo's argument lies in the fact that he has begun by saying, *"Thou canst not speak,"* then proceeds to show that truthful speaking is only allowable in certain circumstances—the "mightst" refers back to, and springs off from "canst not": "Then mightst thou speak." Each time he says "mightst" it springboards the emotion further from the strong beat of the iamb. Having shown the Friar what it takes to speak with feeling, it is as though his emotion escalates and throws him into a frenzy of grief: "Then *mightst* thou **speak**,/Then *mightst* thou **tear thy hair**/And **fall upon the ground as I do now**."

I have gone into this moment in some detail. Your performance will benefit from paying similar devotion to any line of Shakespeare.

The variations of rhythm and their effect on meaning are exemplified in how the syllable "-ed" changes its behavior within the iambic pentameter. The novice Shakespeare speaker sometimes gets the impression that "-ed" is always pronounced because that is "correct" for classical speech, but this is not the case. It is not the *pronunciation of the word* that is in question but the *rhythm of the line*. Most modern editions are quite reliable in their use of an apostrophe (') to indicate where the "-ed" is *not* sounded as an extra syllable, thus suggesting that when you see "-ed" at the end of a verb you *must* sound it in order to fill out the iambic pentameter. My advice is not to be pedantic about sounding the "-ed" when it feels schooled and old-fashioned. You will develop a feeling for rhythm that will tell you when the verse is destroyed if the word is sharply cut off and when the verse is more satisfying with the added syllable rounding it out. Taste and good sense should prevail. In the above passage Romeo repeats the word "banished" three times—in the first seventy lines of this scene (Act III, Scene ii) the word "banished" is spoken thirteen times and "banishment" five times. In line 19 Romeo says:

        -    / - / - / -   / - /
Hence ban I ished I is ban I ish'd from I the world.

Juxtaposing the tri-syllable with the di-syllable makes poetry happen, and the actor will find that his emotions will cry out through the extra syllable he is afforded by the iambic demand. Clinging to an everyday pronunciation for the sake of personal familiarity will unconsciously jolt the listener in the wrong way. The verse is so regular within this play that the constant repetition of "banished" without the sounded "-ed" where it is necessary for the iambic beat will be merely irritating when its intention is emotional transcendence.

Discretion, however, is the watchword, and in the line

> An hour but married, Tybalt murdered . . .

discretion should rule over law. According to the syllable count, "married" has two syllables, "murdered" has three. Yet here, the skilled speaker can negotiate rhythm, and "murdered" has enough weight in it to stretch through the final beat in the line with modern pronunciation. Actors who find it perfectly acceptable and artistically satisfying to say "ban-ish-ed" may balk at the anachronism of "mur-der-ed." In the *playing* of the *feeling* in "murdered" the word can reach to the final stress. Much of this kind of judgment depends on the soul-feeling of the speaker who, equipped with the knowledge of the options of her/his expression, will choose a truthful mode for her/his particular artistry. For another example of negotiable artistic option over the rule of prosodic law we can look at Juliet's rhymed couplet towards the end of Act I, Scene v:

> Go ask his name. If he be married,
> My grave is like to be my wedding bed.

It is not unjustifiable to pronounce "married" as we would today, but if the actress playing Juliet pays heed to what she says next:

> My only love sprung from my only hate.
> Too early seen unknown, and known too late.
> Prodigious birth of love it is to me
> That I must love a loathed enemy.

she will find that rhyming has some significance. The Nurse asks her:

> What's this? What's this?

To which she answers:

> A rhyme I learn'd even now
> Of one I danc'd withal.

A moment before this she met and fell in love with Romeo in the course of a sonnet with its strictly elegant rhymes and harmonic structure. If the actress meets this part of Juliet's romantic-poetic soul she will want to make a rhythmic rhyme of "mar-ri-ed" and "wedding bed."

To speak Shakespeare's verse well is to act Shakespeare better. A natural ease and familiarity with the regular rhythm develops sensitivity to the irregularities which, in turn, lead to the discovery of emotional shifts within the character. In order to speak verse well there is no substitute for practicing verse-speaking, therefore I suggest that you use the examples given in this chapter to practice marking random passages with the iambic stresses, - /. As your inner ear becomes accustomed to the marriage of pulse and meaning, gradually test your ability to take in the irregularities and mark them with an *.

When you have done a few, rather mechanical practice runs, choose a speech that you think you will *never* play and work it first for **content**—vowels, consonants, images, phrases, movement, personalization. Then mark in the iambic rhythm and practice the application of this first element of **form**.

Here are a few suggestions of speeches to work on:

King Henry VI, Part I: Act IV, Scene i, line 134 (King Henry)
King Henry VI, Part III: Act V, Scene iv (Queen Margaret)
Coriolanus: Act III, Scene ii, line 72 (Volumnia)
King John: Act I, Scene i, line 182 (Bastard)

Remember: The iambic pentameter is a pulse; it is the heartbeat of Shakespeare's poetry. Like your pulse it does not keep a steady, dull pace; it races with excitement, dances with joy or terror, slows down in contemplation. The iambic pulse is already there in the poetry and, like all rhythm, it has its origins *inside* the human organism. It was not invented by a clever, external cerebrum. There is nothing mechanical about the rhythms of great poetry. If they seem mechanical, *you* have made them so. And if you let the pulse of Shakespeare's poetry enter your veins, it will quicken and calm you, hurtle your spirits toward frenzy, give your organs an aerobic workout, make you sweat, pump your heart, bring you to inner peace and harmony.

Sonnet 18 is the sonnet I speak to Shakespeare himself:

> Shall I compare thee to a summer's day?
> Thou art more lovely and more temperate:
> Rough winds do shake the darling buds of May,
> And summer's lease hath all too short a date;
> Sometime too hot the eye of heaven shines,
> And often is his gold complexion dimm'd,
> And every fair from fair sometime declines,
> By chance or nature's changing course untrimm'd.

The third quatrain belongs particularly to him:

> But thy eternal summer shall not fade,
> Nor lose possession of that fair thou ow'st;
> Nor shall Death brag thou wand'rest in his shade,
> When in eternal lines to time thou grow'st.

I would like to speak the final couplet to you, as you absorb his eternal lines, his pulse, his voice:

> So long as men can breathe or eyes can see,
> So long lives this, and this gives life to thee.

7

◆▶ Rhyme ◀◆

S hakespeare's earlier plays are composed with obedience to and delight in the rules of verse-making. Rhythmic patterns are regular and rhyme abounds. The earlier plays include *Love's Labour's Lost*; *Two Gentlemen of Verona*; *Comedy of Errors*; *Henry VI, Parts I, II, III*; *Romeo and Juliet*; *Richard III*; *Richard II*; *Titus Andronicus*; *A Midsummer Night's Dream*; *The Merchant of Venice*. These plays were all written by the time Shakespeare was about thirty years old. As his craft deepened, the regularity of Shakespeare's verse yielded to the arhythmia of emotional truth and he used rhyme much less frequently, saving it for special effects, comic interpolations, and final flourishes. In *Twelfth Night*, for example, although blank (unrhymed) verse prevails, every scene that is in verse ends with a climactic rhyming couplet:

> Orsino:
>> Away before me to sweet beds of flowers!
>> Love-thoughts lie rich when canopied with bowers.
>>> *Act I, Scene i*

> Captain:
>> Be you his eunuch, and your mute I'll be:
>> When my tongue blabs, then let mine eyes not see.
>>> *Act I, Scene ii*

> Olivia:
>> Fate, show thy force; ourselves we do not owe.
>> What is decreed, must be: and be this so.
>>> *Act I, Scene v*

And so on throughout the play. *Twelfth Night* is from Shakespeare's middle period and is full of luscious poetry, brilliant prose, occasional rhyme. The great late tragedies are written in blank verse with very little rhyme. Edmund, in *King Lear*, ends two scenes with rhyming couplets:

> Let me, if not by birth, have lands by wit:
> All with me's meet that I can fashion fit.
> *Act I, Scene ii*

> The battle done, and they within our power,
> Shall never see his pardon; for my state
> Stands on me to defend, not to debate.
> *Act V, Scene i*

Kent and the Fool twice use rhyming couplets to end a scene and Edgar (as mad Tom) and the Fool sing and recite in rhyme; but rhyme is rare in *Lear*, *Macbeth*, *The Winter's Tale*, and *Hamlet* and almost non-existent in *Antony and Cleopatra* which has only four rhyming couplets:

Anthony
> Our separation so abides and flies,
> That thou, residing here, goes yet with me;
> And I, hence fleeting, here remain with thee.
> *Act I, Scene iii*

Antony:
> Fortune knows
> We scorn her most, when most she offers blows.
> *Act III, Scene xi*

Cleopatra:
> Ah, women, women! come, we have no friend
> But resolution, and the briefest end.

Caesar:
> Come, Dolabella, see
> High order, in this great solemnity.

Rhyming couplets give a satisfying final stamp to a scene and they are used to ring down the curtain at the end of twenty-seven of Shakespeare's thirty-five plays. Twelve of the plays end with two or more sets of rhyming couplets.

Rhyme is used, somewhat unexpectedly, for comic effect in *Othello*. Iago makes "witty" conversation with Desdemona and Emilia as they await the arrival of Othello's ship:

> Nay, it is true, or else I am a Turk,
> You rise to play, and go to bed to work.

> . . .

> If she be black, and thereto have a wit,
> She'll find a white, that shall her blackness hit.

This continues, interspersed with unrhymed exchanges, allowing

Iago to say outrageous things under the guise of comedy. Iago also makes good exits on rhymed couplets:

> I ha't, it is engender'd; Hell and night
> Must bring this monstrous birth to the world's light.
> *Act I, Scene iii*

> 'Tis here, but yet confus'd,
> Knavery's plain face is never seen till us'd.
> *Act III, Scene i*

> Ay, that's the way,
> Dull not device by coldness and delay.
> *Act II, Scene iii*

> This is the night
> That either makes me, or fordoes me quite.
> *Act V, Scene i*

Fashions in recitation come and go, accompanied by "rules" as to how the verse-speaker is supposed to handle rhyme, and for a long time in the twentieth century the fashion was not to point up the rhymes but to do everything possible to disguise them, hide them, bury them, as if they were embarrassing. But rhyme should not be ignored—Shakespeare used rhyme with intent both in his early plays where he reveled in his ability to make it work dramatically, and in his later writing where its use is spare and effective. Practice will develop the sensibility that allows rhyme to be heard—sometimes even pointed up to add comedy or pathos or power—but to take second place to sense.

I am often asked the question, "What am I meant to do with the rhymes?" The simple answer is, "Enjoy them." The question probably is prompted by fear of the power of rhyme. Rhyme works by balancing a word with another word that has the same sound. The repetition of sounds can affect both speaker and listener on a plane deeper than sense, can arouse nonrational responses that defy academic analysis. Some rhymes and rhythms are incantatory:

> A drum! A drum!
> Macbeth doth come.
> The Weird Sisters, hand in hand,
> Posters of the sea and land,
> Thus do go about, about:
> Thrice to thine, and thrice to mine,
> And thrice again, to make up nine.
> Peace!—the charm's wound up.
> *Macbeth, Act I, Scene iii*

Some rhymes are vicious:

Off with the crown, and, with the crown, his head;
And, whilst we breathe, take time to do him dead.
Henry VI, Part III, Act I, Scene iv

Some are deliciously silly:

Adriana *(Within)*:
Who is that at the door that keeps all this noise?

Dromio of Syracuse *(Within)*:
By my troth, your town is troubled with unruly boys.

Antipholus of Ephesus:
Are you there, wife? you might have come before.

Adriana *(Within)*:
Your wife, sir knave? go get you from the door.

Dromio of Ephesus:
If you went in pain, master, this knave would go sore.

Angelo:
Here is neither cheer, sir, nor welcome; we would fain have either.

Balthazar:
In debating which was best, we shall part with neither.

Dromio of Ephesus:
They stand at the door, master; bid them welcome hither.

Antipholus of Ephesus:
There is something in the wind that we cannot get in.

Dromio of Ephesus:
You would say so, master, if your garments were thin.
Your cake here is warm within; you stand here in the cold;
It would make a man mad as a buck to be so bought and sold.

Antipholus of Ephesus:
Go fetch me something, I'll break ope the gate.

Dromio of Syracuse *(Within)*:
Break any breaking here and I'll break your knave's pate.

Dromio of Ephesus:
A man may break a word with you, sir, and words are but wind;
Ay, and break it in your face, so he break it not behind.

Dromio of Syracuse *(Within)*:
It seems thou want'st breaking; out upon thee, hind.

Dromio of Ephesus:
Here's too much "out upon thee!" I pray thee let me in.

Dromio of Syracuse *(Within)*:
Ay, when fowls have no feathers, and fish have no fin.

Antipholus of Ephesus:
> Well, I'll break in; go, fetch me a crow.

Dromio of Ephesus:
> A crow without a feather; master, mean you so?
> For a fish without a fin, there's a fowl without a feather;
> If a crow help us in, sirrah, we'll pluck a crow together.

Antipholus of Ephesus:
> Go get thee gone; fetch me an iron crow.

Balthazar:
> Have patience, sir; O, let it not be so;

The bouncy energy of these irregular hexameters is heightened by the containment of the rhyming climaxes. The actors must know the meaning of what they are saying and must accurately perform the physical scenario, but the comedy lies in the rhymes. A word is served, like a tennis ball, and the rhyme zings back to score a point. The comic intention works when the actors play with rhyme-slinging virtuosity. *Comedy of Errors* is an arsenal of comedy routines from which rhymes are sprayed about like bird shot.

Acknowledging the power of rhyme and mastering it as one of the instruments of one's craft, removes the fear. *How* to do this is simply to do it—by means of rhyme-consciousness-raising.

In the two instances I have just given, the *sound of the rhyme* plays on the audience as effectively as does the *sense of the word*. Most of the time when Shakespeare writes with a deliberate rhyming scheme, the speaker must be aware of the *sound of the rhyme*, but must think and speak the *sense of the word* in a proportional awareness that favors meaning. The rhyme will then look after itself, providing a subliminally musical accompaniment to the sense. In a passage that is consciously musical it takes a great deal of effort to suppress the sounds of the rhyme, and yet some directors and actors have such an antipathy to the musicality of Shakespeare's verse that they spend their energies on suppression. Better to accept the music, let it lift one almost to the level of song and *then*—from that—discover what to make of it conceptually. Oberon, contemplating the magic flower brought to him by Puck which will afford him exquisite revenge on disdainful Titania, soars into an aria of wicked joy:

> I know a bank where the wild thyme blows,
> Where oxlips and the nodding violet grows,
> Quite over-canopied with luscious woodbine,
> With sweet musk-roses, and with eglantine.
> There sleeps Titania sometime of the night,
> Lull'd in these flowers with dances and delight;
> And there the snake throws her enamell'd skin,
> Weed wide enough to wrap a fairy in;

And with the juice of this I'll streak her eyes,
And make her full of hateful fantasies.
A Midsummer Night's Dream, Act II, Scene i

The rhyming couplets are the wings on which his anticipatory fancy flies. If the rhymes are dwelt on, however, beyond the sustaining power of the image or the thought, they will backfire and thump him and us down to earth.

Rhyme is intrinsic to our experience of language. We grew up with nursery rhymes and rhyming playground games, and the airwaves confirm the revived popularity of rhyme in the form of rap. Noticing rhyme schemes in Shakespeare adds a sheen to the actor's speaking and gives an edge to her/his comprehension of a character's intent and condition.

We have already looked at the sonnet within which Romeo and Juliet meet, touch and fall in love. The rhyme scheme is that of the classical sonnet and the pleasure sparked by their consciousness of rhyming with each other is a potent ingredient in their rapture. Our Master Sonnet, Sonnet 65, will demonstrate how the pattern of the rhymes is constructed, and I will then transfer this pattern to Romeo and Juliet's sonnet.

The rhyme scheme for a Shakespearean sonnet alternates rhymes line by line, with a new pair of rhymes for each quatrain until the last two lines which are a rhyming couplet. These rhymes are usually designated thus:

A B A B for the first quatrain,
C D C D for the second,
E F E F for the third
and G G for the couplet.

Applying this alphabetical designation to Sonnet 65 highlights the rhymes.

Since brass, nor stone, nor earth, nor boundless *sea*,	A
But sad mortality o'ersways their **power**,	B
How with this rage shall beauty hold a *plea*,	A
Whose action is no stronger than a **flower**?	B
O how shall summer's honey breath hold *out*	C
Against the wrackful siege of battering **days**,	D
When rocks impregnable are not so *stout*,	C
Nor gates of steel so strong, but Time **decays**?	D
O fearful meditation! Where, ***alack***,	E
Shall Time's best jewel from Time's chest lie **hid**?	F
Or what strong hand can hold his swift foot ***back***?	E
Or who his spoil of beauty can for**bid?**	F

O none, unless this miracle have *might*,   G
That in black ink my love may still shine ***bright***.   G

To develop your consciousness of rhyme, apply this scheme to several other Shakespeare sonnets. Practice them, letting the rhymes inform your thought and influence your interpretation.

Speaking sonnets is good training in general for speaking Shakespeare but the opportunity for direct application of sonnet-speaking is rare. A prime case is in the meeting of Romeo and Juliet. What does it do for the actors playing Romeo and Juliet to know that they meet and fall in love within a sonnet? Most importantly, it compels an acting choice: love at first sight.

Within the fourteen lines of a classical sonnet the poet is challenged to compact a powerful emotion that must deepen or change palpably between the octet and the sestet. The three quatrains of the sonnet must escalate emotionally and intellectually until their resolution in the final couplet. The sonnet form concentrates and intensifies emotion through forces encoded in its geometry, and although the form is so strong and clear that it can easily be construed as an intellectual artifact, its energy is plugged into the psyche.

Here now is the Romeo and Juliet sonnet which we have already looked at in terms of the clear stage directions it embodies. The first step we take here is "rhyme-consciousness-raising."

Romeo:
If I profane with my unworthiest *hand*   A
This holy shrine, the gentle fine is **this**.   B
My lips, two blushing pilgrims, ready *stand*   A
To smooth that rough touch with a tender **kiss.**   B

Juliet:
Good pilgrim, you do wrong your hand too *much*,   C
Which mannerly devotion shows in **this**;   D
For saints have hands that pilgrims' hands do *touch*,   C
And palm to palm is holy palmers' **kiss.**   D

Romeo:
Have not saints lips, and holy palmers ***too***?   E

Juliet:
Ay, pilgrim, lips that they must use in **prayer**.   F

Romeo:
O, then, dear saint, let lips do what hands ***do***:   E
They pray: grant thou, lest faith turn to **despair**.   F

Juliet:
Saints do not move, though grant for prayers' ***sake***.   G

Romeo:
Then move not, while my prayer's effect I ***take***.   G

The final words in the line leap out both as rhyme and signs: "hand stand, this kiss," says Romeo; "much touch, this kiss," answers Juliet; "too," says Romeo; "prayer," says Juliet; "do," cries Romeo, then "despair"; "sake," offers Juliet, and Romeo responds with "take."

In the first quatrain Romeo approaches with a sense of humor and of trespass. He sees Juliet as divine and knows that he is unworthy (he has, after all, been afflicted with impure thoughts about Rosaline). The second line has a word in it that appears differently in different editions—"fine" often becomes "sin." The choice between the two words seems evenly balanced, as both make sense. Choosing "fine" in this instance, Romeo says that although his hand may be unworthy, he offers his lips as humble pilgrims who can pay the fine for his hand's profanity by repairing its rough touch with a smooth and tender one. Within the first four lines he tells Juliet he wants to kiss her hand.

Entering into the form and language he has initiated, Juliet tells him he has gone far enough already. "*This* kiss," she says, of hands touching hands, is perfectly appropriate to saints and pilgrims; no fine is necessary. The second quatrain puts the young woman on an equal footing with the young man.

Romeo has been rebuffed. Leaving the octet, the sestet brings him onto a deeper level of feeling and he begs for her lips to touch his lips. One line is enough, ending on a plaintive "too," rising in a question; she keeps him at arm's length for one more line, telling him he must ask with the heartfelt fervor of prayer before she can trust him; his next rhyme is a firm "do," as he draws her attention to the touch of their hands and tells her that when their lips touch she will understand that prayer is sensation. His final appeal comes from the recesses of his soul, "Grant thou, lest faith turn to despair"—her word "prayer" elicited the rhyme and in the ring of its truth she hears his love.

The final couplet resolves and seals their love as, unable to move, she receives his kiss.

The solemnity of the sonnet is immediately offset by an ecstatic little coda:

Romeo:
  Thus from my lips by thine my sin is purg'd.

Juliet:
  Then have my lips the sin that they have took.

Romeo:
  Sin from my lips? O, trespass sweetly urg'd!
  Give me my sin again.

Juliet:
                    You kiss by the book.

Some editions will suggest, in an interpolated stage direction, that Romeo kisses Juliet after "Thus from my lips by thine my sin is purg'd." If there is a real experience of the sonnet, the end of its final couplet is the only emotionally true place for the kiss: "Then move not while my prayer's effect I take."

The sonnet form is used more cavalierly by Berowne in Shakespeare's earlier play, *Love's Labour's Lost*, a veritable reference book of verse and prose forms. The following exchange between Berowne, the King of Navarre, and his friends gives a good example of the conscious virtuosity with which Shakespeare, as a young playwright, exploited poetic conventions for dramatic effect.

Berowne:

Study me how to please the eye indeed,	A
By fixing it upon a fairer eye,	B
Who dazzling so, that eye shall be his heed,	A
And give him light that it was blinded by.	B
Study is like the heaven's glorious sun,	C
That will not be deep-search'd with saucy looks;	D
Small have continual plodders ever won,	C
Save base authority from others' books.	D
These earthly godfathers of heaven's lights,	E
That give a name to every fixed star,	F
Have no more profit of their shining nights	E
Than those that walk and wot not what they are.	F
Too much to know is to know nought but fame;	G
And every godfather can give a name.	G

King:

How well he's read, to reason against reading!	H

Dumaine:

Proceeded well, to stop all good proceeding!	H

Longaville:

He weeds the corn, and still lets go the weeding.	H

Berowne:

The spring is near when green geese are a-breeding.	H

Dumaine:
How follows that?

Berowne:

Fit in his place and time.	I

Dumaine:
In reason nothing.

Berowne:

Something then in rhyme.	I

First comes a classic sonnet, combining in its content both flippancy and philosophy. This is followed by a defusing device in the next four lines.The comic effect of the rhyming quatrain, followed by the rhyming couplet and capped by Berowne's *coup-de-grâce*, is not only a very clever trick but has the added fillip of the author applauding his own cleverness. The actor who feels this may arrive organically at a moment where Berowne goes just too far and risks losing the company of his friends, as show-offs sometimes do:

> King:
> Well, sit you out: go home, Berowne: adieu!

It is important for the actor to realize that, even when Shakespeare is using rhyme because it was the convention to do so, he used it with grace and art to underline dramatic points, comic points, philosophical points, to score in arguments, win verbal battles. The actor must assume that if the character s/he plays speaks in rhyme, that character has the wit to exploit and manipulate rhyme along with antithesis, puns, alliteration and all other figures of speech. A heightened state of being engenders heightened language and Shakespeare's characters are not performing a soap opera. The language is not separate from the story, it *is* the story.

There is, therefore, some reason for the actor playing Olivia in *Twelfth Night* to ask herself why in Act III, Scene i Olivia suddenly breaks into runaway rhyming couplets, having hitherto expressed herself in richly imagistic and well-managed blank verse. She has shown Viola (Cesario) her heart and her hopes and Viola has utterly rejected her. With a huge effort she pulls herself together and says, still with ladylike control:

> Be not afraid, good youth, I will not have you,
> And yet when wit and youth is come to harvest,
> Your wife is like to reap a proper man.
> There lies your way, due west.

With her famous would-be exit line—"Then westward-ho!"—Viola almost escapes but makes the mistake of asking Olivia if she has any message for Orsino. At this point Olivia loses control. She asks Viola to tell her what she thinks of her, a riddling exchange ensues, and then Olivia's adoration breaks the dam of her self-respect:

> A murd'rous guilt shows not itself more soon
> Than love that would seem hid. Love's night is noon—
> Cesario, by the roses of the spring,
> By maidhood, honour, truth and everything,
> I love thee so that, maugre all my pride,
> Nor wit nor reason can my passion hide.
> Do not extort thy reasons from this clause,
> For that I woo, thou therefore hast no cause;
> But reason thus with reason fetter:
> Love sought is good, but given unsought is better.

Viola uses the verse form initiated by Olivia to solidify and under-line her refusal. She is firm and fair and does her best to persuade her wooer that the rejection is impersonal:

> By innocence I swear, and by my youth,
> I have one heart, one bosom and one truth,
> And that no woman has; nor never none
> Shall mistress be of it, save I alone.
> And so adieu, good madam; never more
> Will I my master's tears to you deplore.

Olivia's final couplet is utter humiliation:

> Yet come again: for thou perhaps mayst move
> That heart which now abhors, to like his love.

This scene can be played in many ways but the clue to Olivia's behavior lies as much in the sudden rush of rhyme as in the sense of the words she speaks. The actor who is oblivious to such evidence will not find the organic key to playing the scene.

Rhyming couplets and, indeed, triplets, pepper the comedies:

Helena:
> Your hands than mine are quicker for a fray:
> My legs are longer though, to run away.

Hermia:
> I am amaz'd, and know not what to say.
> *A Midsummer Night's Dream, Act III, Scene 2*

And let me note the rhyming couplets that spill out with Richard II's blood:

> That hand shall burn in never-quenching fire
> That staggers thus my person. Exton, thy fierce hand
> Hath with the King's blood stain'd the King's own land.
> Mount, mount, my soul! thy seat is up on high,
> Whilst my gross flesh sinks downward, here to die.

If the rhyme were to dominate, the death would be ludicrous, but when the actor's performance is convincing, the background music of the rhyme strikes a plangent, properly climactic chord.

Rhythm and rhyme are the deep and delicately human elements of verse that ask for a responsive pulse in order to be realized. It may seem odd that these elements of form should be handled on subtle energy levels whereas language and imagery should physically inhabit and activate the body. In my experience, if rhythms of verse are physi-

calized too grossly, if rhymes are exaggerated, the psycho-physical circuitry, at once overburdened and under-differentiated, is rendered
incapable of illumination. The balance of form and content is the balance of head and heart, of soul and body, of order and chaos, and it
lives best—we might say it lives only—in the speaking.

8

◆▶ Line-endings ◆▶

When you look at a page of a Shakespeare play you see that some lines run on until the margin stops them or until a paragraph ends; these lines are called prose. Other lines on the page are stopped, not by the margin, but because the iambic pentameter determines the length of the line. The iambic pentameter arranges and orchestrates thoughts and speech in a particular way for a particular purpose. This purposeful arrangement intensifies the energy of thought and speech, generates an electrical charge which can burn through the daily lassitude of our prose-ridden minds to revive imagination and creativity in both speaker and listener. The relationship forged between actor and audience by poetry is different from that formed in prose.

There is, therefore, a vital discovery to be made about the place where the line ends in Shakespeare's verse. It is not arbitrary. It goes beyond the expression of poetic craft. The choice of the final word in the pentameter line is intentional and the actor who pays attention to how the line ends taps into a rich seam of acting information.

I owe a great deal to John Barton of the Royal Shakespeare Company for my understanding of how line-endings work and even more to his student Tina Packer, now Artistic Director of Shakespeare & Company, for her years of practical work on the text in the classroom and on the stage which rooted this understanding in the acting process and proved its application in performance.

There is much controversy about the treatment of line-endings. I will offer my opinion on the subject, but you must practice, and apply whatever makes you a better actor. Do not abdicate your authority to "experts." Be open to experiment. In the field of Shakespeare training you will find opposing truths about how you MUST speak the verse as you go from teacher to teacher and director to director. Take what works for you, adapt to the different aesthetics and styles, and over the years you will accumulate a mass of information and experience that will develop into the way *you* speak Shakespeare. There will always be more to learn, and always it will be important to trust your own sense of truth.

To illustrate the folly of handing one's judgment over to the "expert," listen to two pronouncements from two acknowledged authorities, pronouncements I have had repeated back to me as gospel by countless students, teachers and experienced actors:

> "You must be able to say twelve lines of Shakespearean verse on one breath."
> *Sir Tyrone Guthrie*

> "You must breathe at the end of every line."
> *John Barton*

Another piece of advice from an eminent school of Shakespearean acting is: "Get on the horse [of the verse], dig in your heels and gallop. If you can pluck a few flowers on the way, well and good, but don't stop."

Then there is the myth of "enjambement," which suggests that there is a special Continental artistry in attaching the end of one line to the beginning of another. And there are those who emphasize the "caesura," which allows you to breathe in the middle of the line. If you put together the "enjambement" and the "caesura" you might as well rewrite all Shakespeare's iambic verse, putting the middles of the lines at the end and the ends in the middle.

The overburdened acting teacher in a drama department whose syllabus includes *Acting Shakespeare* may find it easier to drill his/her students in the absolutism of the Guthrie Rule or the Barton Rule than to dig into the causal thinking that gave rise to the original pronouncement. I was faced directly with the problem of being asked to teach actors something I did not believe in when I worked at the Guthrie Theater in Minneapolis from 1964 to 1967 under Tyrone Guthrie himself. Young actors would come to me and say, "Teach me how to say twelve lines on one breath; 'Sir' says I've got to do it." And I would say, "No, I won't."

Guthrie was a formidable figure, very tall and very tart, but he was fundamentally benign. I remember meeting him in a corridor of the theatre one day. I'm sure I did not knock at his chest as at a door, but I see myself doing it, craning my neck back to look up at his distant domed head and saying, "I wanted to ask you, Sir, about this thing of speaking twelve lines on one breath that everyone wants me to teach them. Surely you mean that they should be able to maintain a long *thought line* throughout twelve or more lines." "Ah yes," he said, with a distant smile, "of course, of course. But, you see, they'd never understand that. It's much simpler to tell them to do it on one breath."

I will try to explain the Barton Rule in terms that make it a contribution to emotionally effective acting. To say "Breathe at the end of

every line" is a shortcut that shortchanges the power of the pentameter line-ending The argument for such a breathing pattern is that the
natural arc of a thought in the English language lasts as long as a pentameter. However, there are within us long thoughts, medium-length
thoughts, and short thoughts. There are short emotional phrases
within the long arc of a thought and there are long outbursts of emotions within which short thoughts twist and turn. Shakespeare has
chosen the shape of the thought/feelings of the characters he has created and when they speak in verse he has chosen that the arcs of their
thought/feeling energies go from the beginning of a pentameter line to
the end, each line serving a larger, longer arc of thought/feeling that
goes from the beginning of a speech to the end.

We get to know a person not so much through how s/he looks or
dresses as through how s/he thinks, feels and speaks. We get to know
Shakespeare's characters when we allow our thought/feeling waves to
be inflected and shaped by the character's thought/feeling patterns as
they are revealed in the verse-form. WHY does that person's thought
end at the end of the line? WHY does the emotion switch suddenly in
the middle of a line and then apparently run on for three more lines
without punctuation? WHY is that little weak word at the end of a
line? What do these patterns reveal about the character's inner state?

You will find, as we proceed, that the end of a line is not just a breath
change—it is an emotional change, a thought change, an impulse shift.
These will often spark a breath change, but not always. You will find
that, by allowing the end of the line to alert you to inner change, you
will think freshly all the time. You will avoid the phony attempt to
sound as if you are thinking the words for the first time by seeming to
search for the word which the audience knows you know. The searches
are built into the structure of the lines which figure forth the alive
thinking, the moment-to-moment impulses of the human mind.

You are now very familiar with Sonnet 65. I would like you to look
at it as if it were prose, its thought processes governed only by the
punctuation.

> Since brass, nor stone, nor earth, nor boundless sea, but sad mortal-
> ity o'ersways their power, how with this rage shall beauty hold a plea,
> whose action is no stronger than a flower? O how shall summer's
> honey breath hold out against the wrackful siege of battering days,
> when rocks impregnable are not so stout, nor gates of steel so strong,
> but Time decays? O fearful meditation! where, alack, shall Time's
> best jewel from Time's chest lie hid? Or what strong hand can hold
> his swift foot back? Or who his spoil of beauty can fobid? O none,
> unless this miracle have might, that in black ink my love may still
> shine bright.

Looking at this prose paragraph what does its shape convey? Does
the linear sense seem to dominate? The rhymes are still so strong that

the arcs of thought remain intact, but the lift of the arc is flattened, particularly in the second sentence/quatrain when the question, "O, how shall summer's honey breath hold out," runs so easily into "Against the wrackful siege of battering days." We lose the urgency of "holding out." The last words in the verse lines have a vitality that they are denied when they merely serve grammatical sense. If we look at those last words by themselves we see how much of the heart of the sonnet is carried in them:

> SEA, POWER, PLEA, FLOWER, HOLD OUT, DAYS, STOUT,
> DECAYS, ALACK, LIE HID, BACK, FORBID, MIGHT, BRIGHT.

I referred in Chapter Six to the twentieth-century speaking ailment called "falling inflections." The ability to drive one's thought through to the end of the line must not be taken for granted. We are not accustomed to the mental follow-through that the iambic pentameter requires and the importance of the line-endings demand. It is all too easy to get by with:

> Since brass, nor stone, nor earth, nor boundless sea,
>
> But sad mortality o'ersways their power,
>
> How with this rage shall beauty hold a plea,
>
> Whose action is no stronger than a flower?
>
> O how shall summer's honey breath hold out
>
> Against the wrackful siege of battering days,
>
> When rocks impregnable are not so stout,
>
> Nor gates of steel so strong, but Time decays?
>
> O fearful meditation! Where, alack,
>
> Shall Time's best jewel from Time's chest lie hid?
>
> Or what strong hand can hold his swift foot back?
>
> Or who his spoil of beauty can forbid?
>
> O none, unless this miracle have might,
>
> That in black ink my love may still shine bright.

This is a travesty, but one that is all too often perpetrated on this sonnet and on others by speakers unconscious of their inflectionary habits.

Now see what happens when you restore the final words in the lines to their rightful place in the arc of the thought/feeling—each one is a pot of gold at the end of the rainbow and, to mix the metaphor, each is a springboard that propels the thought/feeling onto the beginning of the next line.

Allow yourself the time, as an exercise, to stop, think and breathe at the end of every line:

> Since brass, nor stone, nor earth, nor boundless sea,

STOP. Think about these images, contemplate, breathe two or three times.
NOW admit the thought of the beginning of the next line and let it INSPIRE your next breath so that you can speak—

> But sad mortality o'ersways their power

STOP. Think about death overpowering even the earth and the sea, breathe two or three times.
NOW allow access to the next thought which INSPIRES you with the breath to speak it—

> How with this rage shall beauty hold a plea

STOP. Contemplate, breathe, until the next thought MUST be admitted—

> Whose action is no stronger than a flower.

And so on through the sonnet.

Repeat this process until you can honestly think/speak each line on **one** breath, allowing the next line/thought to INSPIRE you with a new breath which takes you through that thinking/speaking line. Gradually speed up your **thinking until you hardly experience the change of breath as breath, ONLY AS CHANGE OF THOUGHT/FEELING at the end of every line.**

IN FACT, THE INSPIRATION OF BREATH IS AT THE BEGINNING OF THE LINE.

By this time, your breath should be inaudible, dropping deep inside as thought experienced in the body. You will probably find that, at the beginning of lines 2 and 4, the thought/breath impulse is swift, almost snatched, and at the beginning of lines 3 and 5 there is a deeper, longer inspiration, filled with poignancy, as the question "How with this rage shall beauty hold a plea?" is redoubled in "O how shall summer's honey breath hold out..." And the breath/feeling that enters before one speaks "O fearful meditation" has a very different quality from the one responsive to "That in black ink my love may still shine bright."

Practice this until the thoughts can speed up while maintaining real feeling transitions between the lines. Do not lose connection with your personal love-loss source for the content of the meaning of the poem. Eventually, the sonnet should take about one minute to speak. All your work should culminate in a deeply-felt "telling" of the thoughts and feelings within the poem at the natural pace of real, but intensified, speaking.

Here is an experiment which I would like you to perform on the Chorus which forms the Prologue to *Henry V*. Write it out *in prose* for

yourself or work from these pages and then spend from thirty min-
utes to an hour working through the words and images in the manner
outlined in the first three chapters of this book. Absorb the vowels
and consonants into your body; drop the images deep inside you letting them stimulate emotion, associations and actions; let the phrases
gradually build and the "story" emerge. Look up in the dictionary any
words you do not know.

> O, for a Muse of fire, that would ascend the brightest heaven of
> invention; a kingdom for a stage, princes to act and monarchs to
> behold the swelling scene! Then should the warlike Harry, like him-
> self, assume the port of Mars; and at his heels leash'd in like hounds,
> should famine, sword, and fire crouch for employment. But pardon,
> gentles all, the flat unraised spirits that hath dar'd on this unworthy
> scaffold to bring forth so great an object: can this cockpit hold the
> vasty fields of France? Or may we cram within this wooden O the
> very casques that did afright the air at Agincourt? O, pardon! since a
> crooked figure may attest in little place a million; and let us, ciphers
> to this great accompt, on your imaginary forces work.
>
> Suppose within the girdle of these walls are now confined two
> mighty monarchies, whose high upreared and abutting fronts the
> perilous narrow ocean parts asunder: piece out our imperfections
> with your thoughts; into a thousand parts divide one man, and make
> imaginary puissance; think, when we talk of horses, that you see
> them printing their proud hoofs i' the receiving earth; for 'tis your
> thoughts that now must deck our kings, carry them here and there,
> jumping o'er times, turning the accomplishments of many years into
> an hour-glass: for the which supply, admit me Chorus to this history;
> who, prologue-like your humble patience pray, gently to hear, kindly
> to judge, our play.

The images that arise are of a small, round, wooden stage, a god-
like King Henry, mythic personifications of a Muse, of Famine, Sword
and Fire, the hounds of war. Having looked up "casques" if necessary,
you see how the glittering helmets on the field at Agincourt seem to
make the air shiver with fright. You must have seen an audience,
because you appeal to them, and when you talk about being "ciphers
to this great accompt" you see zeros written on a page signifying
1,000,000 and compare the ciphers who are the actors to the gigantic
story they must enact. You then paint the scene and encourage the
audience to fill in with their imaginations whatever is physically lacking on the stage to fully represent great historical events.

When you are reasonably familiar with the passage, take the following words and let them animate and activate you imaginatively
and physically:

ASCEND INVENTION ACT SCENE SELF HEELS FIRE ALL
DARED FORTH HOLD CRAM CASQUES AGINCOURT MAY MIL-

LION ACCOMPT (account) WORK WALLS MONARCHIES FRONTS
ASUNDER THOUGHTS MAN PUISSANCE THEM EARTH KINGS
TIMES YEARS SUPPLY HISTORY PRAY PLAY

(The first four words and the last four are excellent kindling for the beginning of any performance: "ascend invention—act scene—supply history—pray, play.")

Now look at the first four lines of the speech as it is written, with the final words in the line highlighted:

> O, for a Muse of fire, that would **ascend**
> The brightest heaven of **invention**:
> A kingdom for a stage, princes to **act**
> And monarchs to behold the swelling **scene**!

These are not the most *important* words in the lines. "A Muse of fire," "the brightest heaven," "A kingdom for a stage," "And monarchs" are more *important*. But if you attend to the function of the final words and allow their meaning to play a part in the way you beg for inspiration, you will lift the energy to another level.

Practice saying the lines slowly enough for you to see the images clearly but DO NOT BREATHE IN THE MIDDLE OF THE LINE. SAY EACH *LINE* AS A SINGLE THOUGHT/FEELING ARC. You can do this lightly whispering or speaking with an introverted energy.

Continue with the next four lines:

> Then should the warlike Harry, like **himself**,
> Assume the port of Mars; and at his **heels**,
> Leash'd in like hounds, should famine, sword, and **fire**
> Crouch for employment. But pardon, gentles **all** . . .

Again, "warlike Harry," "the port of Mars," "hounds," "famine," "sword" and "employment" are the essential images, with the last words in the lines drawing us on and telling us something special, telling us that Harry does not need to be more than "himself" to stand like the god of war, holding the scourges of war "at his heels."

In the second and fourth lines the thought seems to finalize grammatically in the middle of the line ("Mars" and "employment"). This is the device of "caesura" further clarified by punctuation. However, explore what happens *dramatically* when you **don't** breathe as the thought changes after "Mars" and "employment"—your voice, your energy, your thought, the image, your mood shifts—but **do not breathe** until the end of the line. There is no *logic* to this, it is sheer *drama*. You do not have to do it. It is not a rule. But if you follow the hint that each pentameter *line* is a thought/feeling arc with the breath changing on an impulse that is more human than grammatical, you will find some exciting acting possibilities.

Continuing from your apology to the audience coming on the heels of the image of war, the next six lines offer further exploration of the

drama of letting the line-ending dictate the impulse shift. I will now
mark the crucial images that dominate the line so that, visually, the
last word in the line does not get mechanically emphasized:

> The **flat unraised spirits** that hath *dar'd*
> On this **unworthy scaffold** to bring *forth*
> So great an **object**: can this **cockpit** *hold*
> The **vasty fields of France**? Or may we *cram*
> Within this **wooden O** the very *casques*
> That did **affright the air** at *Agincourt*?

What happens to you if you do not breathe after "object" and
"France" and do breathe at the beginning of each line? I am assuming
that by "breathe at the beginning of the line" we understand that it is
not just breath that is involved, but a felt transition **from** the thought
implications of "dar'd" ("how dare we"), "bring forth" ("give birth to"),
"hold" ("contain without bursting"), "cram" ("the audacity and impos-
sibility of the physical act"), "casques" ("thousands of soldiers' helmets shimmering in the sunlight"), "Agincourt" ("England's proudest
victory over France") **to** the contrasting images of the small stage and
the huge battle that must appear on it. Continue through the whole
speech, finding out how an observance of the line-endings dramatizes
your speaking and at the same time makes it more natural.

The natural drama of the iambic pentameter form is its glory.
When you observe the form you do not sound as though you are
spouting poetry, you sound as though you are in the grip of heightened reality, expressing yourself eloquently but comprehensibly. Good
verse-speaking sounds like real talking.

In the later plays it becomes even more dramatically worthwhile to
master the art of line-endings. In the more conversational moments
the end of the line may not be charged enough for an actual new
breath, but there will always be some subtle edge to the thought that
sits just there. In Act I, Scene vii of *Cymbeline*, when Iachimo is again
in Imogen's good graces after his outrageous attempt to seduce her,
he says, casually:

> I had almost forgot
> T'entreat your grace, but in a small request,
> And yet of moment too, for it concerns:
> Your lord, myself and other noble friends
> Are partners in the business.

Imogen:
> Pray, what is't?

Iachimo:
> Some dozen Romans of us, and your lord
> (The best feather of our wing) have mingled sums
> To buy a present for the Emperor:

Which I (the factor for the rest) have done
In France: 'Tis plate of rare device, and jewels
Of rich and exquisite form, their values great,
And I am something curious, being strange,
To have them in safe stowage: May it please you
To take them in protection?

Imogen:
                    Willingly:
And pawn mine honor for their safety, since
My lord hath interest in them; I will keep them
In my bedchamber.

Iachimo:
                    They are in a trunk
Attended by my men: I will make bold
To send them to you, only for this night:
I must aboard tomorrow.

The conversational tone is supported by the line-ending
thought/breath transition after "I had almost forgot" and before
"T'entreat you," and at "for it concerns"—impulse transition—"Your
lord." These are moments which can be picked out and played with the
intimacy earned in the preceding moments of the scene. Running-on
from "Your lord" to "myself and other noble friends" downplays the
significance of the request, making it hard for Imogen not to respond.
The next time Iachimo says "Your lord" it comes at the end of the line,
allowing a breath to think about him and compliment him ("the best
feather in our wing"); and from here the explanation and the requested
favor are lightly and easily presented. Breaths are not necessary
between all the lines to underscore the edge of "jewels," "values great,"
"protection," although "Emperor" probably merits a good breath.

"Willingly" is an audience-grabber. "And pawn mine honor for their
safety" is dramatic irony rampant. For the actor playing Imogen, the
run-on into "Since" is a deliciously dramatic opportunity—slightly
coy, a little dreamy perhaps, a little sexy with the magnetism of
Iachimo arousing a memory of Posthumus, welcoming the entry of
the jewels into her bedchamber—"I will keep them"—at the end of
line. Iachimo is hanging on a thread, everything depends on where
she will "keep them" . . . "In my bedchamber." This does not need to
be underlined, the drama is intrinsic. And what does Iachimo go on to
say, finishing the line as though nothing momentous has happened?
"They are in a trunk." This is the very stuff of drama.

The "Since" at the end of Imogen's line is an elegant demonstration
that the little-big words can carry a major charge of dramatic responsibility when they arrive at the end of a verse-line. And listen as
Imogen admonishing Pisanio about the leavetaking he took of her
husband, at the same time mourns her loss:

> I would have broke mine eye-strings, crack'd them, but
> To look upon him, till the diminution
> Of space had pointed him sharp as my needle;
> Nay, followed him, till he had melted from
> The smallness of a gnat, to air and then
> Have turn'd mine eye, and wept.

I suggest that you take in the circumstances of a newly wed young woman whose father has sent her husband into exile and say (or whisper) these words, letting the emotion breathe only at the end of the lines. "But," "from" and "then" are little words that speak largely, hauntingly, from this position.

Again in *Cymbeline*, there is a speech of Posthumus's after Iachimo has convinced him of Imogen's infidelity which exemplifies the emotional power engendered when it is the line-endings and beginnings that determine breath/feeling transitions rather than the punctuation or the grammar. Differing typeface will mark the speech with proportional emphases which seem emotionally logical to me, given the circumstances—the iambic stresses and the line-endings. I am removing most of the traditional punctuation. Your interpretation may vary, but I hope the pull of the line-endings will influence your choices.

> Is there no way for **men** to **be** but *women*
> Must be *half-workers* **we** are all *bastards*,
> And that most **venerable man** which *I*
> Did **call my** *father* was I know not *where*
> When I was *stamp'd* some COINER with his TOOLS
> Made me a *counterfeit* yet my **MOTHER SEEM'D**
> The **DIAN** of that time so doth my **WIFE**
> The NON-PAREIL of this O vengeance, **vengeance**!
> ME of my lawful pleasure she *restrain'd*
> And pray'd me oft forbearance did it *with*
> A **pudency** so **rosy** the sweet view *on't*
> Might well have warm'd old Saturn that I THOUGHT her
> As chaste as UNSUNN'D SNOW O ALL THE DEVILS
> This **yellow Iachimo** in an HOUR—was't not?
> Or less!—at FIRST? perchance he spake not, BUT,
> Like a full acorn'd boar, a German one,
> CRIED 'O!' AND MOUNTED; **found no oposition**
> But what he look'd for **should oppose** and **SHE**
> Should from encounter **GUARD—COULD I FIND OUT**
> *THE WOMAN'S PART IN ME for there's no motion*
> *That tends to vice in man but I AFFIRM*
> *It is the WOMAN'S PART be it lying, note it,*
> *The WOMAN'S, flattering HERS deceiving HERS*
> *Lust and rank thoughts HERS HERS; revenges HERS*
> *Ambitions, covetings, change of prides, disdain,*
> *Nice longings, slanders, mutability,*
> *All faults that man may name, nay, that HELL KNOWS*

Why hers in part—or *all*; BUT RATHER *ALL*
FOR EVEN TO VICE
THEY ARE NOT CONSTANT, but are changing **still**
One vice but of a minute old for **one**
Not half so old as that *I'll write against them*
Detest them CURSE THEM. Yet 'tis a greater **skill**
In a true HATE to pray they have their **WILL**:
The very devils cannot **PLAGUE THEM BETTER**.

The pace of this speech is so clearly dictated by the internal rhythms and emotional build that it is a stunning exercise for the experienced actor. You cannot fully play this unless your voice is strong enough for the tearing jealous rage that consumes Posthumus. This is not a civilized speech. At the same time, if it were in prose it would be a rant. The form of the verse corrals the content and makes it manageable.

Let us look at one more speech from the later plays—from Act III, Scene ii of *The Winter's Tale*. Hermione, wrongly accused by her husband Leontes of adultery with Polixenes, has given birth to her daughter in a prison cell. The baby has been taken from her to be killed and she, barely recovered from the birth, has been brought to the public court of justice, presided over by Leontes, to be judged. This is how she answers her indictment:

Since what I am to say, must be but that
Which contradicts my accusation, and
The testimony on my part, no other
But what comes from myself, it shall scarce boot me
To say 'Not guilty': mine integrity,
Being counted falsehood, shall, as I express it,
Be so receiv'd. But thus, if powers divine
Behold our human actions (as they do)
I doubt not then but innocence shall make
False accusation blush, and tyranny
Tremble at patience. You, my lord, best know
(Who least will seem to do so) my past life
Hath been as continent, as chaste, as true,
As I am now unhappy; which is more
Than history can pattern, though devis'd
And play'd to take spectators. For behold me,
A fellow of the royal bed, which owe
A moiety of the throne, a great king's daughter,
The mother to a hopeful prince, here standing
To prate and talk for life and honour 'fore
Who please to come and hear. For life, I prize it
As I weigh grief (which I would spare): for honour,
'Tis a derivative from me to mine,
And only that I stand for. I appeal
To your own conscience, sir, before Polixenes
Came to your court, how I was in your grace,

How merited to be so; since he came,
With what encounter so uncurrent I
Have strain'd t'appear thus: if one jot beyond
The bound of honour, or in act or will
That way inclining, harden'd be the hearts
Of all that hear me, and my near'st of kin
Cry fie upon my grave!

By now, I am sure that you can see that there is an oddness to the line-endings in the first few lines. The grammatical sense reads, and the prose phrasing would be:

Since what I am to say,/must be but that which contradicts my accusation,/and the testimony on my part,/no other but what comes from myself,/it shall scarce boot me to say 'Not guilty':/mine integrity, being counted falsehood,/shall, as I express it, be so receiv'd./But thus, if powers divine behold our human actions/(as they do)/I doubt not then but innocence shall make false accusation blush,/and tyranny tremble at patience.

I suggest you read it like this first, in order to get a visceral experience of what happens when you restore the thought/feeling patterns indicated by the verse.

Now let the arc of the pentameter line re-arrange your thoughts and remember how weak Hermione's physical condition is:

Since what I am to say, must be but that
Which contradicts my accusation, and
The testimony on my part, no other
But what comes from myself, it shall scarce boot me
To say 'Not guilty': mine integrity,
Being counted falsehood, shall, as I express it,
Be so receiv'd. But thus, if powers divine
Behold our human actions (as they do)
I doubt not then but innocence shall make
False accusation blush, and tyranny
Tremble at patience.

What did you find? Did you notice that all the words in the first line are small, as if she doesn't know what to say, that ending on "that" allows her to think for a moment, to come up with the strength to "contradict my accusation?" But the effort to articulate this opposition in its Latin-based polysyllables seems to exhaust her, and her thought trails off on a frail "and."

The transition from "and" at the end of the line to "testimony" at the beginning of the next one is monumental. Between those two lines she must really pull her will and her breath into her. After "testimony" her energy again fades almost into defeat, "on my part no other." The end of the line shows her trying to think where else her testimony might come from and falling back on her only friend, herself. "But what comes from myself"—and this hardly seems enough—"it shall scarce boot me." On the verge of defeat she says the words that seem useless, "not guilty." It is the middle of a line. If you don't stop but let the message of that "not guilty" immediately jump to "mine integrity," you will *experience* the tide turning within Hermione. "Integrity" is the first polysyllabic, Latin-based word to come at the end of a line so far; integrity and honor are the most important things in Hermione's life; she is beginning to reconnect with her truest self and, with one more stumble into weakness at the end of the next line, "as I express it," her life force gradually increases, invoking "powers divine" as her support. She confronts the tyrant.

The defense she musters reminds both Leontes and herself that she is of royal blood. We feel her aristocracy when we say with her:

> For behold me,
> A fellow of the royal bed, which owe
> A moiety of the throne, a great king's daughter,
> The mother to a hopeful prince, here standing
> To prate and talk for life and honour 'fore
> Who please to come and hear.

The line-ending on "owe" allows one to play the challenge she throws Leontes on the subject of equality and authority; the significance of "standing" while Leontes sits is playable because of its place at the end of the line; and the humiliation of "prating and talking" about the most precious subjects in public is *felt* in the hesitation after "'fore." It is as though she looks around just then at the rabble surrounding her.

Hermione's assessment of the relative values of life and honor are clear in the place each of those words occupy in the line:

> For life, I prize it
> As I weigh grief (which I would spare): for honour,
> 'Tis a derivative from me to mine,
> And only that I stand for.

The word "honour" comes at the end of a line as she enters upon her personal appeal to Leontes to remember her as she was before the arrival of Polixenes, to remember what an effort it took to continue to please Leontes while his guest remained. The difficulty in talking about such intimate matters is evident in the awkwardness of "With what encounter so uncurrent I," and in the way she seems to search for how to explain that her treatment of Polixenes was more to please Leontes than herself—"Have strained to appear thus."

> I appeal
> To your own conscience, sir, before Polixenes
> Came to your court, how I was in your grace,
> How merited to be so; since he came,

> With what encounter so uncurrent I
> Have strain'd t'appear thus . . .

Then what she has to say becomes strong and direct and defiant:

> if one jot beyond
> The bound of honour, or in act or will
> That way inclining, harden'd be the hearts
> Of all that hear me, and my near'st of kin
> Cry fie upon my grave!

The last words in these lines spell out her position.

In this scene there are many occasions where one person's speech ends on a half-line and the next person begins with a half-line. The clue for the actor here is quite simple. If the two half-lines make up one full pentameter line it indicates that there is no pause between the speeches. The clue is probably that there is some heat in the exchange and the speakers jump in almost interrupting each other.

Hermione finishes:

> Cry fie upon my grave!

Leontes continues:

> I ne'er heard yet
> That any of these bolder vices wanted
> Less impudence to gainsay what they did
> Than to perform it first.

Hermione interrupts his line, as well she might, to rebuke its crudeness:

> That's true enough,
> Though 'tis a saying, sir, not due to me.

Leontes, rather lamely responds:

> You will not own it.

And Hermione finishes his half-line with a dignified rebuttal:

> More than mistress of
> Which comes to me in name of fault, I must not
> At all acknowledge.

And proceeds calmly to say that, yes, she loved Polixenes, but honorably and as she was commanded to do. She denies all knowledge of the conspiracy of which she is also accused, and when Leontes insists that she does know, she says:

> Sir,
> You speak a language that I understand not . . .

The "Sir" stands alone. This means that there is a pause built into the text. Mechanically speaking, Hermione pauses for four-and-a-half feet. Every now and then Shakespeare indicates a pause in the text by giving a character a half-line or less. This is significant because it suggests that apart from these indications there are no pauses. This is worth bearing in mind when weighing the choice of cutting the text against cutting the extraneous pauses some actors may insist are necessary for their "true" playing of a moment.

In Posthumus's speech which we worked on above, there is a striking half-line:

> For even to vice
> They are not constant.

Many possibilities present themselves as to why Posthumus is suspended (for three feet) at this juncture. Emotionally he may have reached his limit. He may see something bitterly funny in the thought that comes to him. He may not know what to say.

According to the circumstances giving rise to half-lines being spoken, the actors' discretion may choose whether they indicate a swift pick-up of the thought or a pause that occupies the missing beats in the line. At the end of Hermione's trial scene the oracle is read to determine her innocence or guilt and Apollo clears her. The Lords unanimously cry out:

> Now blessed be the great Apollo!

And Hermione finishes the beat with:

> Praised!

Leontes, however, stops the celebration: "Hast thou read truth?" he asks the officers, and *either* they answer quickly, finishing his line, *or*, taken aback by his question, with silence descending on the crowd, they pause for two half-lines:

> Ay, my lord, even so
> As it is here set down.

Then there is a definite half-line pause before Leontes announces:

> There is no truth at all i' the oracle.
> The sessions shall proceed: this is mere falsehood.

Most of the next eleven lines are broken. Turmoil reigns. I think that there are options as to which broken lines indicate pauses and which show haste, but my preference in the announcement of the Prince's death would be for a continuous line, the news tumbling helter-skelter from a terrified servant's lips.

> *(Enter a Servant)*

Servant:
> My lord the King, the King!

Leontes:
> What is the business?

Servant:
   O sir, I shall be hated to report it!
   The Prince your son, with mere conceit and fear
   Of the queen's speed, is gone.

Leontes:
                How! gone?

Servant:
                       Is dead.

Leontes:
   Apollo's angry, and the heavens themselves
   Do strike at my injustice.

(Hermione faints)

                How now, there?

Paulina:
   This news is mortal to the queen: Look down
   And see what death is doing.

Leontes:
               Take her hence:
   Her heart is but o'ercharg'd: she will recover.
   I have too much believ'd mine own suspicion:
   Beseech you, tenderly apply to her
   Some remedies for life.

A lighter example of the quickness of response indicated by half-lines in the text is in this teasing exchange between Cleopatra and her attendant, Charmian:

Cleopatra:
               Did I, Charmian,
   Ever love Caesar so?

Charmian:
               O that brave Caesar!

Cleopatra:
   Be chok'd with such another emphasis,
   Say the brave Antony.

Charmian:
               The valiant Caesar!

Cleopatra:
   By Isis, I will give thee bloody teeth,
   If thou with Caesar paragon again
   My man of men.

Charmian:
             By your most gracious pardon,
   I sing but after you.

Cleopatra:

> My salad days,
> When I was green in judgment, cold in blood,

   The line-endings in Shakespeare's verse are actors' clues; they are like internal text coaches, offering wonderful ideas for how this or that thought might go or how to play this or that moment. But *must* you "breathe at the end of every line?" No. Your acting would be in thrall to a rule, and the freshness that brings performance to life would grow stale. The coded information buried in the language and the verse form is there to feed the creativity of the performer, to bring the flesh, blood and spirit of the character vividly into existence. Once the character is alive, with a brain and a heart full of human thoughts and feelings, that character will live and breathe on stage, re-born for each performance.

   If you are Richard III and you are in the penultimate chapter of your life, whipping up the lust for battle in your army, with Richmond's army within an arrow's flight, primed and ready to kill, your line-endings are spurs to your eloquence, seldom breathed transitions:

> Remember who you are to cope withal:
> A sort of vagabonds, rascals, and runaways;
> A scum of Bretons and base lackey peasants,
> Whom their o'er-cloyed country vomits forth
> To desperate adventures and assur'd destruction.
> You sleeping safe, they bring to you unrest;
> You having lands, and bless'd with beauteous wives,
> They would restrain the one, distain the other,
> And who doth lead them but a paltry fellow,
> Long kept in Bretagne at our brother's cost?
> A milksop! One that never in his life
> Felt so much cold as over shoes in snow.
> Let's whip these stragglers o'er the seas again,
> Lash hence these overweening rags of France,
> These famish'd beggars, weary of their lives—
> Who, but for dreaming on this fond exploit,
> For want of means, poor rats, had hang'd themselves.
> If we be conquer'd, let men conquer us!
> And not these bastard Bretons, whom our fathers
> Have in their own land, beaten, bobb'd and thump'd,
> And in record left them the heirs of shame.
> Shall these enjoy our lands? Lie with our wives?
> Ravish our daughters? Hark, I hear their drum.
> Fight, gentlemen of England! Fight, bold yeomen!
> Draw, archers, draw you arrows to the head!
> Spur your proud horses hard, and ride in blood;
> Amaze the welkin with your broken staves!
> *("Britaine" means Brittany, across the channel in France.)*

He probably starts relatively slowly, to gather his soldiers' attention, but if the political content of the oration supersedes the purpose, which is to rouse their fury, not only will his army lose heart but the play will die. The circumstances dictate that Richard speak this speech at fullest voice, with the pace increasing like a horse stretching into full gallop, charging the enemy. Following his "milk-sop" joke—a good orator will always try to win his audience with a laugh early on—the next four lines pick up in energy so that they are spoken on one breath. From "If we be conquered" to "heirs of shame" can easily happen on one breath, the pace accelerated by demagogic fury. "Shall these enjoy our lands?" may well arouse a shout from the soldiers, their rage redoubled by the questions, "Lie with our wives? Ravish our daughters?" And so on to the end.

As it is quite likely that some of you who are working with this book will be playing Messengers 1, 2 and 3 rather than Richard, and may feel that the pressure of racing on to the stage with a vital message which has to be delivered at break-tongue speed utterly precludes any application of the significance of line-endings, here is a favorite scene of mine from Act IV, Scene iv of *Richard III*. I will print it showing the way the spur or springboard of the line-endings can help you build the energy essential to the pace of the scene. I will also contribute my "side-coaching" and "stage directions" in order to suggest where the life of such a scene can be found:

(Enter a Messenger)
(you have ridden at a gallop for three hours, flung yourself off your horse and, on one breath, you gasp out the four lines)

Messenger:
    My gracious sovereign, now in Devonshire—
    As I by friends am well advertised—

                     - / - /

(the correct iambic pronunciation is ADVER|TIS|ED, or you can lengthen the "well" to fill out the beat and use contemporary pronunciation with an added emphasis on the middle syllable, -vert-)

    Sir Edward Courtney and the haughty *prelate*,
    Bishop of Exeter, his elder **brother**,
    With many more confederates, are in **arms.**

(Enter another Messenger [running])
(you start your message at the volume and energy pitch the first Messenger has ended on, and you build it. The "Guildfords" are formidable fighters. The opposition is swelling its ranks)

2nd Messenger: *(in one breath)*
    In Kent, my liege, the Guildfords are in **arms;**
    And every hour *more **competitors***
    Flock to the ***rebels,*** and their ***power*** grows ***STRONG***.

(Enter another Messenger)
(topping the first two Messengers—Good News!)

3rd Messenger:
My lord, the **army** of great ***Buckingham—***

Richard:
OUT ON YOU OWLS! NOTHING BUT SONGS OF *DEATH*?

(he strikes him)

3rd Messenger:
(let the blow arouse in you an appropriately seething reaction which fuels but does not overwhelm the good news. One breath, crackling with reigned in emotion)
The news I have to tell your *Majesty*
Is, that by sudden floods and fall of **waters,**
Buckingham's army is dispers'd and ***scatter'd***;
And he himself wander'd away ***ALONE***,
No man knows whither.

Richard:
(in one breath, excited by Buckingham's downfall)
I cry thee **MERCY**;
There is my ***purse***, to cure that blow of thine.
Hath any well-advised ***friend* proclaim'd**
Reward to him that brings the ***traitor in***?

3rd Messenger:
SUCH PROCLAMATION HATH BEEN MADE, MY LORD.

(Enter another Messenger)
(this messenger must bring back the urgency and present danger of war—fast and full volume)

4th Messenger:
SIR THOMAS **LOVEL** AND LORD MARQUESS **DORSET**
'TIS SAID, MY LIEGE, IN ***YORKSHIRE*** ARE IN ***ARMS***;

(does Richard go to strike him too? or has Messenger 4 come in early and seen the blow delivered to Messenger 3? I have seen a nicely human "moment" made at this line-ending)

BUT—

(he wards off Richard's reaction)

this good *comfort* bring I to your Highness:
The Breton **navy** is dispers'd by **TEMPEST**.

(and the story in the next six lines is very swiftly told in ONE BREATH)

Richmond, in Dorsetshire, sent out a **boat**
Unto the shore, to ask those on the ***banks***
If they were his **assistants**, yea or ***no***?—

> Who answer'd him they came from **Buckingham**
> Upon his party. **He**, mis***trust***ing them,
> **HOIS'D SAIL, *and made his course again*** for **BRETAGNE.**

Richard:

> **MARCH ON, MARCH ON, SINCE WE ARE UP IN *ARMS*:**
> **IF NOT TO FIGHT WITH *FOREIGN ENEMIES*,**
> **Yet to beat down these *REBELS* here at *HOME*!**

Messenger speeches are great acting practice. They depend for their efficacy upon as real a life for the messenger as for any of the "main" protagonists. Your Messenger must have a name, a trade, a childhood, a home, a family and a solid answer to "where am I coming from" and "what is my objective"—that real-life energy is vital to the playing of any character, vital to the playing out of the story on the stage.

Thus, both the Guthrie Rule and the Barton Rule are to be followed as guides to acting Shakespeare—not mutually exclusive, not absolute, but sophisticated instruments in the craft of verse-speaking.

9

◀▶ Verse and Prose ◀▶
Alternation

"You speak the prose twice as fast as the verse" was the first bit of advice I ever was given about how the handling of Shakespeare's verse and prose should be differentiated.

There is a germ of truth in that simple statement because, by and large, the content of the verse passages is emotionally charged, imagistic material to be savored and weighed, whereas we need not linger over the more linear, factual information which prose tends to convey. Prose is usually the preferred style of the lower classes in Shakespeare, and the form in which funny things are said. Most of the bawdy scenes are in prose. Verse, therefore, may be generally characterized as the form that suits the higher and more powerful emotions, prose the form that suits the domestic, often more vulgar content. Unfortunately for those who feel more secure when things are neatly categorized, Shakespeare up-ends the categorization often enough to make it necessary for us to keep a sharp ear open for the refinements of his usage.

Once more, it is in the earlier plays that Shakespeare adheres most to the convention: verse is "heightened" expression and prose "lower" expression, and in general, the histories are faithful to the class rule of thumb—the aristocracy speaks in verse, the proletariat in prose. The whole Cade rebellion, in *Henry VI, Part II*, is in prose. On the other hand, in *Henry VI, Part I*, Joan La Pucelle, the humble shepherdess, speaks in verse—perhaps because her heavenly guidance gives her poetic licence. In *Richard III* the only people who speak in prose are the two semi-comic murderers and the Citizens; elsewhere in the play, Messengers, Pages and Servants take on the heightened form of the verse that surrounds them—the patterns vary.

In *Two Gentlemen of Verona* the servants speak in prose, and when the "upper classes" banter or quarrel with them, they too speak prose. Prose reigns in *The Merry Wives of Windsor*, a comedy about the middle classes, but the sub-plot characters Fenton and Anne Page speak and are spoken to in verse, highlighting the difference between *true* love and the shenanigans of Falstaff and the Wives in the *guise* of love. The only other time verse enters this play is towards the end, when fairies are invoked and something magical enters the imaginations of Mistress Page and Mistress Ford as they devise Falstaff's punishment.

Let us say, then, that the "Rule" is this:

VERSE belongs to the upper classes and to moments of heightened emotion and elevated thought and imagination.

PROSE belongs to the lower classes, to comedy, bawdiness and domestic chat.

Now that we have a *rule* we can tackle the *variations and exceptions.*

One important variant is the tricky one of editorial decision. Quite often the First Folio has verse where a modern editor has mandated prose and *vice versa*. When you compare the choices offered by such a variant, remind yourself that you too are an editor and that your ability as an actor to feel below the surface form to the emotional content and internal meanings gives you the right to make your own decision as to whether the rendition "rises" and/or "deepens" or moves straight ahead to communicate information.

Another *caveat* is that verse is not always elevated and prose is not always prosaic. There is a great deal of poetic prose in Shakespeare's writing which soars on wings as strong as those of verse. There is also some deliberately bad verse. Costard, the Clown in *Love's Labour's Lost*, having rather successfully, he feels, traded naughty, rhyming quips with a gentleman, congratulates himself in bumpy hexameters which try to be elegiac:

> By my soul, a swain! a most simple clown!
> Lord, Lord, how the ladies and I have put him down!
> O' my troth, most sweet jests! most incony vulgar wit;
> When it comes so smoothly off, so obscenely, as it were, so fit.
> Armado to th' one side, O! a most dainty man,
> To see him walk before a lady, and to bear her fan!
> To see him kiss his hand! and how most sweetly 'a will swear!
> And his page o' t'other side, that handful of wit!
> Ah! heavens, it is a most pathetical nit.
> Sola, sola!
>
> *Act IV, Scene i*

Love's Labour's Lost is the play in which Shakespeare has the most fun with verse and language, ringing the changes on every possible convention and style and calling our attention to what he is doing a great deal of the time.

A decade or so later he inspires Hamlet with a vision of the world that sounds like great poetry, that *is* great poetry, but is spoken as prose:

> I have of late, but wherefore I know not, lost all my mirth, forgone all custom of exercises; and indeed it goes so heavily with my disposition that this goodly frame the earth seems to me a sterile promontory, this most excellent canopy the air, look you, this brave o'erhanging firmament, this majestical roof fretted with golden fire, why, it appeareth nothing to me but a foul and pestilent congregaton of vapours. What a piece of work is a man, how noble in reason! how infinite in faculties, in form and moving how express and admirable, in action, how like an angel, in apprehension, how like a god: the beauty of the world, the paragon of animals—And yet, to me, what is this quintessence of dust? Man delights not me—nor woman neither, though by your smiling you seem to say so.

Why is this in prose? Because he is speaking to Rosencrantz and Guildenstern? Because he is pulling the wool over their eyes and does not really believe what he is saying? Because this is the beginning of his loss of balance, his assumed or real madness? Because he is trying to give an appearance of ordinariness or he is too troubled to maintain a poetic flight? Whatever reason you find, there is a reason which must resonate within you as you play this moment in Hamlet's life. The images are deeply moving, the contrast between his knowledge of how beautiful and awe-inspiring the universe is and his loss of connection with that beauty perhaps reveals the collapse of his soul—perhaps that is "why" he speaks in prose.

Hamlet berates Ophelia passionately in prose. He gives his famous advice to the Players logically in prose. Immediately after that he speaks with deep feeling and honesty to Horatio, in verse, and thus finishes his conversation with his friend:

> They are coming to the play. I must be idle.
> Get you a place.

He next dallies dirtily with Ophelia in prose, and mocks Rosencrantz, Guildenstern and Polonius in prose; then when he is alone he shifts into terrifying verse:

> 'Tis now the very witching time of night,
> When churchyards yawn and hell itself breathes out
> Contagion to this world. Now could I drink hot blood,
> And do such bitter business as the day
> Would quake to look on. Soft, now to my mother.
> O heart, lose not thy nature. Let not ever
> The soul of Nero enter this free bosom;
> Let me be cruel, not unnatural.
> I will speak daggers to her, but use none.
> My tongue and soul in this be hypocrites:
> How in my words somever she be shent,
> To give them seals never, my soul, consent.

The poetic verse that follows between Claudius, Rosencrantz,

Guildenstern and Polonius maxintains the intensity of emotions that was built through the Closet scene and Polonius's death until Hamlet defuses the seriousness with his prose ragging of Rosencrantz and Guildenstern and his scintillating disquisition on the way of all flesh:

> King: Now, Hamlet, where's Polonius?
> Hamlet: At supper.
> King: At supper? Where?
> Hamlet: Not where he eats, but where a is eaten. A certain convocation of politic worms are e'en at him. Your worm is your only emperor for diet: we fat all creatures else to fat us, and we fat ourselves for maggots. Your fat king and your lean beggar is but variable service— two dishes but, to one table. That's the end.
> King: Alas, alas.
> Hamlet: A man may fish with the worm that hath eat of a king, and eat of the fish that hath fed of that worm.
> King: What dost thou mean by this?
> Hamlet: Nothing but to show you how a king may go a progress through the guts of a beggar.
> King: Where is Polonius?
> Hamlet: In heaven. Send thither to see. If your messenger find him not there, seek him i' th'other place yourself. But if indeed you find him not within this month, you shall nose him as you go up the stairs into the lobby.
> King *(to the Attendants)*: Go seek him there.
> Hamlet: A will stay till you come.

Prose is, in this play, not *less* than verse but *different*. And, yes, it should be spoken faster, at the rate of energetic conversation. The trick is that the pointing, the phrasing, must be as sophisticated as that of verse. In this regard, verse is easier to speak than prose because the rhythm is such a strong guide. Speaking prose well demands the recognition of and practice in figures of speech.

If indeed *The Tempest* was Shakespeare's last play, he was enchanted by then with the subtle play of verse form upon prose form, and he juggled them expertly to express shades upon shifting shades of mood and influence. Caliban is a suitably innocent student of eloquence to mirror these experiments and his "voice" is always ready for imprint, sometimes drawn prosaically downwards but mostly tending, even under the influence of alcohol, towards the redemption of poetic purity. It is in the conversations of Antonio and Sebastian that the tergiversations of prose and verse show those labyrinths of duplicity that are all too human. Gonzalo is a "good old man" but is easily sucked into prose when goaded by Antonio. In Act II, Scene i the conventional Gonzalo and Adrian are the butts of Antonio and Sebastian's sharp prose ribbing, interrupted by King Alonso's sorrowful verse dirge for the supposed drowning of his son. This is brought back down to earth by Sebastian's bad-tempered response and Gonzalo launches into a paean of the imagination which describes in verse a Utopian, back-to-the-land Paradise.

This is how Sebastian and Antonio puncture his fantasy and deflate the mood. Gonzalo's vision ends:

> No use of metal, corn, or wine, or oil;
> No occupation; all men idle, all;
> And woman too, but innocent and pure;
> No sovereignty;

Sebastian:
>   Yet he would be king on't.

Antonio:
> The latter end of his commonwealth forgets the beginning.

Gonzalo:
> All things in common nature should produce
> Without sweat or endeavor: treason, felony,
> Sword, pike, knife, gun, or need of any engine,
> Would I not have; but nature should bring forth,
> Of its own kind, all foison, all abundance,
> To feed my innocent people.

Sebastian:
> No marrying 'mong his subjects?

Antonio:
> None, man; all idle; whores and knaves.

Gonzalo:
> I would with such perfection govern, sir,
> T'excel the Golden Age.

Sebastian:
>   Save his Majesty!

Antonio:
> Long live Gonzalo!

Gonnzalo:
>   And,—do you mark me, sir?

Alonso:
> Prithee, no more: thou dost talk nothing to me.

Gonzalo: I do well believe your Highness; and did it to minister occasion to these gentlemen, who are of such sensible and nimble lungs that they alway use to laugh at nothing.

Antonio: 'Twas you we laughed at.
Gonzalo: Who in this kind of merry fooling am nothing to you: so you may continue, and laugh at nothing still.
Antonio: What a blow was there given!
Sebastian: An it had not fallen flat-long.

> Gonzalo: You are gentlemen of brave mettle; you would lift the moon
> out of her sphere, if she would continue in it five weeks without
> changing.

The only thing that can deflect this prosaic spiral downwards is magic, and here Ariel enters, laying a musical spell on the prose which puts Alonso, Adrian and Gonzalo to sleep and releases in verse form the passionately wicked ambitions of Antonio and Sebastian. Magic saves the King from their evil intent and, as verse prevails, it galvanizes the shipwrecked group to a further search in hope of finding the King's son alive.

Magical speech is nearly always in verse. The Boatswain is violently possessed by prose at the beginning of *The Tempest*, but at the end he has been visited by magic and speaks in verse.

Why does Prospero, who has spoken some of the most uplifting poetic verse ever conceived, finish his play with mundane quadrameter rhyming couplets? Is it because he has buried his magic, sold his dangerous soul-power for the doubtful security of temporal institutions and domestic comfort? There is something sad and desperate in the unadorned appeal:

> Now my charms are all o'er thrown,
> And what strength I have's mine own,
> Which is most faint: now,'tis true,
> I must be here confin'd by you,
> Or sent to Naples. Let me not,
> Since I have my dukedom got,
> And pardon'd the deceiver, dwell
> In this bare island by your spell;
> But release me from my bands
> With the help of your good hands:
> Gentle breath of yours my sails
> Must fill, or else my project fails,
> Which was to please. Now I want
> Spirits to enforce, Art to enchant;
> And my ending is despair,
> Unless I be reliev'd by prayer,
> Which pierces so, that it assaults
> Mercy itself, and frees all faults.
>   As you from crimes would pardon'd be,
>   Let your indulgence set me free.

No more art from the art master.

What I shall suggest in terms of exercise in the area of verse and prose is that you must *do it*. A classic scene where the shift from prose to verse releases a palpable surge in emotional temperature is Act I, Scene v of *Twelfth Night*. Viola, dressed as a man, begins her first encounter with Olivia with appropriately clever banter. Fulfilling her mission as Orsino's ambassador of love, she mixes male bravado with female wiles and gains a private audience. Her prose is a tribute to her intelligence:

> Viola: The rudeness that hath appeared in me have I learned from my entertainment. What I am, and what I would, are as secret as maidenhead: to your ears, divinity; to any other's, profanation.
> Olivia: Give us the place alone: we will hear this divinity.
>
> *(Exeunt attendants)*
>
> Now, sir, what is your text?
> Viola: Most sweet lady—
> Olivia: A comfortable doctrine, and much may be said of it. Where lies your text?
> Viola: In Orsino's bosom.
> Olivia: In his bosom? In what chapter of his bosom?
> Viola: To answer by the method, in the first of his heart.
> Olivia: O, I have read it: it is heresy. Have you no more to say?
> Viola: Good madam, let me see your face.
> Olivia: Have you any commission from your lord to negotiate with my face? You are now out of your text: but we will draw the curtain and show you the picture. *(Unveiling)* Look you, sir, such a one I was this present. Is't not well done?
> Viola: Excellently done, if God did all.

And here Viola plunges from her brain into a sea of emotion. Olivia keeps her witty intellect in control for a few more sentences and then is swept away by Viola's anguished eloquence. The prose gives way to verse as Viola sees how beautiful Olivia is and, identifying with Orsino's love, taps into the well of her own adoration for him, pouring her words of worship into his plea for Olivia's love. No wonder Olivia's frozen heart is melted and her poetic soul ignited.

> Olivia:
> 'Tis in grain, sir; 'twill endure wind and weather.
>
> Viola:
> 'Tis beauty truly blent, whose red and white
> Nature's own sweet and cunning hand laid on.
> Lady, you are the cruell'st she alive
> If you will lead these graces to the grave
> And leave the world no copy.

Olivia rejects the idea that having a baby is the only way to be responsible to future generations, and her brittle reply breaks through Viola's social manner to ignite a flaming anger, in the heat of which is forged an anthem to love's expressive power that turns Olivia's well-ordered world upside down.

> Olivia: O, sir, I will not be so hard-hearted: I will give out divers schedules of my beauty. It shall be inventoried, and every particle and utensil labelled to my will. As, item, two lips indifferent red; . . . item, one neck, one chin, and so forth. Were you sent hither to praise me?

Viola:
> I see you what you are, you are too proud:
> But if you were the Devil, you are fair.
> My lord and master loves you: O, such love
> Could be but recompens'd, though you were crown'd
> The nonpareil of beauty!

Olivia:
> How does he love me?

Viola:
> With adorations, fertile tears,
> With groans that thunder love, with sighs of fire.

Olivia:
> Your lord does know my mind, I cannot love him.
> Yet I suppose him virtuous, know him noble,
> Of great estate, of fresh and stainless youth;
> In voices well divulg'd, free, learn'd, and valiant,
> And in dimension, and the shape of nature,
> A gracious person. But yet I cannot love him:
> He might have took his answer long ago.

Viola:
> If I did love you in my master's flame,
> With such a suffering, such a deadly life,
> In your denial I would find no sense,
> I would not understand it.

Olivia:
> Why, what would you?

Viola:
> Make me a willow cabin at your gate,
> And call upon my soul within the house;
> Write loyal cantons of contemned love,
> And sing them loud even in the dead of night;
> Halloo your name to the reverberate hills,
> And make the babbling gossip of the air
> Cry out 'Olivia!' O, you should not rest
> Between the elements of air and earth,
> But you should pity me.

Olivia:
> You might do much.
> What is your parentage?

Olivia has lost her heart to the boy. The movement from prose to verse in this scene leads so graphically from the head to the heart that letting the forms into you will do half your acting for you. The shift from crackling prose to the piercing images and mounting rhythm of the verse will alter *you*, if you let it.

As your consciousness awakens to these contrasts, the artist in you will incorporate them into your palette. You will be fascinated that *As You Like It* is written almost entirely in prose, with Rosalind, a Duke's daughter, expounding upon the multifaceted prisms of love in elegantly architected prose while the shepherd Silvius and his love, Phoebe, sigh out their passions in verse. It is said that this play with its brilliant prose owes its style to the fact that two young boys came into Shakespeare's acting company who were exceedingly talented and who had just emerged from a school of law. In those days a legal training started early and incorporated all the refinements of oratorical technique. Students of law were trained to argue according to the rules of rhetoric, matching figures of speech and exercising their skills in debate, point against point, building, capping, scoring according to techniques learnt and respected as rules of a game.

Rosalind and Celia bandy argument and rally with each other like weathered gamesters and they are familiar with rhetorical persuasion. Their feelings constantly threaten to burst the seams of reasonable prose and occasionally do, but prose determines the characters of these sparkling women and gives them a special authority that dominates the play.

Much Ado About Nothing, written in the same period and therefore probably for one of the same two boys as Beatrice, deals also with a love story largely in the idiom of prose. Benedick argues against the madness of love in prose; he also falls in love in prose. Not until he asks the Friar to marry him to Beatrice does he lapse, with difficulty, into verse:

> Friar, I must entreat your pains, I think.

Friar:
> To do what, signior?

Benedick:
> To bind me, or undo me—one of them.
> Signior Leonato, truth it is, good signior,
> Your niece regards me with an eye of favor.

Leonato:
> That eye my daughter lent her. 'Tis most true.

Benedick:
> And I do with an eye of love requite her.

Leonato:
> The sight whereof, I think, you had from me,
> From Claudio and the Prince. But what's your will?

Benedick:
> Your answer, sir, is enigmatical:
> But for my will, my will is, your good will
> May stand with ours, this day to be conjoin'd
> In the state of honourable marriage;
> In which, good friar, I shall desire your help.

The time-stopping scene in Act IV, Scene i within which Beatrice and Benedick admit their love for each other is in prose, but in the final Act, for one minute, they speak to each other in verse, still sparring but caught in love:

Benedick:
Do not you love me?

Beatrice:
Why no, no more than reason.

Benedick:
Why then, your uncle, and the Prince, and Claudio,
Have been deceiv'd—they swore you did.

Beatrice:
Do not you love me?

Benedick:
Troth no, no more than reason.

Beatrice:
Why then my cousin Margaret, and Ursula
Are much deceiv'd, for they did swear you did.

Benedick:
They swore that you were almost sick for me.

Beatrice:
They swore that you were well-nigh dead for me.

Benedick:
'Tis no such matter. Then you do not love me?

Beatrice:
No, truly, but in friendly recompense.

At which ridiculous point, Leonato, Claudio and Hero leap into the breach with incontrovertible proof that Benedick and Beatrice love each other, exhibiting the poems they have written to each other.

Do Benedick and Beatrice then seal their troth-plight in soaring verse? No. Resorting to the prose that is true to their inimitable, cerebral, skeptical characters, they respond thus

Benedick: A miracle! Here's our own hands against our hearts. Come, I will have thee, but by this light, I take thee for pity.
Beatrice: I would not deny you, but, by this good day, I yield upon great persuasion; and partly to save your life, for I was told you were in a consumption.
Benedick: Peace! I will stop your mouth.

The alternations of verse and prose are packed with matter that guide the actor and director to artistic choices.

THE CONTEXTURE

◄►

◀▶

The information in the first nine chapters of this book provides a guide to the actor's experiential understanding of Shakespeare's text. Once one is familiar with the way in which the words and the structure yield their meaning, speaking Shakespeare will be natural and deeply satisfying. *Playing* Shakespeare will require all the art and craft that the skilled actor brings to the creation of any role.

Within these pages I state more than once that when you let the words play you they do half of your acting for you. That is true—but the other half must be fully supportive of the words or the words will only find a half-life. The meaning, emotion, action, character information that you absorb when you approach the text in the way that I have outlined is, to a large extent, the actor or director's homework—everything you must do before you get to rehearsal. In rehearsal, the world of the play, the story-line, the concept, will determine the particular shaping and direction that the textual information must undergo to forge credible life on stage for a particular production. The relationship of the individual actor to her/his words will transform in relationship to other actor/characters; they, in turn, transform as they relate to the events of the play and still more transformations may occur in response to a directorial concept. The presence of an audience is yet another energy that may influence the relationship of thought to word to character. The flexibility of living, breathing, thinking, feeling, real people on the stage is the goal of the work, and they cannot be brought to life solely through speaking the words that Shakespeare wrote.

It would be redundant for me to try to suggest the acting techniques that flesh out reality in performance when there are acting teachers and classes and schools enough to provide that training, but I would like to sketch in some of the framework that I have found useful when the focus of my work with actors goes beyond the immediate text and into the wider scope of performance. In my final chapters I offer some of the points of view I have found to be helpful to today's actors and some opinions that I hold which seem to me significant in terms of providing a context, or a "contexture," within which this approach to Shakespeare's work may be better understood. I present these points of view and opinions as provocation for further study and discussion.

Chapter Ten does not tell the actor everything s/he needs to study to create a character from Shakespeare's plays—it suggests a contexture within which to pursue the study; Chapter Eleven does not offer a clear picture of the place Shakespeare occupies in our theatre—it opens a particular argument about his relevance in our world; Chapters Twelve and Thirteen present some thoughts on the text and the author which are important to me.

The word "contexture" suggests an interweaving of thoughts and ideas and facts into a fabric that can absorb more thoughts and ideas and facts while providing some necessary referential vestments.

10

Today's Actor
◆▶ in Shakespeare's World ◆▶

With any play, film or television drama, the actors enter, to a greater or lesser degree of immersion, the world of that production. It is a world made up of both imagination and reality. Actors study the characters they are playing; they work out like boxers, train like Marines, walk the streets like prostitutes, spend days in hospitals or mental institutions, lose weight, put on weight so that they may observe and *become* the character within that character's environment.

It is the artistic goal of any real actor to become the person s/he is playing. The "serious" actor will admit this, though there are some actors who deny they are doing anything but having some fun and taking the money. The maddening thing for a hard-working student of acting is that there are almost as many very good superficial actors as very bad ones, and almost as many bad "serious" actors as good ones. Mystery remains at the core of acting.

In general, however, it is true to say that the art of imaginative transformation depends upon a craft that can organize a mass of detail: psychological, emotional and intellectual details feeding into action, behavior, motivation and objectives; physical details such as how the character walks, gestures, stands; vocal details—loud or gentle, monotone or wide-ranging, fast or slow, dialect; cosmetic details of hair and make-up. Imaginative transformation takes place as the actor's own psyche rearranges itself, as the neurotransmitters tune in to memory and desire, exposing old wounds and closeted fantasies— problematic in daily life but priceless in the alchemical craft through which the actor becomes the character.

It is the text of any play that sets the investigative and alchemical ball rolling, and most contemporary plays present actors with the task of representing people in the contemporary world. Twentieth-century plays mostly "hold the mirror up" to twentieth-century culture; the resources for studying our own world are visible and within our grasp. When the actor embarks on the Shakespearean adventure s/he must make a leap both of the imagination and the intellect, dig deeper into the storehouse of memory and fantasy to provide the stuff that will make credible the psychology and emotions of, for instance, Cleopatra, Macbeth, Queen Margaret, King Lear, Ophelia, Mercutio, Angelo, Isabella, Falstaff, and Messengers 1 through 16.

The marriage between the twentieth century and the Elizabethan age can be a richly satisfying one or it can be a clashing mismatch. It is rare for a twentieth-century directorial concept to hold the dramatic Elizabethan text in aural and visual balance, but while *Antony and Cleopatra* can only work within the context of Egypt and Rome, *Romeo and Juliet* is an archetypal love tragedy which seems to withstand being uprooted from time and place and grafted on to any location that maintains prejudice beyond human affections. I am not a purist; relocating Lear to Las Vegas, Hamlet to Bogota, the Macbeths to Haiti can work if the actors are good enough to flesh their characters to archetype, but it takes a deliberate act of oblivion to obliterate kingship and the moral exigencies of a belief in heaven and hell. Equally, it takes a deliberate act of understanding the Divine Right of Kings to make sense of, for instance, *Richard II*. This play, along with all the Histories, is a moral tale that moves from particular to universal meaning best when rooted in its true historical detail. Sometimes a modern-dress production works—sometimes it doesn't—but only after a director has fully entered Shakespeare's text within the context of Shakespeare's world can s/he legitimately experiment with time and place, so that incongruities may highlight rather than dilute the story the language tells.

The preceding chapters of this book have shown you how to mine the veins of information that lie beneath the surface of the text of Shakespeare's plays; from this information you will know much of your character's inner life. But without identification with that person's world your creation of his or her psyche will be anchorless. Offsprung from our mothers and fathers, we are creatures of our cultural environment and collective beliefs. Shakespeare's people behave and think in some ways that are common to our common humanity and within the scope of our imaginations, but in other ways they are foreigners. We must look for travel guides for our voyage into their world or we will get lost.

The concentric circles of existence that maintain and contain us, from the breath that animates us, to emotion, thought, body, voice, word, communication, community, city, country, nation, world, cosmos—all form and inform us implicitly. The concentric circles that formed and informed the Elizabethans must be observed and absorbed if the actor who plays the inhabitant of Shakespeare's

Elizabethan universe is to breathe, feel, move and speak with integrity. In Chapter Four I touched on the belief system, inherited from the Middle Ages, that implicitly still supported the ordinary lives of sixteenth- and seventeenth-century men and women.

The philosophy that saw man as a microcosm of the macrocosmic universe he inhabited, organized to withstand the constant threat of chaos by the strict order of the Great Chain of Being, formed an existential circle within which the psyches of Shakespeare's men and women had a particular logic. That embracing circle has been replaced in our world by a patchwork of communal philosophies stitched unevenly together by the political, economic, technological and psychological ideologies that inform the "civilized" cultures of the industrialized nations. Through the seams, the logic of Elizabethan life has seeped away. Embracing chaos may well be our spiritual destiny; we can either let this illumination blind us to the Elizabethans or we can train it as a spotlight from our time to theirs, tracing what we can of that lineage, in part abandoned and in part continued.

The political and psychological upheavals which have marked the twentieth century are similar in effect to those which shook the Elizabethan mind. Science and discovery were remeasuring and reorganizing the world as they had known it, and old beliefs argued with new ones. While in contemporary Western theatre the discoveries we expose are mostly personal, our likeness to the Elizabethans exists in a similar freedom of verbal expression—which is not, I hasten to add, to be confused with equal time on TV and locker-room profanity. Despite a continuing struggle with conflicting values and the responsibilities of freedom, we still have the language for honest, open communication. If we can see through the hypocrisies our culture fosters, we can walk and talk with Shakespeare on familiar ground.

Shakespeare's language is our passport to the Elizabethan world. It introduces us to the expansiveness and exuberance of the Elizabethan spirit. Compare the sheer extroverted verbosity of Shakespeare with the bleak introversions of Samuel Beckett and you will understand a great deal about the evolution and dissolution of Western identity in the last four hundred years. Beckett is the great dramatic poet of our century as Shakespeare was of his. His spare verse-prose, recording dislocation of thought and language and identity, is as true to us and as different in form and content from Shakespeare's confident verbosity as blue jeans are from farthingales. And yet, the encouraging fact about Shakespeare in the twentieth and twenty-first centuries is that it is the first time *since* Shakespeare's time that the plays can be fully realized.

Gary Taylor's *Re-Inventing Shakespeare* gives an overview of the treatment Shakespeare has received at the hands of theatre managers, publishers, editors and actors throughout the changing socio-political scene from then until now. Not until the twentieth century were the plays respected as what they are rather than what someone wished they were, but more than the restoration of literary integrity, it seems to me significant that not until the present time has society been in tune with the Elizabethans on a fundamental human plane, allowing today's actors to enter Shakespeare's world with a real chance of representing its essence accurately.

In brief, I would like to suggest the following areas of similarity between them and us: openness of expression, lack of false prudery, sexual explicitness, belief in astrology, fascination with the "dark side," determination to push the boundaries of science and human knowledge as far as they can go, and, in inverse ratio, the balance of the male and female principle, Jung's *animus* and *anima*. Whereas the Elizabethan man balanced a vigorous, athletic, outdoor existence with the cultivation of the "feminine" arts of music, dance, poetry and singing, today's women combine their sensitivity and affective values with vigorous authority in hitherto male arenas. Men and women can now understand and experience androgynous mind while retaining biological difference. If we can dust off some misconceptions and banish false reverence, Shakespeare's poetry and with it the life of his characters have more of a chance now of being really spoken and heard than for four hundred years.

The post-Elizabethan, post-Jacobean culture was Puritan. Pleasure was condemned, theatres closed, freedom of speech denied, dance and song forbidden. Those twenty years of Puritanical suffocation took three hundred years to heal. The Restoration opened the London stage again—to froth. The theatre fluctuated between babble and bubble and corrective moralization for another hundred years or so until the emotions, locked up in nineteenth-century manners, began to cry out for emancipation. Freud, tapping into unconscious motivation, was an influence in their liberation, and Chekhov and Ibsen, raging against the dying of the light, found a language that brought the stage back to life and into the twentieth century where it has wrestled with the challenge of clarifying the inner human journey with more success than that of expressing the drama of the world.

In many ways the Elizabethans were less muzzled by propriety than we still are. The sexual explicitness, the bawdy scenes in Shakespeare's plays, are only protected from today's Puritanism by the distancing nature of his language. To the educator, Shakespeare is "classical" and therefore as beyond reproach as beyond understanding much of the time. His "classic" stature earns him a place in the classroom canon, but for the schools the very passages which would endear him to teenagers—because of their genital, low-comedy references—are often deleted, confirming schoolchildren in their idea that Shakespeare is a snobby, academic waste of time.

This hypocrisy is supported by too many unintelligible Shakespearean productions posturing in yards of distancing costumes. The Elizabethans were not classical, boring or academic, and I long for the day when red and blue velvet is banned from the Shakespearean stage. However, there is one important lesson for the actor to learn from Elizabethan costume—the boldness of its wearers. Today's actor must exercise honesty and openness and confidence when s/he is to channel twentieth-century freedom of expression through the Elizabethan body and mind.

How confident those men must have been who puffed out their hips with ballooning knickers slashed with ribbons and bright colors, who emphasized their genital value with stiff codpieces and strutted their calf-muscles, as if bestriding the globe like Colossus. Both women and men propped up their necks with stiff, lacy collars so that they might never cease to gaze out above and beyond a common scope or droop in weak despondency. Women's stomachers, breast-plated with embroidery, jewelled with promise, V'd straight down to the pubic bone; and from each hip a small table, hung with curtains, swung out, underneath which it was perfectly possible to hide a lover should a husband return home inopportunely. Underwear was not a requirement under a farthingale.

The doorways that accommodated such clothing were wide, the mansions expansive. The harmonies that accommodated in song the generous passions of these broad-spirited people were rich and dense. Their dances would put most of us into traction. It is said that Queen Elizabeth danced six voltas, the most vigorously leaping social dance of all time (barring some Highland and Cossack dancing) before breakfast every day, a sixteenth-century version of aerobics that takes the breath away. Deodorant had not been invented, bathing was a weekly event, the bejewelled clothing could not be washed; so perfume was important.

Food was rich and abundant for the middle and upper classes. The entree at a dinner in 1552 for over a hundred people consisted of "sixteen raised pies, fifteen joints of beef, four of veal, three of pork (including a whole sucking pig), three geese, a brace each of partridge, teal, capons and coneys, a woodcock and one dozen larks, with a whole sheep and much else that night" (*Elinor Fettiplace's Receipt Book*, Hilary Spurling, Penguin Books, 1987). Sweetmeats, sallets (salads), preserves, conserves, puddings, tarts, fritters, buns and breads were flavored and garnished with almonds, rose petals, rose powder, saffron, coriander, crystallized fruits, orange water, marchpane and gilliflowers.

The five senses and all the appetites were abundantly nourished. We sorely underestimate and underplay the inhabitants of Shakespeare's plays when we behave "well," speak "well," move "nicely," stand and sit uniformly, and generally adopt a "style" that we erro-neously think to be "classical" because it is stiff and unreal, superfi-cially gracious and as far from ourselves as possible. We need to rec-ognize that our most fundamental selves are "classical," belonging as they do to a universal fabric of humanity. By reaching back we can liberate ourselves through the robust and creative lives of Shakespeare's men and women. Their clothes, their social habits, their food, their recreation and their homes all merit a voyage of dis-covery by today's actors—a voyage that must go as deep into their own inner being as it travels far back in time.

The exercise of awareness that is this book's intent can help you gain access to your larger, more robust and classical self, whose natu-ral language is poetry and heightened prose. The practice of that awareness may be slow and painstaking, like the careful scales and arpeggios with which a musician prepares to enter Beethoven's world, but sooner or later, so grounded, all care must be thrown to the winds and you must enter the living breathing life of your character in the story of the play.

Once you have laid down the tracks, you let the train gather speed towards its destination. The animation and speed of real living and talking will be the result of imprinting one's cortex with the minutiae of the text. Speaking Shakespeare in an excited and energized way is not so much the goal as it is the natural result of taking everything to bits and building it back into your own system so that the thoughts and feelings are as if authored by you, spoken—in the largest sense of the word—with "authority."

The music of the vowels and consonants serves the words and images, the words and images serve the phrases, the phrases serve the meaning, the meaning is danced by the rhythm, the rhythm is chan-nelled by the form—all of this serves the character's objectives and actions and all of those serve the story. The characters in Shakespeare's stories are products of their time as we are of ours, and for their lives to have authenticity on stage today's actor must not be afraid to inhabit fully the personal, psychological, political, philosoph-ical, passionate reality of Shakespeare's world.

11

◀▶ Shakespeare's Voice ◀▶ in Today's World

At some point in their careers most English-speaking actors will confess to the thrill they get playing Shakespeare or admit they have a longing to experience the thrill and I hope that this book will help both the veteran and the novice to fulfill their artistic ambitions. But some feel they must justify the indulgence of their own artistic appetite by checking out Shakespeare's relevance in today's world. As a teacher of Shakespeare I too must satisfy my social conscience and constantly question, and constantly answer with evolving insight, the value of supporting this cultural icon. It must be clear by now that I believe that if the voices of today's actors are true to his voice, Shakespeare will illuminate our time as thoroughly as he did his own. In this chapter I would like to range more widely over some of the reasons I think Shakespeare should remain at the center of our culture, not as a museum relict but an active contemporary. My interest focuses on Shakespeare's writings in relation to questions of language, culture and identity. Shakespeare's stories are enlightening as stories but the story in which Shakespeare and the English language co-star is a drama with no foreseeable end.

English is rapidly becoming the first global language. Trade and convenience combine to make this so. English is convenient because it is such an adaptable language; versions of English are used in several countries where the multiplicity of local languages make national communication almost impossible without a *lingua franca*, and English, the language of colonization, has become the preeminent language of international trade and politics. English is also the international language of computers. International air traffic control is conducted in English. International economic reality presumably underlies the Japanese government's mandate that every Japanese schoolchild must be literate in 7000 English words by the year 2000. *The Story of English* tells us that at least 750 million people use

English in the world today, of whom barely half speak it as their mother tongue. "Some estimates have put that figure closer to one billion. Whatever the total, English at the end of the twentieth century is more widely scattered, more widely spoken and written, than any other language has ever been" (*The Story of English*, McCrum, Cran and MacNeil, Faber and Faber, BBC Publications, 1986).

In the teaching of English as a second language, Shakespeare's plays are often used as guides to understanding the language on a creative level rather than as a purely utilitarian tool. However, there are strong arguments both in postmodern criticism and in the multicultural movement that the deification of Shakespeare as the genius of the English language bolsters a conscious or unconscious Western, white, cultural-supremacist attitude.

A large part of the power of Shakespeare's writing lies in his archetypal stories and characters, and his plays have been translated into and performed in all of the major languages in the world. Countries which are secure in their own cultural heritage explore these stories and characters without fear of losing their identities. Kurosawa's *Throne of Blood* and *Ran* take *Macbeth* and *King Lear* and transplant them brilliantly into Japanese culture. Ingmar Bergman's *Hamlet* is Swedish. Kozintsev's *King Lear* is Russian, more accurately Georgian. The inspiration that comes from the original does not depend on Elizabethan clothes and music to bring it to life. Shakespeare translated is not a threat but a resource. His themes weather well and travel well.

However, the sheer poetic power with which Shakespeare wields words intensifies the drama tenfold when these stories are told in their original language. In English-speaking countries there are many citizens whose mother-tongue is English but whose ethnic origin is not, and for them Shakespeare may feel like a threat. He can seem a threat to less vocal cultures which, transplanted into an English-speaking world, have lost their own languages and with them a direct link to their ancient traditions. Tradition, culture, language are sources of identity, and when one's identity is shaky one feels powerless. It is not entirely illogical to imagine that if the powerful, secure English of Shakespeare were to be removed, other cultures might better blossom. It has been argued that teaching Shakespeare in the schools perpetuates a prejudice favoring the Western cultural heritage over other equally valuable and venerable traditions, that it is detrimental to other cultures to insist that African-Americans, Asian-Americans, Native Americans, and Hispanic-Americans study Shakespeare because he co-opts their imaginations and separates them from their own cultural heritages.

Shakespeare can certainly be taught and studied in such a way that the cultural mainstream reduces all other sources to trickles. But I would hope that an educational way of life can evolve that allows the co-existence of many cultures and that, within an English-speaking community, the humanity of Shakespeare's plays is recognized and his language heard. If the plays are spoken and performed, not academically studied, and if the sounds of the words and the rhythms of the language are felt, Shakespeare's voice will call to the voices of eloquence that live in everyone, encouraging their hearts and lungs and resonance. His voice is the voice of individuality, of iconoclasm. It comes from the soul of the English language, and once the soul of the language has been discovered by the speaker, the soul and voice of that speaker is liberated to tell her or his own story.

Within an English-speaking country, diverse cultures originally maintained in diverse languages will have to express themselves in English if they are to have any widespread currency. But not just one kind of English. Not just one grammar, because English is not contained by grammar; and not just one spelling, because English spelling changes all the time. Rather an adaptable English, new-coined again and again, rooted in its origins and branching out into as many different versions as there are different people and different cultures.

Shakespeare's stories tell the stories of the everyday lives of millions of people who suffer painfully the effects of an unequal society, people who feel powerless in the face of the random cruelty of poverty. The fact that the stories are embodied in kings and queens and placed in Rome, or ancient Britain, or Denmark, is the least important element in them. The most important element is that Shakespeare provides a speaking language in which vast pain can be articulated—the *lacrimae rerum*. And his articulation is as accessible to the educationally underprivileged as it is to the college graduate. Time and again I have seen, heard and felt Shakespeare's words enter and restore power to a boy or a girl, a woman or a man, whose sense of worth has been obliterated by childhood abuse, social inequality or racial bigotry. This happens *not when they read Shakespeare, not when they hear Shakespeare, but when they speak the words themselves*. They speak the words and hear their stories told, recognizing that their experiences are part of the fabric of human experience. The words make them part of society when they had felt themselves to be apart from it. The story is no longer hidden, an internal nightmare or private shame, but externalized, seen, heard by a community that recognizes these stories as its own.

Speaking Shakespeare leads us to the sources of our own power because we find a language which expresses the depths of our experience more fully, more richly, more completely than our own words can. Pain, which seemed inexpressible, *can* be expressed. In its expression, feeling returns, and with feeling comes renewed life. It is a sort of alchemy. Unexpressed pain poisons the system. It congeals and turns to lead within us. It anaesthetizes. But words can begin to penetrate scar tissue and drain the poison from the wounds. And poetic words do more. They heighten inner consciousness, operating like ultra-sound or laser surgery. They stimulate the energy states that enable emotions to release.

Shakespeare's words are channels that allow anger to flow until it gives way to grief; the expression of grief is the admission of the loss of love. Experiencing the loss of love admits the potential for love to be reborn and with it the option of joy. The poison of pain can transform to a life-restoring elixir through the alchemy of speaking Shakespeare's words.

The words and the stories they tell are big enough to carry the huge, calamitous events that shatter the lives of ordinary people. It is not just the meaning of the words that convey these events, it is the sounds. The vibration of the sounds travels through the bodies, meeting and merging with the vibrations of the feelings. Once having experienced the psycho-physical possibility of expression through Shakespeare's words, one's own voice and one's own language are stimulated. The inner, psychic world discovers the means by which it can reach the outer world, can penetrate other psyches. This process might be likened to jump-starting a car when the battery has died, and when the engine starts humming on its own, the journey into relationships with oneself, with others and with the world is eloquently enlivened.

Playing Shakespeare is therapeutic at all ages and I am often more moved by Shakespeare performed by 8th graders or high schoolers than by professional actors. When young actors have been led to an enjoyment of the text that helps them understand it as their own, there is a raw energy and direct truthfulness in their acting that create immediacy and excitement. The idea of theatre as therapy is no different from the ancient idea of theatre's healing role, its ability to provide catharsis within a community. "The central meaning [of *catharsis*] is roughly one of 'clearing-up' or 'clarification,' i.e. of the removal of some obstacle (dirt, or blot, or obscurity, or admixture) that makes the item less *clear* than it is in its proper state . . .The medical use to designate purgation is a special application of this general sense: purgation rids the body of internal impediments and obstacles, clearing it up. And the connection with spiritual purification and ritual purity appears to be another specialized development, given the strong link between such purity and physical freedom from blemish or dirt" (*The Fragility of Goodness*, Martha Nussbaum, Cambridge University Press, 1986).

Nussbaum goes on to elaborate on the function of pity and fear in the illumination of who we are, the emotional elements in perception, judgment and ethical choice. Her definition of *katharsis* helps to explain why, when *anyone* speaks Shakespeare's words and enacts his stories, light shines into the obscure corners of the human condition and an option to clear them up emerges. This clarification can occur on a personal level, in the school classroom or upon the professional stage. This book is dedicated to the pursuit of *catharsis* and the consequent therapy/healing. Good theatre is the objective of the work. The highest quality art and the deepest healing go hand-in-hand.

The state of the art of theatre in the final decade of the twentieth century leaves much to be desired. Live theatre has yielded pride of place in the performing arts to film and television and now ranks, in my opinion, well below music, dance, visual art and film. I believe that this is so partly because the instruments of live theatre—voice, body, emotion, intellect, words—have been overshadowed by the grandiloquence of technology. Miking "live" performance has become so accepted that actors apparently need not train their voices at all as part of their craft. The sophistication of microphone technology is such that an actor with a "weak" voice can play opposite an actor with a "strong" voice and, in a 1500-seat auditorium, both actors will be heard equally well. There might be some question about the imbalance of acting energies but, given that audiences are conditioned to listening to technologically adjusted sound all the time from their television sets, they may not notice. David Mamet, in an essay entitled "Against Amplification," expresses as well as anyone could why this is a matter of concern:

> Let's be serious for a moment. If you are an actor and can't make yourself heard in a thousand-seat house, you're doing something wrong—you should get off the stage and go home. Go back to voice class or wherever your instincts lead you, but get off the stage.
>
> Dramatic works are meant to be *acted*. They concern themselves with commitment and its consequences.
>
> They cannot be delivered conversationally and then amplified— that is not *drama*, that is *television*.
>
> Any actor, producer, writer, or director who thinks that transistors and circuitry can fill the gap between the ability of the artist and the needs of the audience is degrading all concerned.
>
> The correct, necessary, and only amplification needed in the theater is the commitment of the artist (and here I mean primarily that of the writer and the actor)—commitment sufficient, if the case is that they cannot be heard, to send the one back to the typewriter and the other back to the studio . . .
>
> The actor who permits him- or herself to be miked on the dramatic stage is destroying both art and livelihood—destroying the profession in much the same way that television has, which says to the artist, "It's sufficient for you just to get up in front of the cameras and say the lines."

The art of theater is action. It is the study of commitment. The word is an act. To *say* the word in such a way as to make it heard and understood by all in the theater is a commitment—it is the highest art to see a human being out on a stage speaking to a thousand of his or her peers saying, "These words which I am speaking are the *truth*—they are not an approximation of any kind. They are the God's truth, and I support them with my life," which is what the actor does on stage.

Genuinely alive theatre is unmistakable and unmatchable both as entertainment and enlightenment, and there are unavoidable disciplines involved in accomplishing the art that can claim to be Live Theatre. Here, I am suggesting that "truth of the art" can be found in a disciplined dedication first to developing a voice that can tell the truth, and then in searching out what truths Shakespeare intended to tell. The clues to the search are laid out in the analysis of words and the forms of language that Shakespeare uses. To some it might seem that this is nothing but an old-fashioned adherence to old ways that have little to do with today's mentality. Insistence on the rule of words and the structure of the text is on the surface the very thing to condemn because it can appear to make an icon out of Shakespeare and have as its goal "museum" performance clad in ruffs and codpieces and spouting verse. In practice, exactly the opposite occurs. The more deeply the roots of the language are penetrated and the more deeply the roots of the twentieth-century human being are connected to the language, the more individual, idiosyncratic and relevant will be the resultant performance.

Paradoxical as it may seem, the more truly Shakespeare's text is spoken, the more diverse will be its utterance by different speakers if the speaker is true to her/himself. The same clues to understanding a particular passage in Shakespeare can be conveyed to ten different actors and ten different interpretations will emerge because ten different biographies supply the psychological ground that receives these clues and processes them into an emotionally accurate rendition. Thus, without imposing a "concept," fresh and culturally apposite interpretations can emerge from the combination of being wholly true to oneself and wholly true to Shakespeare's text. No actors playing Juliet and Lord and Lady Capulet today could play the scene in which Juliet is brutally berated by her father without being conscious of the issue of parental abuse, either from their own experience or from the climate of our times. Knowledge of the psychological damage inflicted by it must be implicit in any contemporary enactment of this scene. Juliet is first betrayed by a mother who fails to support her daughter's determination not to marry a man she does not love:

Lady Capulet:
Here comes your father, tell him so yourself,
And see how he will take it at your hands.

And later:

> I would the fool were married to her grave.

Juliet's rebellion sparks savagery in her father:

Capulet:
>   Mistress minion, you,
> Thank me no thankings nor proud me no prouds,
> But fettle your fine joints 'gainst Thursday next
> To go with Paris to Saint Peter's Church,
> Or I will drag thee on a hurdle thither.
> Out, you green-sickness carrion! Out, you baggage!
> You tallow-face!

Lady Capulet:
>   Fie, fie. What, are you mad?

Juliet:
> Good father, I beseech you on my knees.
> Hear me with patience but to speak a word.

Capulet:
> Hang thee young baggage, disobedient wretch!
> I tell thee what—get thee to church a Thursday
> Or never after look me in the face.
> Speak not, reply not, do not answer me.
> My fingers itch. Wife, we scarce thought us blest
> That God had lent us but this only child;
> But now I see this one is one too much,
> And that we have a curse in having her.
> Out on her, hilding.
>
>   . . .
> hang! Beg! Starve! Die in the streets!

The mother's final words are:

> Talk not to me, for I'll not speak a word.
> Do as thou wilt, for I have done with thee.

To play this in a removed style that hides the violence behind a smokescreen of "period" behavior would be patently untrue.

Equally, I do not think that today's young actor playing Miranda in *The Tempest* could be unaware of the patriarchal assumptions dominating Prospero's behavior toward her and everyone else. We first see Miranda full of anguish at the sight of the storm and the suffering of those she saw drown. She is in a state of high empathy and longs for the power to do good:

> Had I been any god of power, I would
> Have sunk the sea within the earth, or ere
> It should the good ship so have swallow'd, and
> The fraughting souls within her.

Prospero assures her that there is no harm done and that he is in full control of everything that happened. He then proceeds to tell her a very long story about himself at the end of which he puts her to sleep calling it "a good dullness." His magic arranges for Miranda, innocent of the ways of the world, to fall in love with Ferdinand, able to give her heart to him without guile:

> Hence, bashful cunning!
> And prompt me plain and holy innocence!
> I am your wife, if you will marry me;
> If not, I'll die your maid:

Our final view of Miranda is when she is playing chess with Ferdinand, a game that depends entirely on guile and intellectual sharpness. The ensuing four lines strike a chill to the heart:

Miranda:
> Sweet lord, you play me false.

Ferdinand:
>   No, my dearest love,
> I would not for the world.

Miranda:
> Yes, for a score of kingdoms you should wrangle,
> And I would call it fair play.

She has learnt already the wiles of woman in society. When she looks around at the assembled company of would-be murderers and deluded princes she says:

> O, wonder!
> How many goodly creatures are there here!
> How beauteous mankind is! O brave new world,
> That has such people in't!

She has joined their level of consciousness and lost for ever her true self. Twentieth-century consciousness of psychology and politics offers overtones and resonance to Shakespeare's voice when his parents and children, rulers and subjects speak to each other in his words activated with the breath of our lives.

Hierarchy and class structure are personified in Shakespeare's plays in Kings and Queens, Dukes, lords, gentlemen and gentlewomen, merchants, captains and lieutenants, soldiers, servants and simple country folk. In the United States today, within what is said to be a classless society, such hierarchies and status variations still exist. Money has replaced birth as the determinant of who is up and who is down, who is in and who is out, and the opportunity to switch status has made nonsense of the Great Chain of Being, but status is a fact of our lives and we do not have to make a big leap of imagination to know how to behave as a King or a courtier or a servant. It's a question of who has the power, in what degree, and who does not, to what degree. When we bring to Shakespeare's hierarchical world our own experience of feeling powerful or powerless, psychologically and socially and politically, we breathe real life into what might otherwise seem a distant and unfamiliar social structure.

One must not diminish the size of Shakespeare's expression in order to accommodate contemporary truth, but rather must allow personal and contemporary truth to expand to be given the fullest life in Shakespeare's expression. Our present-day issues of economic inequality, race, prejudice, corruption in high places—political intrigue, family squabbles, murder for gain or passion—are all living in Shakespeare's plays. To understand another culture deeply, one must understand one's own, and through the absorption of the language and the meaning of the plays we plumb the depths and scale the heights of our culture.

Actors of cultural origins other than the Greco-Roman/Western one will not be disappointed in meeting Shakespeare's language on this organic level. The absorption of the sounds and rhythms of another language deep into one's living systems puts one on the path to an empathic understanding of all cultures. Multiculturalism at its best celebrates difference and is not competitive, though multiculturalism translated into equal rights is a painfully divisive issue within the theatrical profession as elsewhere. However, there is more and more agreement that for the classics, cultural diversity on the stage is a good thing.

Theoretically, right-minded people know that the classics should reveal to the audience a universal message plumbed from depths reverberating deep below national or racial distinctions. They know that holding the mirror up to today's nature means reflecting on stage the racial and ethnic riches of the world we live in. Shakespeare no longer rings true when presented only through a white cast speaking homogenized English. Mono-cultural Shakespearean productions are not only false but dull. Does this mean that Shakespeare is no longer valid, or that we must bridge the cultural divides and forge an alliance between his truths and the truthful resonance of different cultural voices?

A present-day dilemma in the English-speaking theatre is this: on one hand, there is a battle being fought for nontraditional casting; on the other hand, actors who belong to ethnic or racial traditions other than white and/or Western are torn between a desire to play the "classics" and a longing to be true to their own cultural roots. They are often wary of training for Shakespeare because they feel such training will seduce them away from their true selves.

It would be folly for me to pretend I can resolve this dilemma. However, the fear of folly cannot prevent me from offering this point of view. If an African-American or Asian-American or Hispanic actor goes to London, learns to speak with an English accent and studies with the Royal Shakespeare Company how to play Shakespeare in the very best way that England can teach, s/he will have acquired the style but not the substance of the plays. If that same actor, recognizing the unique artistic excitement to be found in playing Shakespeare, is willing to undergo the rigorous training it takes to free her/his voice from inhibition and limitation so that it has the two to three octaves necessary to express the full gamut of emotion and all the subtleties and nuances of thought, and is then able to explore the anatomy of words and the forms of language not as the outer clothing of style but as the inner guide to understanding, s/he will marry Shakespeare's words to the roots of African-American English, Asian-American English, Hispanic-American English or Native American English, and will liberate Shakespeare from the shackles of a narrow Anglo-Saxon tradition into the wide universal arena where his archetypal works find new life.

Both the United States and Britain have rapidly growing interracial populations. It is estimated that within the next twenty years the United States will no longer be predominantly white. Does this mean that Shakespeare will have had his day? Or does it mean that, with English still the accepted national language, he will be even more vital to our understanding of each other? Will Spanish be an equally important language? Could we look forward to the soul of the Spanish language communing with the soul of the English language through the plays of Lope de Vega and the plays of William Shakespeare, so that we may find mutuality in our common breath and common relationship to the earth we inhabit? Will the cultures that have preserved oral traditions into the age of technology be able to join and enliven the written cultures? Does the new vitality of the English language in African-American writing have to deny the old vitality of the English language in Shakespeare? Could not all these cultural expressions, old and new, oral and written, seek to express the soul of human beings so that the souls of other human beings may hear and understand and join together?

The debate will rage and time will be the referee, but meanwhile I am convinced that the evolution of a civilized humanity that revels in the different strands of our interwoven cultures, repudiates homogeneity and embraces otherness, should argue *for* Shakespeare's achievement not against it. As the global village extends its boundaries to include our own neighborhoods, the sound and sense of the geniuses of other cultures are heard and seen and tasted and felt. When we receive these stimuli on the level of spirit we can only be enlarged, and for those of us who speak the English language, Shakespeare is a powerful guide to our spirit life and empathic consciousness. Shakespeare does not belong in a museum or a library, he belongs on the streets of the global village, hobnobbing with the other cultural storytellers and spirit guides. We need past guides and present guides and future guides to help us find a collective global consciousness that reminds us that we breathe air, bear children, weep for our losses, laugh at jokes, sing and die together on this planet— and with this planet.

12

◆► Which Voice? *The Texts* ◆►

Shakespeare's voice has been preserved and delivered to us in words on a page. Typescript. In this book I have tried to show you ways in which you, the actor, can penetrate beneath the print and reach the voice itself—a voice made up of breath and vibration and emotion, borne by rhythm and pitch in the vessel of the verse through the waves of sound to our ears and hearts.

Who were the middlemen between Shakespeare's voice and ours? Who set the type in the early seventeenth century? Who composed the Folios? Who put the Quartos together? And who has been editing these scripts for the more than three hundred fifty years since then? What do we have in our hands when we go out and buy a copy of the Shakespeare play we are about to rehearse? What are we to do about the fact that the scholars have now come up with two "authentic" versions of *King Lear*?

These are not questions which I am in any position to answer. A major industry exists that is sustained by the detective work done to track down compositors, compute word and rhythm variants, and analyze stylistic inconsistencies. The only real guarantee is that this scholarly industry will continue to flourish as will the controversies surrounding it. While the scholars come up with intriguing alternatives for this word or that word, the actor must not be lightly seduced away from her/his choice, whose study should be the clarification and development of character.

Today's actor is a beneficiary of the research, in that there are several editions of the plays to choose from when s/he begins serious study. Different directors, teachers and actors have their different favorites; most work from more than one edition. All serious Shakespeareans refer to the First Folio and some swear by it as by the Bible.

The First Folio edition of Shakespeare's plays published in a large handsome volume is now available to anyone who can afford to buy it. The First Folio is venerated by actors because legend has it that secrets of the actual performance readings of Shakespeare's actors are encoded in the punctuation, the spellings and the capitalizations of the Folio script. Some simple lessons in decoding will yield much, and a very sophisticated deciphering is available (see the end of this chapter). When I was a student, my teacher Michael MacOwan, who owned a First Folio that we handled with reverence (they were rare and precious at that time), told us that the actors themselves relayed Shakespeare's words to the compositors for publication. Periods, semi-colons, colons and commas indicated their thought patterns and breath patterns; words spelt differently indicated the relative emphases placed upon them; and a capital letter at the beginning of a word showed its importance in the phrasing and pointing of meaning. We were listening in on the readings of Shakespeare's first actors. Although modern scholarship has shown that the legend may be apocryphal, actors revel in the detailed acting information that can be gained from a close reading of First Folio clues.

For those interested in scholarship for working purposes, I would like to recommend some modern editions that I have found useful, and also alert you to a future First Folio publication. The *Riverside Shakespeare* is as comprehensive a Complete Works as is currently on the market. I like the Arden Shakespeare single paperback editions because they have excellent comparative notes at the bottom of every page. And I like the Signet and the Pelican because they are easy to handle on the rehearsal floor, well set out on the page, with good print. *The New Cambridge Shakespeare* is an easy-to-read text with simple notes and theatrical illustrations, and *The Oxford Shakespeare* paperback series provides a working text with excellent scholarship and notes. The Oxford *William Shakespeare: The Complete Works* (which comes in a modern-spelling version and a so-called original-spelling version) is of little use to the actor as it omits scholarship and notes and leaves its "updated" editing unexplained.

You will get a great deal of history and textual information in the Riverside, wonderful illustrations and notes on the text which show the variations in the texts of the Folios and Quartos. I quibble with many of the editorial choices of words in the actual text which often seem calculated to make it *less* likely that the audience will understand what is being said rather than *more*, but on balance it is a treasure-trove.

The Arden editions are a little irritating in rehearsal because they offer so many variants in the notes at the bottom of the page that there is often only a third of the page left for the text itself. But it comes close to a handy version of a Variorum (a scholarly, hard-to-find volume giving every available editorial choice and offering lengthy interpretations of disputed passages by critics and scholars).

I still have a tattered *Complete Works* from my drama school days, edited by Peter Alexander, published in 1952 with a scanty Glossary in the back and no great compendium of notes, and I realize how deeply

I am conditioned by that when I correct an actor on a word s/he has said in a Shakespeare speech only to be shown that word in the Riverside text. As I have already complained, I seldom agree with the Riverside choice and I wince when a well-known speech is "upgraded" by corrective scholarship.

For instance, I cannot understand the argument for "sallied" in Hamlet's first great soliloquy. Riverside has "sallied" and Arden has "sullied." The old editions have "solid." "Sallied" is First and Second Quartos, "solid" is First Folio and "sullied" is an editorial amendment by Wilson. Hamlet is numb and almost dumb with grief and rage at his father's murder and his mother's quick remarriage. The actor, embodying the words, will discover from the first two lines of the soliloquy that he feels literally frozen:

> O that this too too solid flesh would melt,
> Thaw and resolve itself into a dew . . .

To use "sallied" distances the understanding of the audience; to use "sullied" is a cerebration inappropriate to the emotional moment. Wishing that his too solid flesh would thaw and become dew tells us that he wants to weep but cannot.

One other example of a modern emendation of an earlier editorial choice that always makes me jump is when Lady Anne is cursing Richard III over the dead body of Henry VI. She says, in the Riverside and the Arden:

> More direful hap betide that hateful wretch
> Than I can wish to wolves—to spiders, toads,
> Or any creeping, venom'd thing that lives.

"Wolves" is First Folio, but Peter Alexander chose for his edition the word found in the Quartos:

> More direful hap betide that hated wretch
> Than I can wish to adders, spiders, toads
> Or any creeping, venom'd thing that lives.

Adders are venomed and creep, wolves belong to another order of being. The actor's choice, knowing that creeping, poisonous creatures are closest to hell and that Richard is a devil, a minister of hell to Lady Anne, will surely find "adders" more aptly venomous than "wolves" in the creation of her curse. The actors playing Hamlet and Lady Anne, as they read the above words, should not feel obliged to follow my counsel—they have access to the possibilities and will make their choice.

So this is the dilemma of the actor and the director: how to make use of scholars and editors without being in thrall to them; how to make educated, artistic choices that support their own interpretations, not that of the scholars; and how to find the material from which to make the decisions without having to go back to school for a year or employ a dramaturg and three assistants to do research. The problem is that new editions of Shakespeare's plays are often at several editorial removes from the original and that the First Folio "Bible" is hard to decode and does not always make the best sense.

Neil Freeman, currently on the faculty of the University of British Columbia, Vancouver, is for many actors the best champion of the First Folio. He has done exhaustive work on the interpretation of Folio punctuation, spelling variations, capitalizations, line variants, verse and prose variants, and the analysis of rhetorical devices. All of this clarifies the inner and outer world of the actor—her/his thoughts, emotions and actions. Freeman will supply the actors' and directors' needs in spectacular fashion with the publication of First Folio versions of the whole canon in compact, paperback, single edition, "user-friendly" acting texts.

The Folio Scripts, as Freeman's texts are called, are designed for theatre people. Printed on an 8 x 11 page, the opposite page is left blank for working notes. Based on the First Folio only, they are in modern print and offer all significant Quarto and other Folio variants in footnotes. Line structure alternatives are shown, significant punctuation is in bold print, and rhetorical development is visually presented. Two line-numbering systems are shown—one for the Norton facsimile and the other for the *Riverside Shakespeare* edition for easy cross-reference. Visual devices allow the reader to make judgments between split-line choices, between Folio line-structuring and modern line-structuring, and they show where the Folio is in prose and modern editions in verse or *vice versa*. All spellings and capitalizations are explicated.

With this in one hand and a modern edition in the other, the actor will have all s/he needs to know about the text. For the director, there is yet another possibility. The Freeman/Nichols scripts (Neil Freeman is scholar/editor/actor-coach/director and researcher, Jane Nichols is the enlightened patron whose financial contribution facilitated the work) can be purchased on floppy disk so that, working with other editions, a director may cut and paste together her or his own edition and print it up for any particular production. This might seem heretical, but people have always rewritten, rearranged, revised, cut and reshaped Shakespeare, so he will certainly survive the word processor. As of this writing half the plays for *The Folio Scripts* have been completed.

Here, to give you a hint of the kind of detailed textual analysis the Folio affords in Neil Freeman's handling, is a reproduction from *King Lear*.

Scena Tertia

Enter Gonerill, and Steward

Gonerill	Did my Father strike my Gentleman* for chi- ding of his Foole?[1]
Steward	I Madam.
Gonerill	By day and night, he wrongs me, every howre He flashes into one grosse crime, or other, That sets us all at ods: Ile not endure it; His Knights grow riotous, and himselfe upbraides us On every trifle. When he returnes from† hunting, I will not speake with him, say I am sicke, If you come slacke of former services, You shall do well, the fault of it Ile answer[2].
Steward	He's comming Madam, I heare him.
Gonerill	Put on what weary negligence you please, You and your Fellowes: I'de have it come to question; If he distaste it, let him to my Sister, Whose mind and mine I know in that are one, Remember what I have said. }
Steward	Well Madam.
Gonerill	And let his Knights have colder lookes among you*: what growes of it no matter, advise your fellowes so*, Ile write straight to my Sister to hold my course*; pre- pare for dinner*[3].

5

10

15

20

{EXEUNT}

0506 - 0529 : 1.3.1 - 26

[1]though Q/F set a long (15 syllable) line to express Gonerill's indignation, most modern texts amend the
text to a more careful opening statement (9/6 syllables), as the symbol * shows
[2]most modern texts add a stage direction for offstage horns to sound
[3]though Q/F set this passage in prose as if Gonerill is talking hastily or less gracefully, most modern texts
remove this shift by resetting the text as verse (11/12/11/5 syllables, as shown)

13

◆▶ Whose Voice? *The Man* ◀◆

The purpose of this book is to provide a methodology which can help the speaker detect the sound of the author's voice and to establish meaning through an authentic replaying of that voice. But whose voice is it really?

The authenticity of the voice we hear depends in some part on the authenticity of the text that has survived, and despite editorial disagreement the major portion of Shakespeare's text is not in question. The important unsolved mystery does not lie in the realm of scholarly research on the plays, but rather in the historical and biographical search for the man who wrote them.

I cannot, in all conscience, end this book which trumpets so loudly and so often the word "Truth" without bowing my head and my knee in the direction of Edward DeVere, the 17th Earl of Oxford. Whenever I say in public that I am "an Oxfordian," I find myself either defensively jocular or in tears. Nothing in the Shakespeare establishment arouses so much ridicule and rancor as the suggestion that "the man from Stratford" did not write the plays. While I am in general agreement that what is important is not *who* wrote them but that they exist—that the plays, not their author, are what matter most—every now and then I think about Edward DeVere, and I look at his portrait and remember the story of his life, and I passionately care about *him*.

Converts to the Oxford theory are those who like to see the connection between a writer and his work. They not only are interested in knowing something about an author's life but find that the text is often clarified when the light of biographical detail is trained on obscure passages. The man from Stratford, whose name was spelt Shaksper, Shaxper, Shakspere, or Shackspere—but never Shakespeare—left the mere outline of a recorded life behind him, within which there can be found little connection with the thirty-six great plays attributed to him.

This acknowledgement that I believe that Edward DeVere, Earl of Oxford, is the true author of the plays, is intended to encourage those whose curiosity is piqued, so that they may look at some of the fascinating material already available and keep on the lookout for new evidence as it is unearthed. I was introduced to the subject in 1978 through a lecture given by Dr. Ruth Miller, one of the most dedicated and successful searchers for proof of Oxfordian authorship.

I have permission from Dr. Felicia Hardison Londré, Professor of Theatre at the University of Missouri, Kansas City, to reproduce a short biographical sketch of the Earl of Oxford which she wrote for the *Backstage Banner*, a magazine published by the Missouri Repertory Company.

The "Oxford" Theory
by Felicia Hardison Londré

The attribution of the world's greatest plays to the actor/grain merchant William Shaksper of Stratford-upon-Avon is supported primarily by two factors: the weight of a 350-year tradition, and the romantic notion that dazzling artistry and erudition can burst full-blown from the meanest environment.

Space does not permit refutation of the various myths linking the Stratford man to the authorship of the plays and sonnets of William Shake-speare. Suffice it to say that the many incongruities in our received knowledge about Shaksper as the purported author have long incited perplexed scholars to look for other possibilities—like Christopher Marlowe or Francis Bacon. However, in 1920, a systematic study of prominent Elizabethans by J. Thomas Looney traced the evidence back to a previously overlooked candidate: Edward DeVere, the seventeenth Earl of Oxford. Suddenly, everything clicked into place. The dates, the personality, the educational formation, the intimate knowledge of the court, the stylistic data, everything we know about the author from the works themselves fits perfectly when we attribute those works to Oxford.

Edward DeVere (1550–1604) inherited his title at the age of twelve. His mother married shortly after his father's death. As Hamlet observes, "the funeral baked meats did coldly furnish forth the marriage tables."

Young Oxford became a royal ward in the household of William Cecil (Lord Burghley), Queen Elizabeth's right-hand man, who was recognized even in his lifetime as the personality upon whom the character of Polonius in *Hamlet* was based. Fluent in French, Latin and classical Greek, the boy was tutored by Arthur Golding, the acclaimed translator of Ovid's *Metamorphosis*, from which the great majority of the classical allusions in Shake-speare's plays are drawn.

Oxford then studied at Cambridge and Oxford Universities, receiving his M.A. degree at the age of sixteen. Enrolled at one of the Inns of Court, he gained an intimate knowledge of the law. (As Mark Twain observed long before Looney published his findings about Oxford, whoever did write the plays clearly had formal training in law.) The plays abound with images of falconry, a sport accessible only to aristocrats, and Oxford was an expert falconer. At court he led one of the two literary factions that gave rise to so many in-jokes in *Love's Labor's Lost*. His military service in 1570 gave him the direct experience of war that is evoked so vividly in the history plays. His eighteen months of travels in Italy followed the same routes that are described in plays like *The Taming of the Shrew*. On his return to England, he cruelly refused to see his wife for about two years, since he believed the malicious gossip that their child had been born more than nine months after he left. His repentance is evident in the frequency with which his plays depict husbands rashly suspecting their innocent wives of infidelity: *Othello*, *Much Ado About Nothing*, *The Winter's Tale* and *Cymbeline*.

Among his many theatrical activities, Oxford ran a company of actors and wrote plays for court performance, many of which were—judging by their titles (the texts have not survived)—earlier versions of Shake-speare's plays as we know them. As an aristocrat, Oxford could not publish or perform in public under his own name, but he must have enjoyed acting under a pseudonym—perhaps the same as the pen-name he chose: Shake-speare. (The Oxford family crest is a lion shaking a broken spear, and a contemporary referred to Oxford as a prolific poet whose "countenance shakes spears.") Oxford also held the hereditary honorific title Lord Great Chamberlain; the company for which Shake-speare wrote his plays was the Lord Chamberlain's Men.

Oxford incurred the Queen's wrath when she discovered his affair with black-eyed seductress Anne Vavasor (the "dark lady" of the sonnets), especially when Oxford gave to Vavasor a little talley-book (or "tables") that the Queen had given him. Oxford expressed his apology to the Queen in Sonnet 122: "Thy gift, thy tables, are within my brain . . ." Sonnets 37, 66, and 89 refer to the serious leg-wound he received when he was ambushed by Vavasor's relatives. In 1588 he was one of two men who had the high honor of carrying the canopy over the Queen in a procession celebrating England's victory over the Spanish Armada; Sonnet 125 begins "Were't aught to me I bore the canopy . . ."

There are many excellent sources of further information about Oxford's eventful life. Among them are Charlton Ogburn's *The Mysterious William Shakespeare*, J. Thomas Looney's *"Shakespeare" Identified*, B.M. Ward's *The Seventeenth Earl of Oxford*, Dorothy and Charlton Ogburn's *This Star of England*, William Plumer Fowler's *Shakespeare Revealed in Oxford's Letters*, and Eva Turner Clark's *Hidden Allusions in Shakespeare's Plays*.

Even from this condensed version of a life full of action and incident, one sees a man from whose pen the plays might more easily have flowed than from the pen of a man from Stratford whose only six extant possible signatures are written in a hand that seems to have never held a pen in it before. William Shaksper's parents were illiterate, there is no evidence of their son having attended the local school, the only solid facts of his life that are on record is a marriage, births and deaths of children, a series of legal actions over money, the purchase of a house, the acquisition of a coat-of-arms, and a will within which there was no evidence that the deceased was either a reader or a writer. He did leave Stratford and go to London and the name "William Shakespeare" appears on the cast list of several of the plays later attributed to "William Shakespeare" and produced by the Lord Chamberlain's Men. He also became a shareholder in the Globe Theatre. The story behind these facts is convincingly told in Charlton Ogburn's *The Mysterious William Shakespeare*. The facts themselves do not constitute any proof of authorship of the plays. If you read any "biography" of William Shakespeare, notice how many variations of "he must have," "by now he would have," "from this we can confidently speculate that . . ." fill out the account; in contrast, Mr. Ogburn's account of the life of Edward DeVere, Earl of Oxford, gives the satisfaction of a Rubik's cube puzzle settling into its solution. The details are riveting, and mate gratefully with the texts and stories of the plays. Heard or read with an open mind the response to it all is a deep sigh of relief—the "Ah-ha" that greets the ring of truth. For a man whose family motto was "Vero nihil verius"—"nothing truer than the truth"—the sigh is long overdue.

The reason Oxford could not publicly acknowledge his authorship of the plays is partly that as a high-ranking nobleman prominent in Court circles his reputation would have suffered. Playwrights and actors were from a very different walk of life. But politics, court intrigue, the character of Queen Elizabeth and Oxford's relationship with her provide a complex of reasons for anonymity which go far beyond the mere protection of his name by the adoption of a pseudonym which was probably at the time not much of a disguise. *Noms de plumes* were not at all uncommon, and his coat-of-arms depicting a lion holding a broken spear in its paws gives an obvious suggestion for "Shake-speare." The choice of "William" for his first name seems appropriate for the man who enjoyed playing with double meanings: "Will I am." That it was vitally necessary to keep the authorship secret is shown by the lengths to which many went to perpetuate the myth of the "Stratford man," and those who like a good mystery story will be rewarded by one of huge cultural significance if they tackle Charlton Ogburn's *The Mysterious William Shakespeare: The Myth and The Reality* (Dodd, Mead & Co., 1984).

As I continued to read about the Earl of Oxford, I wondered how on earth this "theory" could not have been adopted as the true story. It seems evident, however, that it is more comfortable to perpetuate old myths than to entertain new facts, particularly when the myth supports our apparent need to believe that "genius" can transcend the rule of education or learning, as indeed it sometimes does. There is an investment of faith in the "incomprehensibility of genius." The fact that a multimillion-dollar-a-year industry is invested in the preservation of the myth of the Stratford man may also, in this instance, dilute enthusiasm for biographical clarification.

The cool and often scornful reception originally given the exhaustively-argued claim to Oxfordian authorship in J. Thomas Looney's two-volume *Shakespeare Identified* may have been partly due to the fact that it was published in England at a time when, because of current history and social politics, his story was least likely to be heard. The volumes came out in 1920, when a romantic cult of the working man, inspired by the Russian Revolution, was in full bloom. Everything was possible for everyone no matter what their birth. Class was a dirty word, and the suggestion that the icon of this universal potential—the illiterate from Stratford-upon-Avon—was a fiction— that the true genius was an aristocrat—was an iconoclasm that could not be entertained.

The twentieth century is the century of the "common man," and class is still a prickly subject. But perhaps we are now at the point where we can allow that a man can be of noble birth and yet be in touch with and sympathize with the lives of the less privileged classes. It would seem more likely that that sort of insight could come from the top down rather than from the bottom up, as we have been persuaded was the case. We have been asked to take on blind faith the astonishing ability of the man from Stratford to penetrate the mysteries of Court life and politics and the intricate relationships among the aristocracy.

Oxford's life seems to root and anchor the plays, and I include this glimpse of Edward DeVere because of the delight and excitement I experienced when the man behind the plays came to life in my mind. He was a passionate man, romantic and rash and intellectually profound. His story brings flesh and blood and breath to the voice I hear throughout the plays of William Shake-speare. His cousin Sir Horace Vere survived him and, as many Oxfordians have suggested, it is perhaps to him that Hamlet/Oxford's last words are spoken:

> O God, Horatio, what a wounded name,
> Things standing thus unknown, shall I leave behind me.
> If thou didst ever hold me in thy heart,
> Absent thee from felicity awhile,
> And in this harsh world draw thy breath in pain
> To tell my story.

The story is being told and "the truth will come to light":

> Time's glory is to calm contending kings,
> To unmask falsehood and bring truth to light.
> *The Rape of Lucrece*

With the truth shedding light on the word we will see the word more clearly. Its meaning will penetrate deeper into our hearts and, trusting the word, we will be wooed and won to love and to renewed life:

As an unperfect actor on the stage,
Who with his fear is put besides his part,
Or some fierce thing replete with too much rage,
Whose strength's abundance weakens his own heart,
So I, for fear of trust, forget to say
The perfect ceremony of love's rite,
And in mine own love's strength seem to decay,
O'ercharg'd with burthen of mine own love's might.
O, let my books be then the eloquence
And dumb presagers of my speaking breast,
Who plead for love, and look for recompense,
More than that tongue that more hath more express'd.
  O, learn to read what silent love hath writ;
  To hear with eyes belongs to love's fine wit.

Sonnet 23